Drawn by Strube, the famous
" Daily Express " cartoonist.

THE YARN
OF A YEOMAN

By
S. F. HATTON
(MIDDLESEX IMPERIAL YEOMANRY)

Foreword by
FIELD-MARSHAL VISCOUNT ALLENBY
G.C.B., G.C.M.G., D.C.L., LL.D.

The Naval & Military Press Ltd

in association with

The National Army Museum, London

Published jointly by

The Naval & Military Press Ltd

Unit 10 Ridgewood Industrial Park,
Uckfield, East Sussex,
TN22 5QE England

Tel: +44 (0) 1825 749494
Fax: +44 (0) 1825 765701

www.naval-military-press.com
www.military-genealogy.com
www.militarymaproom.com

and

The National Army Museum, London

www.national-army-museum.ac.uk

I

DEDICATE THIS BOOK

TO

THE YEOMEN OF ENGLAND

AND

THE LIGHT HORSEMEN OF AUSTRALIA,

THEIR LIVING, AND THEIR DEAD.

FOREWORD

THE author introduces us to the Middlesex Yeomanry as they lie in a pre-War camp on the bank of the peaceful Thames.

There came the call to War; and the Regiment volunteered, as one man, for Foreign Service.

Weeks of training were followed by a winter spent in guarding the East Coast; and in the spring the Middlesex Yeomanry sailed for Egypt.

No unit of our armies, probably, had a more varied experience; and nowhere is to be found a truer picture, than is here given, of War as the fighting man sees it.

In Egypt, the Regiment underwent a further arduous course of training, after which it was sent, dismounted, to Gallipoli. Here it saw real War; and " from the moment of landing . . . there was neither a place nor time when we were out of range of the enemy's guns and snipers."

After months of unceasing warfare, under distressing conditions, the order was issued for evacuation; and " less than fifty strong the remnants of the Regiment embarked."

Back in Egypt—and, to their joy, reconstituted as horsemen—the Yeomen did frontier duty on the Canal and beyond, until they were despatched to Salonica.

After much rough work in that theatre, the scene was changed to Sinai and the Palestine frontier.

Here it was that I came across this " splendid body

of sportsmen " ; and I hold myself fortunate in having had them with me, thenceforward, to the end of the War. Gaza, Philistia, Judæa, Jerusalem, the Jordan, Megiddo, Esdraelon, Damascus, are some among the many names of historic localities where their prowess was shown.

In the hard schools of Gallipoli and Salonica, the Regiment had learnt what War is ; and these veteran campaigners could face with calm confidence whatever the future might bring ; a confidence that was quickly proved to be well founded.

Severe as had been the trials hitherto undergone, great as had been the perils and difficulties met with so far, trials as hard and perils as great were to be theirs and to be as bravely overcome.

And the history of it all is written here, in words to stir our hearts.

Read, in Chapter VI, the " Outpost Story " of Karm, a battle of which the author says : " In the general scheme of things it was perhaps little indeed, but it was great to us, and, although we lost heavily of the dearest and best of our comrades, we covered ourselves with glory and brought honour and renown to the Regiment." Here died Lafone, the " hero and gentleman," than whom no man ever more worthily earned the Cross of Valour.

It is a story, brilliantly told, of heroism unsurpassed.

Throughout, the writer fixes our interest and attention.

Characters are clearly drawn and scenes vividly presented.

True to life is the tale about General Barrow, in action. " Sir, shall I move your bivy ? A bullet, just gone clean through it, Sir." " No, that'll be all right,

Pyle, there'll be plenty more through, I expect, before nightfall."

Very moving is the account of the death of " Bully," in Chapter XI.

Eloquent is the description of scenery on entering the harbour of Salonica.

The narrative is never dull ; unaffected and easy, it abounds in anecdote and sparkles with humour. There is no attempt at fine writing, and the style is occasionally careless ; but in many passages it rises to effortless beauty and dignity.

The spirit pervading all the book is well expressed in these—the author's—words : " It was glorious to be alive." " The good times and jokes are more readily remembered than the disasters and discomforts of campaigning, and a carouse recalled more often than a battle."

F.M.

PREFACE

THIS book was conceived in the Hollybush Inn, a tavern tucked away in one of the crazy nooks of Old Hampstead Town, " Better one glimpse within the tavern caught than in the Temple lost outright." It was a Sunday morning in September, and after our walk across the Heath, a number of us were arguing on the plethora of war books and the German view-point in particular.

We definitely came to the conclusion that " All Quiet on the Western Front " was not a real picture of the War as it only portrayed one aspect, and we deplored its lamentable lack of humour. We decided that " when two or three of us were gathered together " discussing old times. it was the pranks we played the jokes we made, the quaint cussedness of it all. that came back to memory more quickly than the actual horrors of battle. We felt that none of the war books had paid sufficient tribute to that great spirit of comradeship, sacrifice, kindliness and consideration for one another that so characterized troops of men, drawn from all ranks and professions, who found themselves suddenly living together under conditions of hardship and danger.

The soldiers we knew and fought with were neither hysterical nor given to introspective analysis. According to several morbid modern war books, the appearance of a " Jordan boil " on the nape of the neck would demand a soliloquy—" This deep yellow canker

gnawing away my flesh, my own flesh, flesh that is me
—this pool of pus, these millions of virulent micro-
cocci eating away down to my very bones,—perhaps
even to my soul," whereas what the British Tommy
actually said was, " Gawd, I've got another beauty."

It was first intended that I should make a collection
of all the humorous stories of the War I had heard
or could gather, but the daily papers about the same
time, curiously enough, conceived the same idea, so
that the theme of this little book was immediately
changed. It is now largely a personal reminiscence.

There is no attempt to deal with the military significance of the campaigns—I leave that to the historian ;
neither have I essayed any such perfection of literary
style as may be seen in Compton Mackenzie's *Gallipoli*,
where he contrasts the brown skin of the Australian
soldiers with the olive-green of the trees and shrubs.

I simply tell the story of the life of a Yeoman in
England, Egypt, Gallipoli, Sinai, Salonica, Palestine
and Syria ; and I tell it to you as if we were sitting
over a pipe of baccy and a pint of beer. You will find
here no " nerve-shattered padres," no " weeping
colonels," nor do my troopers take away their love-
letters to the latrines to read. This story is true, the
men are real, and like the rest of life this yarn is made
up of humour and pathos, comedy and tragedy, sacrifice, courage, heroism and lost-endeavour—in a word,
it is human.

I am greatly indebted to my General, Field-Marshal
Viscount Allenby, for his generous and appreciative
Foreword ; and to my friend Sid Strube for his gift
of a Frontispiece.

I must formally acknowledge my thanks to
Mr. G. S. Odam for his maps, to V. H. Porter and

A. J. Talbot, editors of the *Middlesex Yeomanry Magazine*, for permission to use Corporal Meering's narrative, and their valuable record of the adventures of the Regiment during the War, and also to S. S. M. Dixon for the use of his excellent photographs, and to Mr. J. S. Judd for the loan of several blocks from the *Records of the Middlesex Yeomanry*.

Lastly, I thank all Yeomen and Light Horsemen with whom I ever came in contact, for their splendid comradeship, their cheerful steadfastness, their high endeavour in hardship and danger, and for the honour of having known personally a body of men so utterly devoid of any narrowness of mind or meanness of soul.

CONTENTS

LIST OF MAPS AND ILLUSTRATIONS

The Yarn of a Yeoman

CHAPTER I

AUGUST 4TH, 1914, AND COAST DEFENCES

"Oh ! we don't want to lose you
But we think you ought to go."

VIEWED through a vista of after-experiences, having "smelt it and felt it and seen," the Yeomanry of pre-War days comes back to memory like the lighter scenes of the *Balkan Princess*, or the *Chocolate Soldier*. The Annual Camp was the married man's retreat, and the single man's paradise. I am no longer single, and there is no longer any Yeomanry.

Imagine the peaceful beauty of the scene of my first camp in 1914, with the splendid body of sportsmen—that laughing, swaggering, beer-quaffing, lusty, robust gathering of men—the Middlesex Yeomanry.

Tents aligned on one of the most beautiful reaches of old Thames, just above Cleeve Lock, by Streatley and Goring ; the Berkshire Downs with their curious clumps of trees, like solitary tufts on a bald pate, stretching way up behind the camp, to form that long straight ridge and perfect gallop, the Fair Mile.

Immediately in front of the camp the river itself, and conveniently opposite on the other shore—" The Leather Bottel." The Yeomanry Commanding Officer was ever thoughtful ; though perhaps if any of his men were to become exuberant, he would as soon

have had them under his eye as further afield. Young
men are so often misunderstood.

A day's soldiering—pardon the word—I knew no
better then—under such conditions was something to
be remembered. Réveillé about 7 a.m., hot coffee by
specially engaged cooks ; then early grooming, water
and feed. A two-course breakfast in the Troopers'
mess—(the damned waiters are a bit slow this
morning)—and then dress for parade. Oh yes, we
wore khaki for parades, and saddled up our own
horses with " posh " civilian saddles. A morning's
drill or manœuvring on the Downs, and back to camp,
grooming, watering, feeding ; the regimental band in
full-dress uniform playing all the popular tunes
during " stables." A wash, and change into mess
kit, a dark blue tunic with steel epaulettes, enough
to make anyone throw a chest. Luncheon, beautifully
served by hired mess waiters on spotless linen—
I think there were napkins, but I cannot remember
whether the band was still playing. Anyhow, it
should have been.

In the afternoon saddlery and equipment were
given over to a batman to clean for the morning—
it was customary for four or five Troopers to run a
" civvy " batman between them during the camp—
and then change into flannels for the river, lounging,
sleeping or anything else Satan found one to do.

It was a bit of a bore that at least half a troop had to
remain in camp for evening " stables," but after
that, with the exception of night guards, everyone's
time was his own.

Some would dress in full " lion-tamer " rig-out,
and swagger down to the " Miller of Mansfield " or
" The Swan " in Streatley, and possibly pick up a
spare village maiden *en route;* or by train to
Reading where the choice was greater. Others,
preferring to take their beer in greater comfort,
loosened their mess tunics and strolled to the " Beetle
and Wedge," crossed the river to Bill Davis's at the

" Leather Bottel," or stayed in the canteen, paid less
for more, and sang in chorus songs of praise to Bill,
a nautical gentleman of great physical prowess.

To prohibitionists, I regret to say there were no tee-
totalers in the pre-War Yeomanry—and the beer
really was " bitter " then, why, you often found hops
in it, especially on the last knockings at eleven o'clock
or so.

And so to bed ; four to a tent, plenty of comfort
though not overmuch room for your trunks, which
had, of course, been sent " luggage in advance."

This was soldiering indeed—I was only twenty-two
at the time, and I could have joined at eighteen—
S'truth, I'd missed it all those years.

On the night of August 2nd, 1914, I was on night
guard. A dreadful thing, you know, being out there
all alone from, say, 12 till 4 a.m., with all those horses,
and the owls hooting in the trees around old Moulsford
churchyard. One of our long-faced friends might have
got loose, or anything happen ; and if you'd ever seen
a Yeoman " rookie " try to catch a horse at night by
holding a lantern in his face, you'd appreciate what I
mean.

I was strolling up and down the horse lines, thinking of a thousand and one things. What a fine fellow
I was ; to-morrow was August Bank Holiday, we were
to have special sports, and the batman I shared was
so good—been in the 10th Hussars—that I was being
paraded as best turned-out trooper for my troop ; my
girl was coming down to the sports, and I was going
to ride my mare in the local steeplechase—and—what
a fine fellow I was—and oughtn't she to think herself
jolly lucky !

The lights were still on in the Colonel's tent way
over on that sacred strip of ground, the officers'
quarters, and also in the orderly room—the sergeant-
major was playing poker I supposed—when a car came
snorting through the darkness of the silent lane, and,
turning into camp, pulled up with a jerk at the " Holy

of Holies." An officer who looked like a "real" soldier jumped out and started playing hell ; I realized at once he was " pukka." I knew the same words, but I couldn't say them quite the same way. A banging on officers' tents, a pyjama parade in the orderly room, and then the orderly sergeant and the sergeant of the guard started tearing all over the place.

" Wake 'em all up," the sergeant of the guard rushed at me. I stared at him in blank amazement. Sacrilege—fancy waking up the Yeomanry from a decent night's sleep. He seemed to mean it, so I got busy. Nobody seemed to know what anything was about, and as every officer and non-com. came fresh from sleep, each gave a different order, and we were soon in real chaos. Some shouted " get the horse lines up " ; others howled " get the tents down " ; one or two of the old Boer War men disappeared, and kipped under the hedges till dawn ; but mostly we got in each other's way, mixed up tents and horses, bedding, rifles and trunks, moved things about aimlessly, and then moved them back again, tried to hold five things at once, and generally created an amorphous mass of " quick, dead and the plumbers."

With the dawn, and the help of the old soldiers, we straightened things out a bit, and also our ideas. Rumour had it that there was to be war with Germany ; anyhow, we knew the camp was being struck, we were going back to London, and the French were on our side.

What a lark ! It would all be like this glorious camp, only much more exciting ; real scouting, real trekking, real bullets and real charging. Crumbs ! I was a schoolmaster. No more going back to that stuffy classroom, and those kids, no more trying to write articles, and worse still, trying to sell them to meet my extravagances. Real war : see a bit of the world, have a man's life—this was going to be great fun, one big adventure.

Such were our thoughts as we rode down to Streatley Station about 10 a.m. with all the villagers out cheer-

ing, and the band in the station square playing the
" Marseillaise " ; everyone singing at the top of his
voice, and feeling patriotic to the point of tears.

Papers were eagerly bought and, once entrained,
arguments began to ride high—Germany had violated
Belgian neutrality, and what was England going to do
about it ? The older men understood the political
significance more thoroughly than I did. I could only
speculate what a change would come over my life and
outlook if war became a certainty.

A little cameo remains in my memory. A tent mate
of mine named Diedrichs, a very decent fellow indeed,
was known to be of German origin. I can see him
sitting gloomily in the corner of that railway carriage,
trying to grasp the situation. We, in our youth and
arrogance, had made the conversation pointedly dis-
tasteful to him, and there he sat, feeling that we, who
yesterday had been his boon companions, were pur-
posely shunning him ; and I expect, finding himself
torn between his loyalty to us and the Regiment, and
his innate duty to the home of his family. He must
have had a perfectly wretched journey, and I for one
am sorry for the mental agonies I helped to heap upon
him. He had to leave the Regiment, and I do not
know what became of him, but I remember him as a
very decent chap indeed.

London again ; on a broiling hot Bank Holiday
noon—I guess that I looked the " Sap " all right as
I was immediately placed on saddle fatigue, though
most were dismissed to their homes. I understand
lots of things now, I've been a sergeant myself since
then.

Two of us with the help of a six-foot-two farrier,
one Gillingham, loaded up saddles into a greengrocer's
van, and commenced to drive to Chelsea Headquarters.
Gillingham, one of the largest and stoutest of men I
have ever seen, was by this time very full of beer and
insisted on sitting on top of the van, cheering every
motor that passed by, many already flying little flags

and French tricolours. When I say that Gillingham
was full of beer, I mean something. If you want to
test your powers of endurance, drink pint for pint with
any self-respecting Army farrier, and you'll soon learn
your limitations. From tuneful patriotism, our friend
above sank into less melodious slumber, when suddenly
in the middle of High Street, Kensington, the van
passing over a too prominent drain hole, gave a lurch,
and precipitated fifteen stone of flesh into the roadway. Gillingham woke up with a start and began to
bellow. Some fellows rushed out of a pub, and forced
whisky down his throat. Gillingham's face was a
masterpiece—he appeared in genuine doubt, firstly, as
to whether we had done it on purpose, and secondly
as to whether he was going to get more free liquor
from the crowd by appearing hurt, or by treating his
bruises as nothing, and playing the hero. We left him
to it and no doubt he had a memorable Bank Holiday.

London was a seething pool of excitement that day.
I travelled by the newly opened tube to my home in
Hampstead, and the train was full of real Harriets
with feathers, who insisted on kissing me, and on my
dancing with them. Hampstead still wore feathers in
1914—it was before the famous discovery of silk stock-
ings for working lassies' legs and everything there was
a real beano, but I noticed that some of the older folk,
and especially the women, looked worried and anxious
as if they foresaw parting and bereavement from
husband and son.

The Tuesday passed in anxious anticipation as to
what the Government would do, and rumours of mobilization of the Guards and departure of troops for
France were already in the air.

The ultimatum had been delivered to Germany, and
by the Wednesday morning, August 5th, came the
news to the world that on the previous midnight war
had been declared. I received my mobilization orders,
and reported straight away to Chelsea Headquarters.

There were scenes of remarkable enthusiasm everywhere. Whatever the misgivings of the politicians may have been, the general public went into the War in holiday mood. People could not do enough for anyone in khaki during those few days—Tommy Atkins was " riding on the pig's back " right enough. No fares were accepted from any soldier on either buses or tubes, no one would allow you to pay for a drink in any " pub " anywhere, and invitations to have the best of everything came from strangers and friends alike. If one bought an article in a shop, the shopkeeper would often say he couldn't give it to you, but you could have it at cost price. This generosity did not last long, but it existed everywhere during the first few weeks of the War, and I mention it as evidence of the spirit of the nation in those early days.

Mobilization parade of the Regiment was held in the square. The Colonel read a letter to the troops from Lord Kitchener, who was Honorary Colonel, and the men who did not wish to sign for foreign service were asked to take a pace to the rear. The ranks remained unbroken. Then a thing, which seemed to me stupendous, happened. We filed past the Regimental Quartermaster sitting at a small table, and were handed five golden sovereigns as mobilization money. Gee !—five golden Jimmy-o'-goblins ! You could do something with that in 1914. Officially you were to buy yourself vests, and pants, and things—but every trooper I knew wired home to Mother immediately that he was sorry that he was on night guard that night, and then commenced one glorious " blue."

During the first week we slept at home, and reported for duty daily at about 9 a.m. One of the first duties was to equip the Regiment with horses, and there were visits to all parts of London on this exciting errand. Buying up horses from the stables in Park Lane and the Mayfair districts was a " good conjure " ; rankers were treated like " toffs," and how the officers fared, I can only imagine. The horses were pegged down in Chelsea Gardens, and gave a good deal of trouble to

the men new to the game. I remember a beautiful
chestnut mare bought out of a private stable near
Knightsbridge : I had to lead her in. She somehow
got loose during the night and could not be found anywhere. Next morning I was paraded to fetch some
more horses from Fulham, and as they were bought up,
and led out, I saw a handsome chestnut. I, thinking myself clever, shouted to the sergeant-major,
" Sergeant-major, isn't that the chest . . ." but I got
no further—

" Shut up, you fool," he promptly replied ; so, you
see, I was learning things—one glance at his face, and
I knew I must have been mistaken.

They tell me that saddles fetched a good price about
this time too.

At the end of ten days or so the Regiment was
equipped with horses and saddlery, and we camped on
a dirty field at Hounslow, with our sister Regiments,
the Roughriders, and the Sharpshooters, forming the
London Mounted Brigade.

The allocation of recruits at this time was said to be
as follows : if a fellow couldn't ride they sent him to
the Roughriders, if he couldn't shoot they sent him
to the Sharpshooters, and if he could neither ride nor
shoot they sent him to the Middlesex.

Training began in earnest at Hounslow, and the
number of horses that ran loose going to water must
have made our officers despair of us. Moreover, our
transport was a sight for the gods : bakers' carts,
laundry vans, railway floats, with a preponderance of
vehicles from greengrocers. My chief impression of
Hounslow was dust, loose horses and a gap in the hedge
where you could get back to lines without passing the
guard.

I was sitting just inside a tent here on a blanket in
the gloaming with the lady who is now my wife, when
the saddler corporal put his big head inside, and, not
distinguishing anybody, shouted, " Kilby, where's my
b——y spurs ? "

I, wishing to inform him of the lady's presence, ejaculated, " Ssh, Ssh," at which he exploded, " Don't you b——y well Ssh-Ssh me, Kilby, I want my b——y spurs." The gentleman holds a prominent position in the City to-day, and I'm sure he remembers the incident.

Rumour was our daily portion ; the Regiment was going to Flanders, the Russians were coming through London, and we were going to St. Petersburg—but finally it was all settled—we packed up camp hurriedly and started on a long trek to Southampton, *en route* for France—at least so we all thought. There was tremendous secrecy about all movements of troops at this time, and some of the rumours were beyond belief. Still, the War would be over by Christmas ; the whole of the Guards had gone, and that settled it.

When I think of the continuous advances in flying column, that we were afterwards to experience, this first trek was the most awful affair imaginable. It was one repeated dropping off of nosebags, picketing pegs, water buckets, etc., and galloping back to fetch them. It was damned bad saddle-packing for, of course, none of us really knew anything about the game. Outwardly it was in the nature of a triumphal march. Wherever we halted *en route*, the townsfolk and villagers came out in thousands and made much of us filling our haversacks with cakes and fruit galore— giving us their very best in all the goodness of their hearts.

We camped one night, and the following morning rode through Reading just before church time. It was a glorious September morning, and the streets rapidly filled with folk who heaped gifts of cigarettes, tobacco, home-made cakes and apples upon us. 'Twas a good life being a soldier. Pangbourne, Goring, Streatley, bless my soul ! We turned into the very same fields we had camped on in the summer, and began to put down horse lines. It soon dawned on us that there was no France for us after all. In fact, severe intensive training began and we rapidly found out what a devil of a lot we had to learn.

Several men were passed as unfit for foreign service, and recruits were sent down from London to take their places. The old Colonel retired, and the command of the Regiment was taken over by that genial sportsman, Lt.-Col. Sir Mathew Wilson, Bart., D.S.O.— frequently mentioned in the press as " Scatters." I never dared call him that, yet.

The Regiment was concentrated into three squadrons, instead of four ; and a " pukka " regular officer from British or Indian Cavalry was attached to each squadron. They didn't, perhaps, look as showy as some of our own officers, who were all splendid sportsmen of good stock, but they soon taught us what " Musical Comedy " soldiers we were ;—saddle packing, so that things didn't slip and bump about, saddle fitting, different methods of blanket folding, real sword drill, reconnoitring, map-reading and making, night marching and general care of horses.

Captain Bennett, from Jacob's Horse, I believe, was one of the smartest, quietest, yet most deadly efficient officers I have ever served under. He was attached to my squadron, and, though the training was severe, the troops were kept happy, and it began to shape us into soldiers. Through a glorious September, troop drill, squadron drill, brigade drill, and even divisional parades on the beautiful Berkshire Downs form glorious memories of physical fitness, and care-free days of happy manhood.

The feeding of the Regiment at this time was not of the best. One of the lesser humours of the piece was the fact that all the " Odds and S——s " attached to the Regiment during the summer training, such as cooks, waiters, batmen, etc., had found themselves in an awkward position. Nominally they had signed on the Regiment for a fortnight's camp, but as war had broken out during the camp, they had automatically come under mobilization orders, and were now part of the Regiment.

A cook may be excellent with all the paraphernalia of a peace-time camp about him, and equally rotten when he has raw rations, a field kitchen and dixies to depend on. Still, they did their best for us, and things gradually improved, but, my oath—for weeks it was always stew.

My squadron leader was the Marquis of Aylesbury, a very kindly gentleman, and my troop officer was no end of a boy—a medical student whose training had been interrupted. He was always very keen, but very tired in the mornings ;—but more of him anon. My sergeant was Bob Thompson, of the fierce moustaches, with a devil of a bark on parade, and a faculty for not quite knowing when his leg was being pulled ; but one of the dearest and most generous-hearted fellows in the world.

Three recruits from Chelsea Art School, Joy and Latham, with the well-known artist, C. Q. M. Orchardson, had joined the Regiment as privates. Joy and Latham were short and stout, and rather alike. Poor old Bob could never learn one from t'other, and they, soon tumbling to it, if perchance Bob addressed Joy as Joy, Joy promptly answered, " No, Latham, Sergeant," and, of course, Latham would do the same.

A typical early morning stables scene :

Bob, rather sleepily, " Get your dandy brush, Latham."

" My name's Joy, Sergeant."

" Joy ! You told me yesterday your name was Latham."

" No, Joy, Sergeant."

Bob would stroll up the lines, keeping half an eye on Latham, then look at the real Joy, and, coming back, address a remark to Latham :

" Put your back into it, Joy."

With the slightest twinkle and rather doubtfully—

" Latham, Sergeant."

"Latham, you told me your name was Joy only a few moments ago."

"No, Sergeant, you called me Joy, but my name's really Latham."

"Latham or Joy, I don't give a damn, you're Joy this morning, and don't argue."

But these lads, champion leg-pullers, were afterwards killed on Gallipoli, and Orchardson, who became Captain in our Regiment, a magnificent fellow, died of wounds with the Camel Corps.

Another bright lad we had was O'Reilly, who hardly ever put his head inside the canteen but he would be greeted by a shout from all :

"Are you the O'Reilly who keeps the hotel ?
Are you the O'Reilly who does us so well ?
'Cos, if you're the O'Reilly they speak of so highly,
Gawd blimy, O'Reilly, you are looking well."

His favourite excuse to Bob Thompson when late for any parade was, "Sure, I've been looking for mushrooms, Sergeant."

I remember O'Reilly riding in troop line behind Bob on one occasion, when his horse insisted on being a head out of line to the rear. O'Reilly had spurred and kicked him, and, finally, to keep up, every few yards went "Cluck-cluck-cluck-cluck" with his mouth. Bob stood it for a time, and, finally, turning in the saddle, shouted, "O'Reilly, you're in cavalry now, d'ye think you're driving your b——y cab horse ? "

Sergeant Thompson slept in a tent at the end of the lines, and, after his evening pint or two, slept very heavily. All recruits looking for a bed, or strollers or drunks, we sent to his tent ; some of them bundled in at midnight. Once, whilst he was out, we filled his tent with a complete set of ten new recruits with equipment, who were all well asleep by the time he came home. The scene was good to behold, and listen to. We were never dull, I assure you.

Always being a mimic, I was very popular with the

canteen as a " turn," doing imitations of the various officers, and singing many charming ditties which were much in request.

There should be an anthology—not an emasculated one—of all soldiers' ballads. Those chiefly in favour at this time concerned a tinker of abnormal physical proportions and procreative powers ; a charming ballad of one " Nellie " who was not as good as she should have been, a celebrated " Ram of Derbyshire," " A monk of high renown," and the nautical gentleman previously mentioned.

Who could fail to be moved by the genuine sentiment of that classic :

> " She was poor, but she was honest,
> Victim of a rich man's whim, etc."

Those of you who have not bawled in slow pathetic rhythm this most moving of all choruses :

> " It's the same the whole world over,
> It's the poor that gets the blime,
> It's the rich what 'as the pleasures—
> Isn't it a . . . shime ! "

know nothing of community singing at all.

The tinker song caused me a little trouble, as on one occasion a troop of men singing on return from a parade—they would crescendo on the " yards "—let fly rather badly, and I was paraded before the Marquis, who told me he'd always thought I was a nice quiet fellow, and that I'd been recommended as a lance-corporal, but if I sang songs of that nature he would have to reconsider his decision. I was, however, promoted lance-corporal shortly afterwards in spite of this ribaldry.

A little yarn at this period tells of a rather nervous trooper, riding in squadron line at the canter, next to his more seasoned corporal. There was considerable buffeting and knee crushing, the horses were getting bad tempered, and as the pace increased the highly anxious voice of the trooper rang out as he tugged

c

furiously at the reins, " My horse is going to bolt, Corporal, my horse is going to bolt."

" If that's so, then take your b——y foot out of my stirrup."

My troop officer, who was called " Pip " to distinguish him from his elder brother in the Regiment, was a man of infinite resource on several occasions. On many a field-day he saved us endless riding by the quickness of his imagination. We would be manœuvring around the Wallingford country, miles from the other troops, when he would set the map, and call his non-com. officers around him.

" There you are," he'd say gruffly, " there's the village we've got to take by 1.30. Damn long way, ain't it, I'm tired, and I expect you fellows are the same."

After some consultation, a message would be sent to the squadron leader to say we'd reached our objective ; then into the nearest village to water the horses, in the courtyard of an inn. " Give these fellows something to drink," he would call, and after a refresher—or several—he'd gather the non-com. officers again around his map, and finding a convenient large hedge near the main road, say, " Guess we'll have a kipp down—God save Ireland—but the squadron is bound to come back this way."

On one occasion he got so fed up with the whole proceeding that, as the squadron deployed on a reconnaissance, he rode us clean off on a joy ride, jumping hedge, ditch and wall as they came, and brought us back some hours after dark, and about three hours after the troops had got back to lines. He was a bighearted boy, and, though eccentric, I liked him. Mark you, my imitation of him in the canteen was one of my most successful, but he'll forgive me, as it was so true to life.

On October 8th the whole Yeomanry Mounted Division with its various Brigade Artillery—our Brigade had the " A and B " Batteries of the celebrated Honourable Artillery Company—and other services, was paraded on the Fair Mile, and inspected by His Majesty the King, Lord Kitchener, and other heads from the War Office.

We moved into billets in Moulsford shortly afterwards—a troop to a barn with the squadron mess in the village hall. Probably as the outcome of the Royal inspection, dozens of horses were cast, and replaced by remounts, our saddlery packed away, and the real cavalry saddle with the long rifle-bucket issued to us. A more modern rifle and other kit followed, so that we were sure we should see active service in France very shortly.

It was here that two notable characters joined the squadron—Charlie and X——.

To tell of Charlie first—there'll be much more about him anon. When I first saw Charlie, he was grey-haired, about 5 ft. 8 in., with a rather wrinkled, wizened face, out of which peered the most twinkling little eyes imaginable. He was fifty-eight years of age at least—I know he'll deny it—the old devil—bandy of leg, with rather bad feet, a strong West-Country accent, and a scrubby moustache from which he was always wiping beer. So much you could see, but what you couldn't see was a heart that never knew when it was beaten ; at his age he went all through the War with us and was seldom ill.

Later he told me how he came to join up—it was something like this : " You see," he would move his fingers at you like a dwarf as he talked, " I was a chef at the Carlton, and there was all this 'ere recruiting business a-going on. I goes out into the Strand to get a pint or two after lunch, and someone trying to take the mike out of me says, ' Charlie, you ought to be a blinking soldier.'

" ' Soldier,' says I, ' why, I knows more about soldiering than all the b——y War Office. Wasn't I five years with the Gloucester Yeomanry, and didn't I serve all through the Boer War with the Worcestershire Yeomanry ? Yeoman I am, none of yer blinking

foot sloggers—everyone down Worcestershire and
Warwickshire knows me. Through South Africa I
was, and old Sal Galloway as kept the ' Coach and
Horses,' she'd tell yer I was the finest man around
there for miles.' They laughed, and ' You ma' laugh,'
I ses. I was having another pint and a band come
marching down the Strand, so I went to the door, and
somehow I don't know what it was, but before I
knowed anything, I held myself up and was marching
along behind. I walked all the way to Chelsea.
    " ' What's this mob ? ' I says. ' The Middlesex
Yeomanry Band out a-recruiting,' they says. ' Yeomanry,' says I, ' sign me on, Sergeant.' He looks at
me old-fashioned like, and says ' What's your job ? '
' Chef,' says I. ' Oh! cook,' says he, ' come on in,
boy.' Yes, I puts thirty-eight instead of fifty-eight
years on my paper, and here I've been ever since. Yer
see, when I heard who they were, well, I just had to
join."
    To any of those who dodged the column—you can
take your hats off to Charlie.
    Owing to the sudden mobilization of cavalry
throughout the country, every regiment found itself
very short of farriers ; and as these " Shoeys " were
earning good money in the local blacksmiths', etc., to
induce them to join up the War Office offered them
5s. a day. The unfair thing, of course, was this, that
the farriers already in the Regiment drew 1s. 2d. a
day, and these new blighters were sent to work beside
them for 5s. Now a farrier does not mince his words
—he hadn't need to—repetition is the soul of his wit,
and there was constant friction between our own
farriers and these new-comers—and rightly so : for
X—— couldn't have shod a lizard ; was perfectly useless in the forge, and a thundering nuisance out
of it.
    I first met him in very charming circumstances ; we
had been round to Mrs. Blewett's, at the " Beetle and
Wedge," having a bit of a sing-song, and we strolled

home late along the river-side. I entered our troop-
barn by the river, and groped across to the corner
where my blanket should have been rolled upon the
floor. I put my hand down, and touched something
hairy. Lighting the lamp, I turned it over and exclaimed, " Who the hell put this b——y Egyptian
mummy in my bed ? " There was a titter or two
from the corner, so I slung a boot at that, and then
realized the thing was alive. I scruffed it up, and,
spluttering and reviling me, I found it to be the real
counterpart of Wagner's " Mimi " of the Nibelungs.
" Gaw'rn," it says, " I'll sleep where I like."

" Not in this bunk," I answered, and seeing that I
meant business, he mumbled off to the middle of the
floor dragging his blanket with him.

He didn't know one end of a horse from the other—
and every time there was a full parade a decent
trooper had to pack his saddle and saddle up for him.
Though we gave him a small Shetland pony to ride,
he could never mount it by himself, and I've frequently
seen him trying to mount with his foot in the sword-
hilt.

We worked a spruce arrest on X—— one night ;
he'd been boasting what he was going to do, so one
evening as he was turning into bed, I entered the barn
with six troopers with fixed bayonets. " X——, you
are under arrest for issuing threats against your
superior officers, which is treason against the King's
Regulations," I informed him, " dress quickly and
come along." We marched him through Moulsford,
and put him in a small outhouse at some stables a
mile away, telling him he was in prison, and would
have to go before the Colonel in the morning. We
left the door just closed to, but he stopped there all
night, and only discovered he was not locked in when
morning came.

Happy days in billets here on peaceful Thames-side
were cut short, for on the night of November 16th a
midnight alarm was sounded, and by early the next

afternoon the whole Regiment and horses were entrained—this time, we were sure, for France.

But no, a chilly dawn found us at Cromer, and by
the following evening troops were billeted in villages
along the Norfolk coast, with the Grand Hotel,
Mundesley, as the Regimental Headquarters. They
say that when the Regiment moved from Moulsford
there was enough kit and equipment left behind to
equip a squadron—and among the debris were not a
few broken hearts. I often wondered whom the pretty
little postmistress felt the loss of the more, the Captain
or the trooper. I think I could tell, but I'd not offend
the vanity of an officer.

The reason for our sudden move to Norfolk was
soon apparent: a German invasion was expected before
Christmas, and it was rumoured that the north-eastern
Norfolk coast was the enemy's chosen landing-place.
Hearsay had it that from Holkham Bay to Happis-
burg were many places where German transports and
battleships could come close into the shore, to facilitate
the movements of their landing parties; and, honestly,
the folk in Cromer, and like towns, were really very
" windy."

My own troop was billeted in the quaint old cliff
village of Trimingham, and here training during the
day was very strenuous indeed. At nights we formed
a series of cavalry patrols all round the coast, with
troops as picquets in private houses. I shall long
remember those winter night rides like smugglers along
the windy cliffs of Norfolk, with the wind singing,
whining rhythmic songs among the trees and telegraph
wires ; the biting cold and the rapid movement making the blood to tingle attune with the merry rattle of
hoofs through the silent countryside.

There was a large house with a flat cement roof
standing right out by itself on the cliff, a mile from
the village, known as Trimingham House. It was
rumoured that signals had been seen from this house
to ships at sea, and the owner, a German, was promptly

interned. The spy was supposed to be rife in Norfolk at this time. Any bearded elderly entomologist riding around with a box in search of specimens became an obvious object of suspicion, and many a stranger to the district was arrested and made to give a thorough account of himself.

My troop was sent to occupy this Trimingham House, and place picquets at night on the cliffs around. The house was beautifully furnished, the garden was well stocked with vegetables for that time of the year, and there was a large chicken-run at the end. I am afraid some of the knick-knacks about the place began to disappear, and I even heard one trooper negotiating to send the grand piano home. " Charlie," who had by this time established himself as the cook *par excellence*, and who could often be seen tramping his way over ploughed fields with a little sack, on what he always called a " foraging expedition," had no need to go far afield, and performed wonders with the vegetables at his disposal. He also looked very handsome in the late owner's dress suit, though the trousers were a little tight under the armpits, and the sleeves turned back four inches. As he said—" he wouldn't half look a lad when he got that back to town."

The second evening the whole troop was to be out on patrol, and come in about 3 a.m., and a meal was ordered for that hour.

My troop officer called me, " Here, Hatton, about those fowls down there, something ought to be done about them, we ought to feed them or something."
" Yes, we shall have to get some corn. Want a lot of corn those fowls will, cost us a bit, won't it ? I think you'd better take Charlie down with you and feed those fowls right away."

At roosting-time Charlie and I fed those fowls as requested, and " a delicate dish they made." A trap was despatched to " The Anchor " for some " pig's ear," and when we came in from patrol at 3 a.m. a rare gargantuan feast awaited us. Charlie had laid table in the hall, a log fire threw out a cheery heat, and the beer was served, for want of sufficient glasses, in delicate finger-bowls.

No feast is complete without its spectre, and this arrived in the form of Captain Bennett, who, efficient as ever, was spending the night visiting all coastal picquets. There was some sort of half-hearted enquiry about those fowls and things, for I remember the village policeman questioning Charlie afterwards in the troop cook-house.

Charlie was saying, " Fowls, constable, fowls, d'say ? Blimy, couldn't my lads just do with a bit of 'em ! Coo, you make my mouth water ! No, they has to have stew, that's all they gets, I do my best for 'em you may know. The other night, down at that very house you were talking about, I bought 'em a couple of pair of rabbits,—here, you can see it in my little mess book ; but fowls—blimy, couldn't I do with a bit, not 'arf ! "

When off duty for an evening—it was seldom indeed—a favourite pastime was to borrow a trap and, harnessing up a troop horse, take a trip to Cromer or Mundesley for a change. Unfortunately most of our troop horses considered it far below their dignity to pull a trap along, and many of them promptly proceeded to give exhibitions of equine pyrotechnics, so that soon there wasn't a trap without a broken dashboard in the whole of Trimingham. One horse left in charge of a small boy outside the " Anchor " decided to go home, and so he took the trap with him. He cantered jauntily up to the stable-yard with one shaft hanging in a trail of harness, with a gleeful expression on his face, as much as to say, " I've had a good day to-day." I hope all the broken traps have been paid for. You could hardly put your head out of a stable door but someone would shout, " What about that trap ? " They stopped asking in the course of time, so I can only presume everything was satisfactory.

Christmas week, the protracted German invasion

was most certainly coming, so that in addition to the
patrols, trenches were dug, and manned nightly.
Christmas Eve everyone was especially windy, and we
all saw the dawn of our first war Christmas standing
to in the cliff trenches ; it was a bitterly cold night,
and the rime was on our hair and moustaches, as
we scrambled out to wish each other " happy
morn."

The local vicar had asked me to sing " Nazareth "
at the Christmas service, and I was afraid the troops
were going to " bird me " in some way. I got through
it all right, the organist only a bar and a half behind
most of the time. I remember the service well, as the
old verger sitting right at the back of the church
always crooned in a high-pitched, goat-like voice
" Aaa-men " well after everyone else. The troops
listened for a time, and then decided to wait and help
him. After each prayer, therefore, there was a long
pause and then a chorus of " Aaa-aaa-men " that
would have done justice to a flock of sheep.

Christmas dinner was held for my troop at 6 p.m.
in the village school-room, and Charlie had risen to
the occasion. Our officer, " Pip," said that as the lads
had not had much sleep for the last night or two, he
wanted them fairly early to bed. I helped to mix the
rum punch ; and so, like good fellows, they all retired
quite early ; many, I presume, the more eager to be
ready for any alarm, slid just off the benches and slept
where they were, without undressing.

Shortly after Christmas our squadron moved to
Bacton, to the east of Mundesley, and my own troop
occupied the famous " White House " on the North
Walsham Road. On this move a new trooper was
noticed riding behind the transport. The Colonel,
coming up in the rear, spoke to this fellow, only to find
it was a woman in full Yeoman kit.

This was " Jack Horton's wife." Anyway, wherever
Jack went, the lamb was sure to go. Jack, a regular
world trotter, had come over from the Argentine and

joined the Regiment. She always did night guard if
Jack was on duty, and slept in the stables with him,
but, unfortunately, like a lot of modern women, she
wanted to be treated like a man-chum and like a lady
as well. She annoyed me considerably once, as, forgetting her presence, I snapped out an oath at somebody.

" I'm surprised at you talking like that in front of
a lady," she exclaimed.

I explained that I could only judge by her be-
haviour, and thus it was easy for me to have made a
mistake.

About this time both she and Jack and the giant
farrier Gillingham disappeared mysteriously from the
squadron, and apparently no enquiries were made.

Fear of a German invasion had subsided, but as
early as February, 1915, the Zeppelins could be heard
and seen over the Norfolk coast. Training was indeed
rigorous, but life was very pleasant, and as the spring
began to break the Regiment spent whole days on
lengthy reconnaissances of the whole countryside.

> " Bacton, Trimingham, Knapton, Trunch,
> These four villages lie in a bunch,"

and were familiar villages to everybody. Trunch was
noted for its brewery.

Our squadron leader, who was exceptionally keen
in all things, had a mania for orderliness of the stables.
It is amazing how easy it is to make work for the
troops when apparently everything is in apple-pie
order. Our troop stable-yard had been occupied by
tremendous Norfolk punches, a notable one of which,
from listening to the farm hands we had learned to
call the " Fir King." The straw and dung had not
been shifted for about three years, and was now some
four feet deep. As the weather seemed bright, it was a
good occasion to mess the troops about, so we were
ordered to clear this out, and it took a solid week of
spare time.

Wishing to impress on us the value of tidiness, in a weak moment, the Major told the squadron that its motto should be " N.L.U."—" never leave untidy." The squadron clutched this inspiring motto to its heart ; chalk became at a premium and, before a week was out, there wasn't a fence, stile, gate, house, wall or signpost that didn't bear these cryptic letters " N.L.U."

Corporal B——, the Regiment's champion heavy-weight, was in " bits and pieces " of trouble from time to time.   One or two pigs disappeared, and as B—— was discovered reading Lamb's *Essays*, the inference was obvious.   There was a little row in the " Ship " one evening, and whether she met a typhoon, or a tidal wave, I'm not sure—the landlord could never quite make out how he received such a severe buffeting.

We played a good deal of games, troops and squadron rugger ; and with boxing tournaments and concerts the months passed pleasantly enough.   There were several good songs to sing, as the first batch of war songs were now sung everywhere.   It is not gener-ally realized by the younger generation that the world-famous " Tipperary " was not originally a war song, but happened to be a popular seaside song at the time the War broke out, and thus became the first march-ing song of the old and new armies.   After, " We don't want to lose you, but we think you ought to go," and " On Monday I walk out with a Sailor," etc., we had such goey tunes as, " Hullo, Hullo, who's your lady friend ? " " Sister Susie's sewing shirts for Soldiers," " Are we all here, Yes," and the ever-popular " Gilbert the Filbert, the knut with a K."   I much regret, of course, that the vulgarity of the troops soon parodied this chorus to describe in detail the career of one Charlotte : the rhyme is not hard to imagine.

Such joyous times were coming to a close, for early in April the Regiment entrained at Mundesley Station for Avonmouth, *en route* for Egypt.   The general

kindness and considerate hospitality of the Norfolk folk
during the whole stay of the Regiment in that county
was only equalled by our splendid send-off, when they
loaded us with provisions and smokes galore, as we
moved off for the big adventure.

CHAPTER II

EGYPT

> " That was the time, in Egypt's sunny clime,
> Reading Sunday papers in an E. P. tent.
> Too hot to work, we couldn't find a Turk,
> So we played ' Crown and Anchor '
> Till our piastres all were spent."

THE main body of the Regiment rested in sheds three days at Avonmouth, and then embarked on the s.s. *Nile*. My own troop, however, with one other, and details, walked straight from the train on to the s.s. *Crispin*, or *Crippen*, as she was soon called, to take charge of about six hundred horses.

If you apply for a job to sell button-hooks to-day they'll require to know what experience you've had ; if none whatsoever, you'll soon be like the lady in the ballad, "selling matches by the box." When there is a war, however, you get all your experience by doing all the damn silly things once—" Once, my ducky, and only once," as Kipling says. Not a single one of our officers, non-com. officers, or rankers, had ever loaded up a horse-boat before, so you can imagine those six hundred horses were not enticed aboard the *Crippen* without considerable difficulty.

She was a small boat, and had been used, so we were told, as a South American cattle boat. The whole of the top, first, second and third decks were fitted up with narrow stalls, 3 ft. 6 in. wide at the most ; the passage-ways were very narrow, and the sloping gang-ways from one deck to another very deep. Each horse, fresh, frisky and frightened, on a head-stall only, had

45

to be run up a gangway, along a deck passage, down a gangway, along another narrow passage and then backed into a stall, which his hips would just go through if you steered him carefully.

The officers were all arguing as to which horses should go on the bottom deck, and which should have the serener air of the top deck, but somehow or other with the help of " brute force and b——y ignorance," those horses were soon all stalled, and with eighty souls to attend them the boat sailed early next morning. Of that eighty men, there were, say, ten to give orders, ten to hang about in an advisory capacity, such as farriers and veterinary staff; ten to look after the ten who gave the orders, ten for ship's routine, and the remainder really to do any work. There was, of course, no grooming to be done, as the horses were packed so tightly together; but every horse had to be watered separately, feeds had to be prepared, and hay packed in hay-nets—like ladies' hair-nets—so that by the time the whole shipload had been watered, fed and hayed-up, it was time to start feeding again.

The bugle sounded almost continuously for something or other all day, and of course, among so few, the night-guard duties were heavy indeed. Moreover, as the horse-boat of the Warwick Yeomanry had been torpedoed just behind us, we travelled without lights at night; which added immensely to our difficulties, for all the portholes had to be closed, and thus it became terribly hot and stuffy below decks after sundown.

Although we had a roughish passage in the Bay, there was no time to be sea-sick on the *Crippen*. They fed us very well with rich, thick Irish stew for breakfast—just one morning I didn't seem to like the look of it; but abstinence from that meal, and a " belly-full " of work all the morning, made the " belly-full " of food at midday welcome.

At Gibraltar we were surrounded by fussy little

naval boats enquiring into our credentials, but after an hour or so were allowed to proceed.

It had all been a wonderful voyage for one who had never left England's shores before ; and I shall never forget the magnificence of that first sunset in the Mediterranean. A slight mist had arisen on the water, and as the sun sank astern in a track of golden glitter, the mountains on the Spanish coast reflected ever-deepening shades of red, orange, mauve and purple, which darkened further into indigo after the sun had gone down.

A day out from Gibraltar a curious illness was contracted by several of the horses. They went off their feed, and developed rapidly a kind of pneumonia, which in many cases proved fatal within twenty-four hours.

It was pitiful to watch some of the best-loved horses in the Regiment taken suddenly with this disease. The symptoms were lack of appetite, a high temperature, a glassy eye and a gasping for breath. Very few horses thus afflicted recovered, and the veterinary staff and the farriers were soon desperately overworked in devotedly nursing their sick charges.

The cause of it was the fœtid heat below decks, and the lack of a clear stream of fresh air through all parts of the vessel. Many of the horses had their heads very near the engine-rooms, and it was in this part of the boat that the greatest fatalities occurred. Throughout the journey, owing to the narrow nature of the stalls, and the general crowding of the horses on the boat, no attempt had been made to clear any of the dung, and the gases from this, accentuated by the heat, may have been a decided contributory factor.

Orders were thus given to clean out the stalls, and for two days we worked continually below decks, stripped to the waist, dripping with perspiration ; breeches, puttees and boots soaked in dung-juice, shovelling horse-dung into baskets by the hundred-weights, hauling them up and emptying them overboard.

Each horse was stood out in a narrow passage way in turn, and his stall thoroughly cleansed and disinfected.

A word of praise for the officers, who, realizing the immensity of the task, readily gave a hand, not with the actual cleaning out, but with the disposal of " the golden balls." It was a sight to see some of them, heavily gloved, hauling up the dung-baskets and slinging the contents overboard. The remarks of the trooper who drew such an eloquent analogy between certain of the junior officers and the material they were handling, if relevant, were hardly in the best of taste.

Another difficult task, and a hateful one, as may very well be imagined, was the disposal of the bodies of the dead horses. There was hardly room for a horse to fall down in its stall as it died, and working in the cramped space it called for great strength to heave the carcases into the passage-ways. If possible we turned the body on its back, for the more easily manœuvring along the gangway to the hatchways, through which the derrick chains could reach it for slinging overboard.

There was a prevalent idea, I believe invented by the farriers, that whisky was good for the sick horses, and several officers, in well-meant endeavours to save their charges, gave half-bottles of whisky to the farrier-sergeants to administer as draughts. A farrier-sergeant, Bert, who always had the suspicion of a twinkle, agreed that this was very kind and thoughtful of them. I asked him once if he really thought it did the horses any good. " Yes," he said, " but you have to be careful not to give it 'em too strong like, I'm very particular about that myself," and he would stroll away muttering something about what sort of a " b——y fool " he'd be if he wasted damned good whisky down half-dead 'uns' throats.

These frequent sea-burials were a melancholy sight, as men who understand know that horses have their

YEOMANRY DIVISION MARCHING ACROSS SALT LAKE PLAIN
Middlesex Yeomen in foreground on Chocolate Hill.

DEAD MAN'S GULLY, SUVLA

characters as well as humans, and some of our very best pals were dumped into the waters of the Mediterranean.

The trip was a hard one indeed, but great physical labour brings added joy to the brief periods of rest allowed. We usually had two hours off in the afternoons, and it was just sheer bliss to lie half-naked on the fo'c'sle deck in the glorious sun with all muscles relaxed ; or seated upon the anchor chains, watch the porpoises playing in the bow-spray as it formed and broke into faery chains of white ladies dancing in the sunshine.

I could enthuse over this, my first Mediterranean trip, but as this is to be a war yarn and not a rhapsody —on with the " muttons."

The good ship *Crippen* sailed into Valletta Harbour, and after an hour or two of back-chat with the bum-boat vendors of Eastern shawls and vases, which could have been won on Hampstead Heath for breaking a clay pipe in an old man's mouth, it was learned that we required a little coal.

A lighter came alongside with about fifty tons of coal, and about a hundred of the noisiest and dirtiest dagoes to load it. I've never heard such a crowd of chattering monkeys in my life, and what with the petty disputes, and the general lack of orderliness, we were fortunate to get the ship away by nightfall.

Malta was a strongly fortified garrison at this time, and it was a memorable sight to watch the twenty or thirty searchlights that flashed from all parts of the town to light us out of the Harbour Bar.

The sickness amongst the horses increased, and by the time we reached Alexandria no less than thirty-two had been thrown to Davy Jones.

Imagine our delight as the boat neared the shore, and we saw the desert for the first time ; passed the old Napoleonic forts in Aboukir Bay, where Nelson had fought his famous Battle of the Nile, passed the Pharos, and into the kaleidoscopic harbour of

D

Alexandria. The harbour was full of craft of every kind ; French and Italian warships, and of supreme interest to us—hospital boats full of wounded Australian and British soldiers from the Dardanelles.

The day following our main troopship, the *Nile*, steamed into Alexandria and disembarkation began. Unseasoned as we were, we found the heat terrific, and here a mistake, possibly from over-keenness on the part of those in command, caused the Regiment unnecessary hardship, pain and subsequent sickness. Instead of waiting until the evening, the Regiment was paraded at noon,—out of condition,—in full kit, leading two horses apiece that had had no exercise for nearly a fortnight ; we marched a full ten miles to the open desert at Sidi Bishr, where we had to get to work at once to lay a camp on the seashore.

This long march, under unaccustomed conditions, took its measure of the men ; for in a few days dozens were badly down with dysentery. It was a pitiful sight to see men who had evacuated some twenty times a day lying almost beside the latrine pails, as they had insufficient strength to trust themselves further afield. I experienced a bad turn of this myself, and know of nothing which will sap away the vitality so quickly and cause such excruciating stomach pains as dysentery. Our Medical Officer, Captain Bristow, performed wonders of endurance during this first fortnight at Sidi Bishr, and it was largely owing to his sympathetic care, added to the natural cheeriness of the men, that the Regiment so soon regained its strength.

At this camp, when fit enough, we bathed daily in the Mediterranean, many of the men taking sun-baths to their cost, for an hour's nakedness would produce water blisters for a week. In the evening, by donkey and train, we visited the town of Alexandria. Well-known sounds at this time were the shrill, " Pip, pip, Sidi Bishr " of the tram-conductors' Christmas-cracker whistles, and the " Donkey goood—Donkey Quaiss "

of the Arab who fain would loan you a milk-white ass
for the last mile into camp.

In about a fortnight's time we entrained for Moascar, an open desert camp on the outskirts of the
charming little village of Ismalia on the Suez Canal.
Only single tents were issued at first, and with the
thermometer sometimes reaching 120 degrees in the
shade, the excessive heat was a considerable hardship.
The Colonel soon, however, made arrangements for
the men's greater comfort, and as the process of ac-
climatization advanced, life became very pleasant
indeed.

Réveille at 3.30 a.m. with parades between 4.30
and 5.30 ; then morning stables, and with the exception of guards we were done for the day. The Sharpshooters had lines adjacent to us, and many new
friendships were made with this Regiment that became further cemented throughout the War.

A squadron of white Arab stallions was pitched
near by for this short period, and they caused us endless trouble, not only by their breaking loose and
paying unofficial visits to our mares, but also by the
consequent jealousy engendered in our own horses.
This episode was duly registered by the inclusion of a
special verse in that popular riding ditty of the time :

> " We are Fred Karno's Army,
>   The ragtime cavalry,
>   We cannot ride, we cannot shoot,
>   What b——y use are we ?
>   And when we get to Berlin,
>   The Kaiser he will say,
>   Hock ; hock ; mien Gott,
>   What a b——y fine lot,
>   Are the London Yeomanry."

Try this to the tune of " The Church's One Founda-
tion," for that's the air to which custom decreed it
should always be sung.

During the heat of the forenoon, and after lunch,
many, instead of sleeping, sat in the rush-matting huts,

and played bridge, poker or patience. Bathing in the Suez was extremely popular, but the silent night bathe was the most joyous of all.

To take a towel, and a companion, and stroll off through the silent date palms, down to where Lake Timsah lay gleaming 'neath a golden moon. To slip silently into the water, and swim side by side to a sand-bank half a mile from the shore, to feel the cooling salt water along the flanks so lately tried by heat of sun. There to stretch one's length in the shallows, prone in the lazy ripples on the sand, and look back at the palm-shadowed shore—this was bathing fit for Grecian gods.

Back through the silent town, past the marshes by the sweet-water canal, where the constant croaking of a myriad frogs made such a merry cackle ; through the acacia-scented groves, watching the play of shadows on the white stone houses ; through the native quarter, with mysterious glints of flickering light and muttered hummings breaking forth from shuttered hovels ; to the fitful flares of the camp— the shouts of laughter from the canteen ; the rattle of dice around the candle-lit " Crown and Anchor " boards, and the shrill chirping of the thousand crickets in the rush-built huts and bivouacs.

The mention of " crickets " reminds me of a little midnight scene I witnessed which has caused me many a laugh. There was a transport driver named T—— who slept in a little rush-matting " bivy," which he was very proud of having constructed himself. He was a man of hefty chest and arms, and a very pug-nacious face, with temperament to match. Having rolled his way home from the canteen, he had settled down to sleep, only to find slumber impossible for the presence of an odd cricket or two somewhere in the matting. As I watched, I saw his ponderous form come out in a little short shirt, leaving his posterior well bared to the desert breezes, and on all fours, go groping round and round his " bivy " with a slipper in his hand. After some moments I emerged from the shadow.

" What's up, T——, lost something ? " I said.

" No, but by God, I'll not sleep till I've killed this b——y linnet," he sleepily complained.

To help with the roughest work of the camp, and to do a deal of the mucking-out, a number of Arab syce were attached to each troop, and quartered in an enclosure some distance from the horse-lines. It was amazing to see the devotion these fellows displayed to any particular N.C.O. or trooper, and also to the horses themselves. They loved to be allowed to help with the horses and saddlery, and would work like the devil for a piastre. They also did washing for the men, and did it tolerably well and cheaply until they began to be spoilt by over-generosity.

These syce, with a few pedlars, were allowed in the lines, and prided themselves tremendously on their power of assimilation of the English language. To hear some of their conversations—a mixture of Arab patois, and English swear-words, was very amusing. The fruit vendors cried their wares throughout the lines, " O-rang-ges, O-rang-ges," " Grape-pes—good for de stummick " ; " Eggs-e-cook-e-breed," followed, and then the newsboys, " Tim-mes of Egypt—Bludder gooder news too-da-ey." Whether the fortunes of England waxed or waned, it was always " Gooder news " to him, and I remember on another part of the canal, just after the Battle of Jutland, a lad crying— " Tim-mes of Egypt—Bludder gooder news too-da-ey —Bludda-gooder news too-day-ey—Lordy Kitchinner dead—Five Engleesh ships zunk—Bludder gooder news too-da-ey."

I can vouch for the following illustrative yarn, although through constant telling it has become fairly well known. Abdul, a syce, with ragged flowing robes and naked feet, was leading four horses to water on head-stalls only. The water was half a mile away, the horses had stood patiently with the afternoon heat on their backs, and were now both rampantly thirsty, and thirstily rampant. Abdul, with many curses, had consistently managed to restrain them, when in spite of his tugging and swearing, as they neared the water-troughs, one of them reared badly, and came down full force with his fore-feet on Abdul's naked toes. This was the last straw. With all the concentrated fury at his command, Abdul looked up snarling with rage and pain, and hissed in the horse's face, "You-you-you-b——y liar."

The syces were, at rock-bottom, good fellows. I had one attached to me, and by mingling little kind-nesses with absolute justice, and severity if necessary, Mustapha Ali became the most devoted servant one could wish for. He would attempt to anticipate my every desire, and would walk many miles a day to provide me with fresh water for washing and drinking purposes.

Bert, our squadron farrier-sergeant, a real tough 'un, with a playful sense of humour, was a man who knew his game from A to Z. Well over sixty years of age to-day, he is still working at the forge, drinking his pints and singing his way home at nights to start again at five o'clock next morning. Hats off, some of you drawling, thoroughly bored young moderns ! Bert, as I was about to tell you, shared a rush hut near the forge with Jim Bly, the Regimental Farrier-Major. Towards the end of a hot afternoon, Jim, portly, slow of movement, and rather dignified, pulled a dirty pair of khaki slacks from under his sack bed, surveyed them, rolled them up carefully and threw them down.

He called across to Bert who lay watching, " Bert, there's no b——y syce about, and I've got to go round with the Colonel in the morning, so I suppose I'll have to wash these b——y slacks myself."

Jim toddled off with two buckets to get water from the troughs more than half a mile away, and came back puffing and blowing from the exertion. He boiled the water in a copper by the forge, and taking up his slacks from the bed, gave them a thorough doing.

Bert was still recumbent, a half-interested spectator, listening to his mutterings—" B——y fine thing when a Farrier-Major has to wash his own slacks, 'cos the damn niggers 'a got a holiday, ain't it, Bert ? "

" Yes, Jim ; still, you'll make a better job of it."

" Not 'arf, I won't, I don't 'arf do a thing when I start it."

" Don't often start, do you, Jim ? "

" What d'ye mean ? "

" Nothing, Jim, I only mean you don't often wash your own trousers."

" 'Course I b——y well don't."

Jim rinsed them, and hung them carefully in the breeze to dry, then lay down again to restore his energy after such violent exercise. In an hour or so he arose, yawning, to survey his handiwork.

" Blimy, Bert, they ain't 'arf shrunk. Why, they must be miles too short—here, look at 'em—'arf a mo' —I hadn't got any white buttons on the top of mine. What's the game ? "

Bert came to inspect them himself.

" Jim, you ain't 'arf a pal—you've washed my old 'uns." Bert's chuckles nearly convulsed him.

" 'Ow the 'ell did I come to make that mistake ? " said the crestfallen Jim in dismay.

" Damned if I know," answered Bert, as, still chuckling, he folded the slacks and placed them away in his kit.

He had, of course, simply put Jim's back under the bed, and substituted his own whilst Jim had gone for the water.

If you're ever in the York Road district, call and see old Bert, and get him to tell you this yarn. The tears in his eyes, and the chuckles in his throat, are good to behold and hear.

The concerts were a great feature of camp life here.

Let me describe a typical one held in the gardens of Ismalia.

Behold the stage improvised from carpeted messing-tables, a background of Arabic tapestries, a canopy erected for the occasion, and tastefully decked with the flags of the Allies lit by the soft seductive glow from a hundred Japanese lanterns. The stalls, some hundred deck-chairs for the officers and their civilian friends ; the pit and the balcony are composed entirely of forms, and in the lounge standing room only.

The audience, a sea of bronzed faces, the dark effect of the khaki interspersed with splashes of white, where the sailors from the battleship out upon the lake mingle with the sister service, and here and there on the outskirts of the throng, the furtive face of an Indian beneath a coloured turban. The orchestra— a popular sergeant-major at the piano, and a flight-sergeant with a violin, burst into the overture, a medley of London music-hall songs. With infinite ease, one tune wends its way into another, and is taken up by the voices from a thousand throats. Dear old songs ; carolled out daily in the streets of London by the tuneless barrel-organ, how strange they sound out here ! As some haunting lilt is taken up, there seems a far-away timbre in the voices, the air is pregnant with visions ; imagination wafts one back to the Homeland. The overture ends ; the spell is broken, and all attention is given to a husky trooper, with a rich baritone voice, who renders, " England, Mother England." A sergeant-major gives us, " I hear you calling me," and gets the boys all groggy ; he will sing " Parted " for an encore. They are in a more sentimental mood than ever ; so follows Gunboat M——, looking little enough like the Mayor of Barnet at this stage of his career. From somewhere he has procured an old " lion-tamer " tunic, and made up with wig and flour paste, representing an old Yeoman of eighty, gives us his latest parody on that celebrated

" Long live the King." The last lines of each verse
and the chorus are sung with gusto :

> " We still kept the old flag a-flying
> A damned long way from the front.
> Yes, we still kept the old fly a-flagging,
> A damned long way from the front.

Chorus—

> That was the time, in Egypt's sunny clime,
> Reading Sunday papers in our E. P. tent ;
> Too hot to work, we couldn't find a Turk,
> So we played ' Crown and Anchor ' till
> Our piastres all were spent."

Then Noel Kilby, one of the most popular and hand-
somest sergeants in the Regiment, gives us the " M.I."
or " War," by Edgar Wallace. (This is the first time
I have heard of him, who was later to become the
national novelist.) Two of the crew from the battleship keep us merry and the audience is led through
" Old MacDougall had a farm-eih-i-eih-i-o." Follows
myself with imitations of well-known characters in
the Regiment—the audience is duly merciful—and
then, the " Star " of the evening. An elderly subaltern
with the heart of a schoolboy, garbed as an out-of-
work tragedian, such as one may find in many a Fleet
Street tavern to-day, recites " A Fallen Star " with
a pathos which is human yet never sentimental. In
answer to the thunders of applause, he replies in
lighter vein with that old Vaudeville favourite, " I like
you in velvet," and finally, to establish his versatility
beyond doubt, he impersonates Harry Lauder in
" Roaming in the Gloaming." Everyone votes him a
" perfect knut," and to judge by his smile as he leaves
the platform he has pleased himself as much as he
pleased the audience.

The last turn of the evening—will he oblige ? —calls
and calls for him again and again,—yes, he rises from
beside the Brigadier, Lord Denbigh, in command of
the H.A.C., will sing " Alouette " and, as he swings
his arms for us to come in with the chorus, we just do,

and he knows what a fine sportsman we think him to be.

At a smaller concert at which a certain " Captain " was in the chair, I was asked to give imitations of the officers. The Captain complained rather naïvely that I had omitted to give imitations of any of those present. I promised to rectify this in the second half, and gave an imitation of a court-martial of a lad who played in the " Manchester town band "—bringing in only one of the officers, the Captain in question himself. I don't think he found his request number quite as humorous as he had expected it to be.

One of these concerts was useful to me in another way ; as the *Egyptian Gazette* accepted an article from me describing life on the canals and the concerts in particular, and sent me a cheque for eighty piastres, which, with my week's winnings at bridge, enabled me to have just a short leave to Cairo—regimental pass from Friday morning to Monday night.

So now to El Khariyeh. I shall never forget the intense excitement of that train journey from Ismalia to Cairo. Here I must introduce you to " Mick,"— we were corporals together and were afterwards to become firmer friends as fellow-sergeants,—who accompanied me. Mick was the son of a major in the regular Army ; had been born, as it were, on the Barrack Square ; and though a civil servant, in civvy life, had an intense passion for the Army in his blood, and the histories of all the famous regiments at his tongue-tip. He was Irish, and therefore temperamental, but a most lovable companion, with a keen sense of the ludicrous, in fact, I have never seen him so happy as when someone else was ridiculing— usually myself, I'm afraid—any of his little vagaries or idiosyncrasies. I can see his mouth puckering into a smile now as, at a later date, I enter a newly constructed " shack " of his, and being amazed to see it, tastefully decorated with reproductions of oil-paintings, ejaculate " You art-collecting little bastard."

Remember we had seen nothing of Egypt as yet—just a fortnight's sickness at Alexandria and then to be stuck out on the desert at Moascar !

It was July and the hottest season of the year, the train was simply stifling, the hot glare of the desert on either side almost painful to the eyes and the dust an abomination. Then the wonderful change after that typically Eastern town of Zag-a-Zig, as the journey took us down the cultivated valley to the Nile. Our intense interest in the crops of " dhura," the little irrigation canals, and the ancient water-wheels, the " sekiyeh," and the " shadoof," primitive contrivances for raising water from one level to another.

Mick asked me what the " fellaheen " were, and, not really knowing, I talked a lot of pseudo-learned rot about the origins of Eastern races. Then with heads craned well out of the window, we saw in the distance the white city of Cairo set in emerald-green ; —the hills of Mokattom, the minarets of the citadel, the domes and towers of this wonder city of the ancient world.

American globe-trotters were nothing to Mick and I. With what earnestness we set out to fill ourselves with Cairo in the short time of our leave. We visited the Citadel with its magnificent mosque, the Mosque of Mohammed Ali. We wondered at the golden mosaics worked into rays of the setting sun, the pulpit of gold and ebony, and the glorious richness and beauty of the roof and windows. We heard the story of the architect, of the years he had spent to build such beauty, and how, on its completion, his eyes had been put out, so that he should never create such another. We gazed at the stone walls and lapped up the yarn of the Mamelukes. Mohammed Ali had invited the lesser chiefs to a banquet and, after feasting them well, as they passed below the upper wall, they had found themselves set upon from above with boiling lead and stones, and had all been killed,—save one,—who jumped his horse over that fearsome height. The horse had been smashed to pieces, but he had escaped unscathed. I care not whether these stories are true, the guide told them to us—I tell them to you—and anyhow, they were just the sort of stories that should have been told of such a wonderpile as the Citadel.

We visited the Mosque of Ali Hassan and the Blue Mosques; we saw the holes in the walls from Napoleon's cannon and the spaces where the golden doors had been before that military genius had stolen them for the melting-pot.

We went to the museum, surely one of the most interesting in the world, and we visited the Coptic quarters and the Coptic Church, and saw the cave where the young Christ lay when the Virgin brought him to Egypt to escape the Herodian massacre.

Then the beautiful Ghersirah Gardens, the Kasr-el-Nil Bridge and the Zoo. Through the old bazaars of the Mouski, with the scents of spices, coffee, perfumes, herbs and humans reeking in our nostrils.

The long journey out to Mena to gaze at the Sphinx, to marvel at the Pyramids, and, of course, to ride on the camel—everyone does that. To enter the first Pyramid by its slide, the stones worn smooth by countless " bottoms," to be taken through those weird low passages to visit the King's chamber, the eerie climb in the dark to the Queen's chamber, the feeling of the eyes of the Arab guides behind you, the extra " backsheesh " for them to light magnesium ribbon so that you can see the alabaster.

Back to the hotel, a real course dinner, served with fresh figs for dessert and wine, and real sheets to sleep in—a happy short leave indeed.

And now a little episode to deal with sex. Gather around some of you modern young snivel-noses, something for you at last. Come with your waisted coats and silly side-whiskers; come from your cocktail drinking and your petting parties, and listen unto me. The soldier is always deadly serious and sentimental about one woman on earth, and his general idea of sex apart from that " the one and only," is that sex is something of a joke. This may be a wrong point of view, but, at least, he doesn't flop about on cushions in an underground " studio," and attitudinize about art and the originality of his outlook. If he feels the promptings of desire, he doesn't begin to psycho-analyse himself and write a book about his silly emotions as if they were something new—as if Chaucer, Fielding, Sterne and Smollett had never lived. No ! my exquisites—remember your origins—whenever you're feeling more " frightfully bucked " or more " positively priceless " than usual ; hang on to Darwin, and don't forget that every 'bus that rumbles homeward down the Strand, is nothing more or less than " a waggon-load of monkeys." No, baggy trousers, the soldier knows what's wrong with him, gets it off his chest and thinks of something fresh like the smell of nice clean stables.

But now to the story. There was a street in Cairo running off old Rue Kamel, parallel with the Esbekieh Gardens, which was one continuous row of brothels. The street was called the " Wassau " and the incident I have to tell of was known throughout Egypt as " the battle of the Wassau." Now, the brothels were licensed houses and the women were supposed to have held certificates of cleanliness from a doctor. One side of the street was bawdy houses, and the other side low drinking saloons. A soldier usually got " tight " before crossing the road ; no man in his sane mind could enter a brothel stone-cold sober. A large number of Australian infantry encamped near Cairo, on their way to Gallipoli, had the misfortune to be rendered inefficient by the contraction of venereal disease. There had been considerable internal trouble, in several battalions, in consequence, and whether the whole thing was preconceived or whether a number of soldiers acted on the spur of the moment, one could never determine. Suffice it to say that on the Satur-day evening of my leave in Cairo, some five hundred

" Cobbers " came down the " Wassau," smashed up a
few of the saloons and then raided the brothels. Every
article of furniture, chairs, tables, bedding, tawdry
hangings, etc., from the houses was pitched from the
windows into the street below. Pianos in particular
were very popular—a small piano dropped from the
third storey into the road makes a good row and a
really decent smash-up. Aussies appeared at every
window throwing clothes, china, anything movable,
amidst the frantic screams of the madams and the
frightened cries of the girls. Many of the girls were
dashing about the streets in various stages of dis-
habille, and the whole scene was a complete sacking.
When the street was well filled with household goods,
the whole lot was set fire to, many of the houses
catching alight as well, and the soldiers were beating
off the hysterical, screaming women as the engines
arrived to deal with the conflagration. A native fire-
engine breaks into a " trot "—going downhill.

Then the authorities did a foolish thing. Instead
of turning out Australian troops to create order again
—they summoned English military police and patrols
to deal with the situation. Now, there is always a
certain amount of latent jealousy between English
and Colonial troops on both sides, and naturally the
Australians became very incensed when British troops
were sent to quell the disturbance. There was a rare
set-to—the saloons were emptied and bottles were flying all over the place. Order was eventually restored
and the men were got back to camp—but the whole
affair had two unfortunate sequences. Leave was
greatly restricted and troops had to be off the streets
earlier, but, worse still, a bad feeling was created
between the English and Australian troops which took
a considerable time, with many tentative overtures
from either side, to eradicate.

It was at Moascar that the Regiment first made
the acquaintance of Bilarzhiosis—introduced to us
through Regimental Orders. It appeared that the

waters of the Sweet Water Canal were inhabited by this little gentleman in germ form, so that if you drank thereof, Bill took such a fancy to you, that he could eat away into your skin in his thousands, and eventually put you "clean out."

Corporal B——'s favourite recreation here was playing ninepins with native policemen, his bag of four tarbooshes in one evening holding the record.

The troops had been inclined to restiveness, wondering when on earth the Higher Command would find them something to do, instead of the everlasting training. Popular belief was that the War would be finished by Christmas, 1915, and here it was August and the Regiment had never been near enough to battle to hear a gun. Imagine then the intense excitement, when on August 1st the Regiment was ordered to draw infantry equipment, and to proceed dismounted to the Dardanelles. Troops were made into platoons and the bandolier and belt gave place to web equipment and entrenching tool ; and, everywhere, great excitement and keenness prevailed.

Three days later, however, the order was countermanded, and the infantry equipment hastily sent back to store. This disappointment almost caused a riot in camp ; such was the amazing keenness of everyone to get into action that the veto created scenes of considerable disorder. The Colonel, realizing the temper of his men, ordered an impromptu concert with free beer, and this only partially pacified the troops. Towards midnight a mock funeral was held, at which the body of the London Yeomanry was buried, and an effigy of the General who countermanded the order was burned. "Fred Karno's Army" was sung all through the night, with a special verse about the G.O.C. canal forces. This was a real riotous night, but by next morning the men saw things more philosophically. As one old Boer War veteran put it, "Can't understand you lads, you'll get all the b——y fighting you want afore this show's over." However, about a week later, infantry equipment was again drawn from the Quartermaster, and this time it was the real business indeed ; for orders were given for the Regiment to leave half a squadron and details with the horses, the remainder to entrain that evening for Alexandria and the Peninsula itself.

That night in camp was a real " barney "—those of you who have lapped up stories of the reluctance of Regiments to be ordered to the Front should have witnessed the scenes of jubilation among our boys. The canteen did a record trade, including four barrels of beer p——, pardon, " borrowed " from under the brailling by Corporal B——, three of which were consumed down the lines and the other he had considerately given to the camp guard and was thus only half emptied ; the guard consisting of a mere dozen men, some of whom were on duty. And thus amid scenes of great rejoicing the London Yeomanry left Moascar to go forward. " On, on to the breach, dear friends."

CHAPTER III

GALLIPOLI

"All the Germans in Berlin Town
Couldn't put those six Australians down."

THE story of Gallipoli really belongs to the Australians. It is their epic ; a wondrous story of undaunted heroism and a surmounting of innumerable difficulties by sheer naked manhood.

It is not my purpose to discuss this splendid failure, either in its political aspect or its military significance. It is not for me to cavil at the misdirected naval engagement of the Dardanelles, which gave the Turks preliminary warning of our design ; nor to complain of the lack of support from those at home, who would not believe in the efficiency of the venture. These aspects of the campaign have been fully chronicled by Mr. H. W. Nevison, and the General commanding the expedition, Sir Ian Hamilton himself.

Nor, again, is it for me to pay tribute to that wonderful body of men, the Anzacs, who gave the flower of their manhood, and the beauty of their youth, with a jest and a song, in this desperate adventure. For all who would read the glorious story of their cheerful courage, their indomitable perseverance, their comradeship and resolve, I commend them to John Masefield's *Gallipoli*, where the soul of the Anzacs is treated with the poetic dignity it demands, and so richly deserves. From the heroic first landing of the British troops from the flanks of the *River Clyde*, like the Trojan horse of old, to the last devastating storm and the final miraculous evacuation, it is there portrayed, with all Masefield's magnificent command of the beauty of our language, that he who runs may read.

This is purely the story of war as seen by a Yeoman and thus, although we were only in at the death, just in time for the last great attempt to break through the impregnable Turkish lines, it is of life on the Peninsula as we saw it that one would wish to tell.

The good ship *Caledonia* took us, and several other Yeomanry regiments, from Alexandria to Mudros harbour. The harbour was one conglomeration of every type of craft imaginable. Battleships towered above tugs, cruisers rubbed bulwarks with Thames paddle-steamers, there were lighters and barges galore. The Russian cruiser *Askold* with its five funnels created considerable interest, and was soon dubbed " Packet of Woodbines."

On board the *Caledonia* it was found that one trooper, Leybourne, well known for his superlative genius in management of the " Crown and Anchor " board, although he had been detailed to stay with the horses, had managed to " Stow-a-way." He was paraded before the Colonel, who, with characteristic naïveté, told him he would " let him off this time, but he was not to do it again."

The following afternoon the Regiment was transferred to the H.M.S. *Doris*, and a perilous transfer it seemed to most of us. For a landsman to clamber up the steep bulwark of a battleship by means of a " Jacob's " ladder, in full pack with rifle slung, was a hazardous performance. This little cruiser was crowded with no fewer than 2000 men, but many of us managed to sleep somehow, to find ourselves at dawn, on the 18th of August, inside the world-famous Suvla Bay.

Everything was very peaceful, with neither sight nor sound of war, and it was hard to imagine that on those grim scrub-covered hills ahead were Turkish battlements and trenches forming a formidable posi-

tion. We were transferred from the ship to the shore
in the dark and vile-smelling hold of an iron lighter,
expecting every minute to be blown to pieces by a
shell. Johnny Turk did let fly at us with a dozen or
so of the best, from the gun we got to know as
" Whistling Rufus," but as we landed they were over-
ranged and fell into the sea.

Let it now be clearly understood that, from the
moment of landing on Gallipoli, there was neither a
place nor time when we were out of range of the
enemy's guns and snipers—in fact, the so-called rest
areas by the beaches were often more dangerous than
the line itself.

We advanced a way inshore, and attempted to dig
ourselves into some sort of position under cover of the
hills. As night fell it was a wonderful sight ; the
ships' guns in the bay, together with the field batteries
on shore, opened fire on the Turkish positions on the
Anafarta Hills, ringed semi-crescent-like before us.

The next day there were ration, ammunition and
water fatigues to be carried out on the beach, exposed
to the attentions of the long-range Turkish guns. The
beach presented a scene of ceaseless activity : the un-
loading of stores, guns, ammunition, mails, etc. ;
dozens of half-clad stalwart, bronzed Australians,
with mule carts and ambulance waggons, working away
at the various dumps, moving the " olla podrida " of
war from place to place.

Out in the bay were battleships and monitors,
flat lighters and tugs, apparently paying little heed
to the occasional shells dropped among them.

On Friday, 20th, at about 8 p.m., we began a long
and tedious march along the beach, alternately over
loose sand and shingle, till we came under cover of the
small hill known as Lala Baba, and early next morning 'bathed in the sea ; to remove both dust and
soreness after the night's journey.

At about 2 o'clock on the afternoon of August 21st we
paraded with full equipment, an extra hundred rounds

of ammunition, two sandbags, a pick or shovel. It
was understood that an advance was to be made, but
none of us had any idea either of the general scheme
of the attack, or our own particular objective. One
thing was pretty obvious to all, that, in order for us to
go forward, we were to march across two miles of open
country without a vestige of cover, in broad daylight.
They kindly told us that we need not take any notice
of the Turkish shells, as most of them were " duds."

In about half an hour's time the battle had apparently begun, for every ship in the harbour, and
every gun on shore, sent forth its hymn of hate to the
Anafarta Hills.

The bombardment lasted only a half-hour, and was
described by Sir Ian Hamilton in his report as " very
inadequate in duration but the most our ammunition
would run to," and then the Division began to move.

To quote again from the report, " The Yeomanry
were also Corps reserve at Lala Baba, where they were
safe. But when they advanced, supposing they had
to, they would have to cross a perfectly open plain
under shell-fire. This was the special blot on the
scheme, but there was no getting away from it."

Immediately, the main attack was launched from
Chocolate Hill, so we moved out in echelon of troops
across the Salt Lake plain. If most of the Turkish
shells were supposed to be " duds," they must have
borrowed some from elsewhere, for we were met with
a murderous fire of shrapnel and high-explosives. We
were led by Captain Watson with Mr. Wedgewood
Benn acting Adjutant beside him. The officers
marched straight on, carrying walking-sticks, and
amongst the ranks several mouth-organs were heard.
Here and there a bursting shell would take toll of
several men—one shell alone accounting for eight.
There was no stopping for the wounded, and so the
march went on in perfect order, until, close on Chocolate Hill, the order was given to double. At the time
there was some suggestion that we were being used as

CAMP BY THE SUEZ CANAL

LAFONE'S CORNER, SINAI DESERT

cannon fodder, to divert the attention of the Turkish gunners ; and in the light of after knowledge it certainly seems absurd that, as reserves, we could not have crossed the plain under cover of darkness the night before. To lose one quarter of your reserves by shell-fire is by no means good Staff work.

I will not dwell—in the modern style—on the severe sufferings of the wounded. The heat was intense, and the warm air over the Salt Lake accentuated the craving for water. It was a long time before stretcher-bearers could be got to them, and thus many died of thirst. A more horrible death still awaited those who attempted to crawl into the scrub by the foothills to get cover from the sun, for the scrub, dried by months of sunshine, was readily set on fire by the shrapnel, and many a poor fellow, suffering in body and mind, saw the sharp-tongued flames creeping towards him, and was finally burnt to death.

A school-chum of mine in the Westminster Dragoons was badly wounded and found cover thus, but was rescued by a stretcher-bearer from the R.A.M.C., and dragged into comparative safety, just before the fire reached him. Turning his eyes up to his rescuer, he found him to be his own fifth-form chum, whom he had not seen since the commencement of the War. The private from the R.A.M.C., realizing that his wounds were fatal, stayed with him all night, and the laddie died in his arms in the early morning.

A Turkish officer, met in Constantinople after the War, said that, " the Division presented a target such as artillerymen thought impossible outside the world of dreams."

Whatever the purpose of the march, and whether or no the sacrifice of such fine human blood was justified, the Yeomen, under heavy fire for the first time, did not let the British Army down. Sir Ian Hamilton's despatch pays an eloquent tribute to the steadiness of all ranks :

" Whilst this fighting was in progress the 2nd

Mounted Division moved out from Lala Baba in open formation to take up a position of readiness behind Yilgin Burnu. During this march they came under a remarkably steady and accurate artillery fire. The advance of these English Yeomen was a sight calculated to send a thrill of pride through anyone with a drop of English blood running in his veins. Such superb martial spectacles are rare in modern war. Ordinarily, it should always be possible to bring up reserves under some sort of cover from shrapnel fire. Here, for a mile and a half, there was nothing to conceal a mouse, much less some of the most stalwart soldiers England had ever sent from her shores. Despite the critical events in other parts of the field, I could hardly take my glasses from the Yeomen ; they moved like men marching on parade. Here and there a shell would take toll of a cluster ; there they lay ; there was no straggling ; the others moved steadily on ; not a man was there who hung back or hurried. But such an ordeal must consume some of the battle-winning, fighting energy of those subjected to it, and it is lucky indeed for the Turks that the terrain, as well as the lack of trenches, forbade us from letting the 2nd Mounted Division loose at close quarters to the enemy without undergoing this previous too heavy baptism of fire."

We were rapidly collected together under the seaward slope of Chocolate Hill and then our objective pointed out to us. The attack on Ismail Oglu Tepe (Hill W) had been repulsed by terrific frontal and enfilading fire ; and we were to go forward to make another attempt at its capture. It must be remembered of the whole of Gallipoli, that every position had to be stormed, as the Turks held the high ground and consequently the strategic points throughout the whole campaign.

We skirted the right flank of the hill until we came to a gap in the hedge, and this we soon found to be well marked by snipers, as the first four through were

shot in the head, and the fifth—a taller man—through
the shoulder. Down on the belly then and crawl for
it ; we then doubled across the open and jumped into
a shallow trench about three feet high. Just like sheep
we followed each other, stooping to gain what little
cover we could ; few having any idea which way we
were to go, or what we were to do. The rattle-rattle
of the machine-guns was incessant, and all the while
a continuous stream of terribly mutilated men, some
walking, some crawling, all cursing and groaning,
squeezed past us.

We then seemed to run from trench to trench, from
bush to bush, from hillock to hillock, several of us
taking cover behind a pile of dead Turks. We could
not see the enemy as a mist was settling on the hills,
we could only guess where his trenches should be, and
more or less aimlessly let off round after round of
ammunition.

When night fell we moved on, and seemed to have
gained our objective, as we were apparently on the
top of the ridge ; here we found ourselves all mixed
up with men of other regiments ; and no one knew
what to do, who was in command, where the enemy
was, or anything about anything, but a desire to sleep.

Many dropped asleep from weariness, and about
1 a.m. the order was given to retire. The Regiment was
thus assembled somehow on a road to the rear and,
with bullets whistling overhead, we started back
across country.

We had continually to jump over shallow and narrow
trenches which were full of wounded men, who cursed
us to hell flames, as we inadvertently stepped on them
or knocked down boulders or loose pieces of earth as
we plundered forward in the darkness. Here and there
we met a lad demented ; his nerves wrecked by wounds
and his last shreds of sanity driven from him by thirst.

Back again, across the Salt Lake Plain we had
crossed with such difficulty the afternoon before, and
even now chance shots from snipers depleted our

ranks ; till, arriving at Lala Baba, we sank down and slept the sleep of the utterly weary.

Thus ended our first battle, and the last big engagement of the Gallipoli campaign. Through the lack of adequate support, and insufficient troops to consolidate the positions gained, another hard-fought venture had failed.

Those who are familiar with the whole story of the campaign will know that three times the key positions of the Peninsula were gained by desperate heroism, only to be given back to the Turks again ; as the G.O.C. had no further troops to throw into the line.

Enough of generalities—to our own particular story.

It was found in the morning that a small party was missing, but they turned up later on. Captain Watson, afterwards D.S.O. and V.C., killed in France, had remained in the firing line all night doing what he could to succour the dying, and the Regimental Medical Sergeant, Sergeant Bird, was out for three days tending those of his wounded who were too badly hit to move. He was afterwards awarded the D.C.M. and, mark you, he richly deserved it.

During the next night, we were marched back again to Chocolate Hill, not across the Salt Lake this time, and here we settled down in trenches, continually digging and bringing up supplies. The trenches for the most part were very shallow, and there were no dug-outs. Johnny treated us to shrapnel fairly continuously and casualties were just pretty frequent.

Water was very scarce and could only be obtained by waiting in a queue at one of the small wells for some hours. A pint a day was the usual ration, and the diet just biscuits and bully, occasionally relieved by our old friend " MacConachie."

For weeks now life was one monotonous drudgery. Stand-to about 3-30 to 5 ; and the rest of the day two hours' digging, two hours' guard, two hours' rest, with occasional listening-patrols and ration and water fatigues into the bargain.

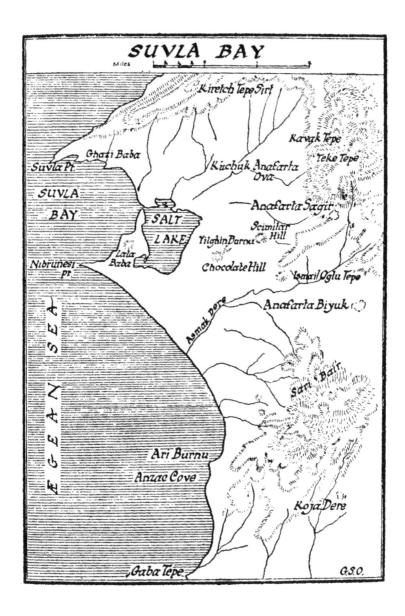

During our rest periods we cooked our own meals—always biscuits and bully, sometimes baked, sometimes raw, sometimes boiled, sometimes mashed; anything to pretend we were having a change.

We became filthy dirty, lice were our constant companions, and, as we could not spare water for shaving, we were soon all " bearded like the pard."

I cannot describe to an ordinary cleanly person the most revolting sensation that a fellow undergoes when first he discovers that he has become the prey of body-lice. I think I was more inclined to be sick at their appearance than at anything I saw or smelt during the whole War. After a time one got quite used to the little pests, and entered into the sport of the daily " louse " with glee.

The heat, the dust and the flies were an abomination. The whole ground to the front was covered with rotting bodies in various stages of decomposition, and the stench of the decaying flesh was nauseating.

Sleep was in two-hour stretches and could only be taken by lying full-length at the bottom of the trench, to be kicked and stepped upon by every officer going his rounds.

Altogether it was a wretched existence and required all one's reserve supply of humour to prevent it " getting you down." The sameness of the diet, the dust, the shortage of the water, took toll of the men through sickness, and many a man who had tried his damnedest to stick it out, was finally evacuated from jaundice or dysentery.

We had a fortnight in reserve trenches by the beach, and here life was much pleasanter. It was more or less safe to walk about singly in the open. There was fresh meat, an occasional egg—a present from the Colonel—and best of all, bathing from the beach.

Those of you who have never been thoroughly dirty of body through no fault of your own, will not appreciate what it means to a man to get a chance of getting clean, after weeks in which dust and sweat have caked together all over the skin, so that every little knock and scratch has turned to a gangrenous septic sore. To us, then, the sea-bathing was a sheer delight, although it could only be undertaken by a few at a time for fear of calling forth wrath from " Whistling Rufus " or " Asiatic Annie."

Back to the front-line trenches again, this time at Tint's Corner, in front of which was the famous Dead Man's Gully. Here the trenches were a little deeper, but were partly under water; there were few dug-outs, and all the discomforts of the previous spell in the front line seemed accentuated.

The days were very hot and the nights were very cold. The drinking water was limited, was chlori-nated, muddy to look at and filthy to taste. In front of the trench in the gully, and up the hill-side were thou-sands of unburied and rotting bodies, lying in fantastic attitudes, there seemed to be at least one a yard, and in many places they were piled into little heaps. The stench from these was appalling, and the flies from all these putrefying corpses came over in their swarms and settled everywhere. At meal-times this was especially unpleasant, one had simply to open a pot of " Pozzy "—jam—to attract them in thousands.

The hardships, the long spells without sleep, the lack of decent food and water, combined with the sapping away of strength from these horrible septic sores, took its toll of the men, and with all the best intentions in the world to see it out,—in fact, most of them held on against approaching illness until they had to be carried down the trenches,—daily, sickness from jaundice, dysentery and malaria overcame them by dozens.

The hospital staff was sadly inadequate in number, though heroic in endeavour, and it was impossible for them to cope with the wounded after an engagement, to say nothing of the constant stream of sick men from the trenches.

In the Battle of Suvla, a chum of mine, Sergeant

Bartlett, was wounded by gunshot in the back of the neck and the base of the skull, a wound near enough to the brain to demand considerable attention. He was taken to the beach by a stretcher-bearer, heavily bandaged by the Field Ambulance and finally found himself lying on his back in the bunk of a hospital ship bound for England. The ship was so crowded and so hopelessly understaffed that his wound was not touched through the whole of the homeward voyage, and he received his first redressing in an English hospital. He is alive and well to-day, but I quote this as an example of the difficulties with which this little force on the Peninsula had to contend.

Searching the corners of one's memory thoroughly, it is yet difficult to find any humours in this part of the campaign—there was precious little funny about Gallipoli.

And yet, the men did laugh, chiefly at their own misfortunes which were manifold, and throughout the worst of it there was always someone who could raise a smile.

Two well-known Tommy anecdotes which owe their origin to " Gallipoli " may well be repeated here.

There is the celebrated story of the illiterate writing home to his inamorata and seeking etymological advice from a more erudite companion.

" Bill, how do you spell ' fought ' ? "

" Which one d'ye mean, Harry, the fought that yer fights with or the fought that yer thinks with ? "

" The one yer ' thinks ' with."

" Oh ! ' f-o-r-t '."

And later—

" Bill, how d'ye spell ' lices ' ? "

" Which one's, Harry, the ones yer has in yer boots or the ones yer find in yer breeches ? "

The Turkish and British trenches were often not more than twenty yards apart and, in consequence, both sides indulged in a good deal of bombing.

The popular Mills' bombs, or hand-grenade, had not

yet made its appearance, and so the troops used to make their own. These were known as the " Jamtin " bombs and were made by taking an empty jam or fruit tin, packing it with gunpowder, little stones, old nails, pieces of flint, anything that came to hand, putting in a long fuse, and then tamping down the top with clay or earth. You lit the fuse and held the tin until the fuse was about half an inch from the top of the tin, and then let fly over the trench.

A certain Cockney who had got a " Blighty one " in the leg and was waiting to be evacuated, amused himself by sitting in the trench making an extra-special tightly-packed bomb with an old tin.

Having finished the task to his satisfaction, he scrambled up on his knees, lit the fuse and, peering over the parapet, addressed the adjacent Turk as follows :

" Hi, any of your blokes like strawberry jam ? "

A pause.

" Well, share this amongst you." Wallop.

Another traditional story concerns a very peppery and unpopular Colonel who was edging his way down a narrow and very shallow trench. The trench was well-marked, and at every movement he made, a sniper's bullet just pinged past his ear.

He got hot and bothered and sent for the Company Commander to give him a roasting.

" What the hell d'ye mean by allowing this sort of thing to go on ? Every step I take a sniper's bullet just misses me."

The Captain roasted the Sub.—the Sub. the sergeant, and, finally, little Private Jones was sent for.

He arrived, blinking from a hurried snatch of sleep, before the Company Commander.

The Captain roared, " Are you the Company sniper? "

" Yes, sir," with a click of the heels.

" Then what the hell d'ye mean ? The Colonel's been down here and says that every step he takes a Turkish sniper's bullet just misses him."

" Yes, sir."

" Don't say ' Yes, sir,' do something ! "

" Yes, sir."

" You'd better get busy and see if you can finish that fellow off."

" Yes, sir."

Private Jones dismissed and, taking his rifle, crawled wearily into his observation post. He waited and, after a time, spotted the Turkish sniper in a scrub-bush. He took careful aim, fired and watched his man topple over.

" Sorry, mate," he expostulated as he turned away, " but that'll b——y well learn yer ter miss our Colonel."

Heard those ? Well, the next one you haven't.

Two troopers driven to desperation by the boredom of a hot fly-stricken September afternoon in the trench, and by the enforced eking out of their water supply, decided to make a dash down the hill some quarter of a mile to where there was a well, known as Little Anafarta. They procured a large empty biscuit tin and, making holes in either side, placed a stick of wood through to act as a carrying shaft. They went down to the trench opening and then began their slow progress in the open, from bush to bush and cover to cover, drawing sniper fire as they ran.

They reached the water supply, filled their tin and began the more perilous ascent. They could be seen dodging about from stone to stone and scrub to scrub. Every now and then the rattle of a rifle would keep them concealed for a space ; but by little short rushes they were triumphantly bringing the burden home. There was a stretch of twenty yards from their last boulder to the communication trench, and their faces were beaming with the joy of the difficult task well-accomplished. The whole distance of that " sticky " climb with their precious freight was safely run, and they were about to enter the final cover of the trench when, worse than death itself—a bullet went obliquely right through the tin and the water fountained out on either side. The look on their faces was wondrous to behold. I am afraid we could only roar with laughter, but let it be said to their credit, they soon saw the joke too. I suppose this isn't really humorous, but it struck us as being funny at the time.

It probably falls into the same category of jocosity as the merriment experienced by a certain boy whom I had asked to write an essay on " The funniest thing I ever saw." It ran—" There was an old gentleman crossing the High Street, Camden Town, in a top-hat, a long black coat and an umbrella. He didn't seem to notice where he was going and a motor-'bus came and knocked him right over. I didn't half laugh."

I suppose it is always as well to be able to laugh, even if it is only at other people's misfortunes. If you can learn to laugh at your own it is better still.

Another little incident comes to mind. We were to be relieved one night by some troops who were to arrive about 11 o'clock. By 1 a.m. the relief had not arrived and we had begun to think they were not coming, when a fellow on a traverse picket rushed in excitedly and whispered, " The Turks have broken in, I can hear them muttering, they're in the next section." Several rushed along with him, only to find it was O.K. It was the Scottish Horse coming up and a number of them were talking their native Gaelic— in fact, I believe there were some who could speak nothing else.

There was a tremendous strafe all over the Peninsula one night as news spread rapidly from trench to trench that there had been a great English victory at Loos. The Scotties played their pipes, mouth-organs were heard and everyone started singing. A sense of jubilation spread around and Johnny, thinking a new attack was contemplated, loosed off every gun and rifle that he possessed all through the night to keep our heads down.

Towards the end of October further physical discomfort was our portion as we were visited by a series of storms with hurricane winds and torrential rain. This meant not only sodden clothes and blankets, but semi-immersion ; as the waters found in the trenches a ready-made river bed down the hill-slopes to the sea. Men stood for hours in raging torrents with all their kit and ammunition in their arms, often having to grasp the crumbling sides of the trench to prevent themselves from being washed away.

Rumours of evacuation came to our ears and these, to our immediate joy, proved to be true :

A farewell message was received from General Peyton :

" The G.O.C. 2nd Mounted Division wishes to convey to all ranks his great appreciation of the soldier-like qualities and fortitude which have been so markedly evinced during the last two months in the face of heavy losses sustained in the action of the 21st of August followed by exposure, often in a cramped and crowded situation. Subject to incessant shell-fire, which caused many casualties, the Division has been called upon whilst continually under fire and suffering from the ravages of sickness to carry out abnormal physical and manual exertions to maintain and improve our defences. The time has now arrived that the troops should be withdrawn and rested, and the G.O.C. feels sure that when reinforcements arrive and the Brigades are reorganized they will return with the same indomitable determination to face all hardships and difficulties which the service of their King and Country demands."

After a few days, a very long night march, which seemed half-way across the Peninsula, brought us to the beach, where we lay down on the cold sand, exhausted, to snatch two hours' sleep before dawn.

The following night we bade farewell to Gallipoli ;

less than fifty strong the remnants of the Regiment embarked on the *Irwin*, a sturdy little Irish cattle-boat bound for Mudros harbour, in the Isle of Lemnos.

Not a man was sorry to leave Gallipoli with its continuous mental and physical strain and yet, as one stood on deck and watched the sombre shadows of those death-strewn hills recede, there was the feeling of regret that such hours of work, such long endurance, such loss of fair young life, such high endeavour in such a desperate venture, should have proved to be of such little avail.

CHAPTER IV

SINAI

" Somewhere East of Suez
Where a man can raise a thirst."

AFTER a brief stay at Lemnos, the Regiment
was transported back to Egypt, and eventually found itself encamped with the entire
2nd Mounted Division on the desert at Mena, on the
opposite side of the road to the Pyramids, with its
horses in squadron standings.

It was a real sight to see the joy with which the men
moved about among the horses again, recognizing
many an old pal until—" *the* " nag—the very one, was
found. A man can be as fond of a horse as of a woman,
and—he doesn't get answered back.

Various drafts, and the now recovered Peninsula
wounded had been formed into a composite cavalry
regiment, which had been sent up the Western Frontier
to fight the Senussi tribes who were giving considerable trouble. These were now brought back, and the
Regiment began to assume its normal aspect. Many,
who had been right through the Gallipoli period, now
fell sick under the reaction ; but the Colonel, Sir
Mathew Wilson, and his officers, did all they could
to give the men adequate leisure and amusement ;
which, added to that innate spirit of cheerfulness
within the British soldier himself, soon restored
the Regiment to its physical and mental health.
Parades were light, and leave to Cairo was frequent.
Sergeants were allowed to take their horses on joy-
rides, and one of the happiest days I ever spent was

one such ride with Nic and Mick, out through the village of Mena—along the valley of the Nile to the ruins at Gezira. Having tethered our horses and consumed our rations—we had each brought a large supply of beer as a surprise to the other two—we lazed and loafed among the old ruined temples, and jogged homeward in the cool of the evening, 'neath a myriad stars; the shadows of the great Pyramids throwing fantastic shapes across the sand.

Another joy-ride we had here was remarkable for its beauty. The Nile valley was in flood. Riding out in the opposite direction to the Pyramids and sometimes skirting, and sometimes wading, through the flood waters, we came to a magnificent palm forest with native villages scattered here and there. This formed a most pleasant ride, the route taking us through the forest, for some while along the banks of a canal, often through the narrow tortuous street of a mud-hut village, to a clearing and a small township in the centre. When the Nile was fully in flood many of the villages were entirely surrounded by water, and, at sunset, with the dense black shadows thrown on white bleached walls, looked like fairy dwellings set in a lake of golden crystal.

Rhapsodizing on such scenes to Nic, he would invariably reply, " Earl's Court on a Saturday night, but you can't get home by District."

You have met Mick, it is time you were introduced to Nic. Nic was a fair young Saxon, with closely cropped hair and moustache—he was really rather good-looking—but if he had any leanings to the poetic he promptly crushed them into the practical. He was perhaps the most efficient sergeant in our squadron ; his troop was never short of a nosebag, headrope or shackle. He had an acute property sense wherever his troop was concerned, and every article of equipment was marked in large black stencilling " A.2." You couldn't pick up a blanket or sandbag, without finding his mark upon it. I used to accuse him of

sharp practice and, after listening patiently to my
tirade at having found nosebags with A.2 marked outside and A.4 marked inside—my troop was A.4—he
would blandly query, "What is sharp practice,
'Appy ? " or " Tell us some more about this practice
business."

He had a whimsical smile when it broke, but he
usually looked very serious. He was the sort of fellow
who, camping up-river after the War, would walk into
the " poshest " fishmonger's shop in Henley and,
without moving so much as an eyelid, would earnestly
enquire the price of salmon, if the oysters were fresh,
could the lobsters be recommended, and then politely
answer, " Thanks very much, I'll have a couple of
kippers.' Withal, he was a lovable character—but,
like " your little Smee, Cap'n," he'd hate to have been
called lovable. Though not much given to words he
was a loyal and faithful friend.

One such joy-ride together we shall long remember
as " The Taming of the Shrew." There was a horse
in the lines known as Pip's Chestnut, though her
real name was Floss ; she was hard on the mouth,
wayward and " scatty " and the most difficult ride in
the Regiment. In fact, owing to her bolting tendencies, she was practically unmanageable but, if in a
generous mood, would consent on occasions to carry
a light pack. Like many of the most wayward and
capricious of her sex, she was beauteous to behold,
having a most imperious set of the head, and a walk
which would have done credit to a princess. Her
colouring was a light golden chestnut, her coat was
soft and silky, and as she stood in the lines tossing her
mane, she was the picture of equine loveliness.

Mick, Nic and I, together with Bert, the farrier-
sergeant, had arranged an afternoon's jaunt together
out through the palm groves. We three started, and
Bert said he would follow on. We crossed the open
desert for a mile or so, and entered the grove by the
banks of a canal. Here, we rode along in Indian file,

watching the play of shadows from the strong sunlight shafting through the trees, and scenting the warm earthy smell which arose from the turgid waters. On and on we rode until we came to a ford, and then crossed the canal. My horse stepped a little too far to the left and got in a pit-hole, much to the amusement of the others. Horse and rider disappeared for a second, and then came up swimming for the other side covered in rich brown mud, hardly pleasant to the taste, however good it may be for the germination of rice.

Anyhow, we rode on and halted outside the central village to wait for Bert, whom we had almost given up, thinking he had perhaps changed his mind. Hearing a monotonous chanting in a white stone building near by, whilst the others slept, I strolled in, and behold it was the village schoolroom.

An elderly father sat cross-legged on the floor and around him squatted thirty to forty brown-skinned little Arab boys. He had on his knees a big book—the size of the family Bible—which I supposed to be the Koran. He would intone a verse and give a command, and then the little fellows would recite long passages in chorus—swaying their tiny heads and bodies backwards and forwards in tune to the monotonous chanting of beautiful words in rhythmic cadence:

" In the name of God, the Compassionate, the merciful.
From the evil therefore of that day hath God delivered them
 and cast on them brightness of face and joy :
And hath rewarded their constancy with Paradise and silken
 robes :
Reclining therein on bridal couches, nought shall they know of
 sun or piercing cold :
Its shades shall be close over them, and low shall its fruits hang
 down :
And vessels of silver and goblets like flagons shall be borne
 round among them
Flagons of silver whose measure themselves shall mete.

And there shall they be given to drink of the cup tempered with
 Zendjebil (ginger)

From the fount thereof whose name is Selsebil (the softly
    flowing),
Aye—blooming youths go round among them. When thou
    lookest at them thou wouldest deem them scattered pearls :
And when thou seest this, thou wilt see delights and a vast
    Kingdom :
Their clothing green silk robes and rich brocade ; with silver
    bracelets shall they be adorned ; and drink of pure beverage
    shall their Lord give them."

I quote this passage at random to show that the
beauty of the rhythm and the richness of imagery
rival that voluptuous love poem in our Bible, " The
Song of Solomon."

To the muttons again. Lolling at the foot of a palm
tree, our horses linked together before us, lazily nod-
ding the flies away, we waited for Bert nearly an hour,
and were about to tighten our horses' girths when up
he rode, covered in perspiration, chuckling for all he
was worth. And he was on Floss, mark you, who
was now snorting and blowing in a muck sweat from
head to foot. Whether Bert had had an extra one at
lunch, or one of these curious innate challenges to his
manhood had arisen in his mind, I know not.

Having listened to our queries he explained himself
somewhat as follows : " I takes a look down the lines
to see what horse I'd ride and seeing her ladyship
standing so scornful like—thinks I to myself, I'll give
her a bit of an outing. So I saddles her up and rides
her out of the lines, she tries a buck and a rear, takes
three bounds and off she goes.

" Well, you know that little hill half a mile from
the camp, 'bout twice as high as Parliament Hill, but
a little steeper and all loose sand. Well, I just heads
her for that and up she goes. She isn't going to be
beaten, oh ! no, she struggles on and on until almost
at the top she's done, so I turns her round and she's
thankful enough to walk down to the bottom. Bless
my heart and soul, she's no sooner down than she
starts her tricks again. All right, thinks I. I've been
up that b——y hill to please you, you'll go up to

please me, so I digs my spurs in and sets her straight at it, and up she goes again.

" I walked her down and then just for luck sent her half-way up again—do you mind me ? —she's come along the rest of the journey at a nice steady pace and remarkable docile like."

Bert gave her a good scrape down and she shook herself and began to show her dignity again.; we rode home together and even then, when a couple of hundred yards from camp, she had a " go " at bolting back to the lines. Oh ! Floss ! " When have I seen thee so put down ? "

The sergeants' mess at Mena Camp was run for us by a native caterer, Mohammed Aziz ; he took all the rations and charged us so much a day messing allowance as well. He certainly performed wonders in varying his menus ; and his mess waiters in white gabardines and red tarbooshes with sashes to match, would have done credit to the most up-to-date night club. He did well on the drinks, and what with adulterating a little and overcharging a little, we must have been worth a small fortune to him, though he insisted he was always " Mafishe verluche."

A number of officers now joined the Regiment from England who in some cases were sadly below the calibre of the men the Yeomanry were used to being commanded by, and there was a little friction between some of these and the senior non-coms. and men.

One of them would persist in attempting to court popularity by being over-friendly with the sergeants, and coming into the sergeants' mess to stand drinks. Now, a sergeant no more wants a young and inexperienced officer in the mess, than a man really wants a woman in a public-house. In fact, you have to be just the right type of officer to ever receive an invitation into the sergeants' mess, to be able to drink with them, and preserve their loyalty and your own dignity.

This officer was not of that " kidney," and thinking he would be welcomed just because he was an officer, he got himself well " tied up " on many occasions.

He was found dead drunk several nights in the horse lines,—I've seldom seen a Yeoman trooper so tight that we couldn't put him to bed,—and so naturally, everyone vied with the other to be the first to kick him. Nic had this honour, as, returning from the horse lines one evening, he found him with his head in the sergeants' mess, hanging on to the tent flaps with a hand on either side and his posterior presenting a splendid target. " Nic " just took one root at him, though, as he said afterwards, " it was just cruelty to kids." If a man can't drink without making a perfect nuisance of himself, he should leave it alone.

The troops treated him properly one night. As the evenings were cold, a number of buckets were put in the tent lines at night for the men to urinate without having to go out of camp. " Very well on," one evening, he went banging about the tents late at night. The canteen had closed, so the buckets were well filled. His ardour was somewhat drenched by the contents of at least a couple of them.

For one thing the Colonel was very quick to tell a man from a mountebank, and many a young officer was quickly shifted to some job on Divisional Headquarters, sanitary duty, transport, or town service, and the troops left in charge of the troop-sergeant.

Two officers who were welcome and who joined us here, were both connected with the musical world, Mr. C. E. Boosey and Mr. Huntley Wright of *Geisha* fame. Mr. Wright, who was by no means a youngster, gave us many a good turn at the concerts. He was very short ; and really one of the best turns he ever did, was to teach us the new sword drill dismounted, though most of the humour was unconscious. He had no sooner squatted on his haunches than a faint humming broke out which finally resolved itself into—" Rootsy Pootsies' twinkling Tootsies waltz across the floor."

CAMEL TRANSPORT IN THE WADI GHUZZE

WINTER IN THE BALKANS

He was a good sort, however, and brightened up many a dull show.

Our second Christmas of the War was spent at Mena, and a real good feed Mohammed put up for us. The Colonel and squadron leaders came into the mess before dinner and took a drink with the sergeants—a half-bottle of " bubbly " for Sir Mathew. He had already brought one horse to run at the Cairo meetings and he was asked if he thought it would win next time out. It was not an Arctic Star or Golden Rain, and he replied rather naïvely :

" No, I don't think it'll win—at least, not unless the reins break."

The H.A.C. produced a splendid pantomime, but I forget whether it was *Cinderella* or *The Babes in the Wood*. It was certainly a very good show ; the beauty chorus were made up perfectly and the songs, if broad, were very witty and called forth roars of laughter.

On Christmas night, acting under the natural seasonal exuberance, a small party of sergeants set out after midnight to climb the Pyramid of Cheops. Something went wrong with the staff work, for when we appeared to be within a hundred yards of the base, a wager was made for a race to the Pyramid. Everyone started off " hell for lick " over the loose sand but in a few seconds we all disappeared rolling, spluttering and cursing down a steep sand-bank. We had walked too far to the left of the causeway, and now found ourselves covered in sand, and huddled at the foot of a steep hill by the Mena graveyards. We abandoned the project, but Nic and I got our " own back " by conducting a similar " tour for innocents " over the same hill on New Year's Eve.

From this happy camp at Mena, the Division split up ; the Bucks, Berks, and Dorsets (6th Brigade) went up the Western Frontier to induce the Senussi tribes to be reasonable sort of fellows, and after several engagements finished up the campaign with a charge. One squadron of the Dorsets, during this charge, suddenly found themselves hurled by their pace over a hidden " nullah " and many a brave lad was smashed to death. It was here that Major Cheape, the world-famous polo player, met his untimely end.

The 7th Brigade, the Sherwoods, the Derbys, and the South Notts Hussars, were sent straight to Salonica where they acted as Divisional Cavalry.

The 5th Brigade, that splendid body of Westcountrymen, the Worcesters, Warwicks and Gloucesters, went to Katia, an oasis on the northern coastal caravan route to Palestine. Here on a misty April morning they were surprised by the Turks in considerable force, and about three squadrons of the Gloucesters and Worcesters after a magnificent fight against tremendous odds were practically annihilated.

The London Brigade, Sharpshooters, Roughriders and ourselves, " Karno's own Hussars," were shifted to the Cavalry Barracks at Abbassia to the north of Cairo on the Mokottam hills.

The ride from Mena to Abbassia in the early evening was beautiful indeed, and I shall long remember the wonderful illusion just after sunset, as the city of Cairo appeared poised in the air across the Nile, the domes and minarets towering one above the other, fading into purple darkness; the crescent moon and stars hung just above the pinnacles themselves—a fairy city beyond the utmost dream of Rackham or the wildest imaginings of Dulac.

The worst of Cairo is that one can never be romantic about it for long.

Romance and ugliness, luxury and poverty are there hopelessly jumbled together—there is many a palace with a hovel on either side.

Arriving at Abbassia, good standings were found for the horses, but the men went into huts that were so lousy and bug-ridden that sleep was a sheer impossibility. Nic, Mick, and I found quarters in a disused Indian hospital. Here you could lay for hours stabbing bugs off the wall with a bayonet and still there were thousands to come. Here we had native beds, a framework made of palm sticks—" bug hutches " we called them. I think they were largely responsible for the majority of our visitors.

I shall always remember this short stay at Abbassia, for a peculiarity developed by Mick. If ever he had a drink or two, one was no sooner into bed, than he would draw a sword, and, clambering over you, he would stand astride of you and shout " lie still." He would then do the pursuing practice over you, watching with fiendish glee the glints of candlelight along the sword-blade as he swayed it either side of your recumbent body, after the manner of Sergeant Troy and Bathsheba. Sometimes one sword would not suffice, two would appear, which he would swing like Indian clubs and, I am thankful to say, with infinite precision.

The foolish young officer previously mentioned, had an uncomfortable evening here, as again poking his nose into the sergeants' mess, we brought him home, and, after a mock storm in which the beds and bedding rolled with the ship all over the place, Nic and I had great difficulty in restraining Mick from standing him against the door, and giving an exhibition of bayonet throwing all around him in the manner of knife throwers, so beloved by circus audiences.

There were some Australian Light Horsemen camped in a large remount depot near us, and one of our officers was soon to learn a trifle of " Aussie " independence. Capt. M——, a tall smart officer, with no small opinion of himself, rode out with a jingle of spurs and bit across the parade ground on to the main barrack road. Suddenly, remembering something he had left behind, he jumped from his horse and, seeing an Aussie strolling by, threw the reins to him, with a haughty : " Here, hold my horse, my man." The Aussie looked at him in surprise as he began to walk off, and then, suddenly finding speech, called after him : " Here, how long are you going to be ? "

" Ten minutes or so."

" Oh ! then you'd better tie your horse to these b——y railings," and, slinging the reins over a spike, he stuck his hands in his pockets and strolled away. The officer was speechless.

After much reconnoitring on the old Suez road, towards those hillocks known as the " Virgin's Breasts," with the beautiful white-towered city of Heliopolis way out to the north, the Regiment moved off by train to the southern zone of the Suez Canal, to join the Canal Defence Force.

We crossed the Suez Canal by a pontoon bridge at Shaluffa and set up a camp on the Sinai Desert itself, near to the Canal. Behind the camp one saw the high sludge banks hiding the Canal and, way out above, the great red rock mountains beyond Suez.

Before the camp lay the open desert, rolling in wave-like billows of sand, away to the white mountains of Sinai. In front of us, obscured from view by the sand-dunes, and about five miles from the Canal, was a chain of heavily-wired outposts held by infantry and labelled affectionately with such names as Ashton, Manchester, Wigan, etc. Beyond these posts and further into the desert were three dried-up rivers, or wadis as they are called, the Wadi El Haj, the Wadi Mukshieb, and the Wadi Gidi. These formed the chief Bedouin routes through the mountains to Nedjel, and any approach to the Canal by Turks or Bedouins in this sector had perforce to be by means of these wadis.

It was curious in this arid desert, with its alternate oceans of wave-like dunes and hard scrub-covered plains to find these wadis, with their pebble and limestone bottoms, clearly marking the course of some rushing torrent hundreds of years ago.

It was the duty of the cavalry to systematically

patrol these wadis, and also to act as patrol links between the various infantry outposts. This routine work was varied by longer excursions into the Sinai mountains themselves, to keep the Bedouani well informed of our proximity and to round up groups of hostile tribesmen.

These long reconnaissances involved considerable organization. For the Regiment to go out for a week, at least 900 camels were required to carry the water supply for men and horses in long tin "fantassies," shaped like large suit-cases. There were many little brushes with Bedouins, and from time to time groups of them were captured, but the expeditions are chiefly remembered by the long hours of riding without rest or water ; the dryness of the biscuit and "bully," and the limit to one bottle of chlorinated water a day, in a temperature that brought the perspiration wringing through the tunic. Terrible heat, terrible thirst and sometimes terrible sandstorms. So terrific were these that one sat down in the open with just a blanket over one's head for hours and waited for the storm to pass. On one such an expedition, in order to get back to water by night, our horses did forty-nine miles in the one day, over loose and shifting sand-dunes—surely a feat of endurance.

It was at Shaluffa that each Yeomanry Regiment furnished sufficient personnel to form a troop of the Imperial Camel Corps. Several good fellows left us to join this branch of the Service, but I think after a while they wished they were back with the " 'osses."

My troop had a fortnight's stay as patrol troop to a battalion of infantry at the outpost of Wigan, and here again, though the routine of early morning patrols was easy and in some respects delightful, we suffered agonies from heat and lack of water. We would saddle up at 2.30 a.m., ride off at 3, so as to reach the Wadi Mukshieb about dawn—riding out of the wired positions in the silent darkness, taking one's course by the stars, no sound but the jingling

of the bit and curb chains, as the horses' hoofs sank
noiselessly into the loose sand. Eastward towards
the mountains of Sinai to watch "the long grey
fingers of the dawn clutch at the fading stars."

There was a most peculiar light on the desert before
the sun rose over the mountains, an unreal opalescence
which overawed one so that one felt chilled, and
"the silence was so heavy you was half afraid to
speak." Then the monarch of the sky would ride
up in all his glory, throwing the base of the mountains into deep shadow, upward, upward, blaring
down his brazen rays.

The patrol would move along the wadi bed for about
four miles and, finding no sign of the enemy, ride
into camp about eight o'clock. Routine stables and
rifle inspections were all that was required during
the day.

We were particularly unfortunate in having three
days of a "khamseen" wind; it was insufferably
hot in the lulls, but when the wind blew it was like
a blast of heat from a ship's furnace. Owing to the
unbearable heat, the camel convoy that was supposed
to visit us every other day with our water supply,
failed to reach us, and although the plight of my own
men was bad, that of the infantry was far worse.
On the third day of this dreadful "khamseen" the
water shortage was becoming very serious indeed, and
I had only a minimum left to water my horses before
the morning patrol. Our water supply was kept in
a long cylindrical tank, let into the sand and covered
over with a wooden top. My own men had suffered
so from thirst, that I had issued out really a little more
than I should have done, and knowing that the ration
for the horses was small, I ordered that not another
drop was to be taken from the tank. A message by
heliograph—in this rare atmosphere this form of
signalling was efficient up to forty miles—had been
despatched, saying that an emergency convoy of
camels had left the Canal, and should be with us by

11 a.m. By three o'clock in the afternoon there was still no sign of them, and the men were in agony—several of my men drank the vegetable water and others aggravated their thirst by drinking tins of Nestlés milk. My second in command, Corporal Staples, " Shorty " he was known as, and a dear kindhearted little fellow he was, played chess with me with a pocket set during most of the day to keep our minds off our raving thirst. Our tempers became very ragged, and though we had hutted together for some weeks, this afternoon we could have murdered each other. Things got worse and worse, until it was difficult to keep one's sanity.

Over in the infantry camp matters were even more serious. The men had raided the officers' lines, and drunk the soapy water they had washed in that morning, and many of the men were nearly mad. The commanding officer of the battalion was one of the old school who believed in curing all ills by discipline, and as the morale of his men was badly shaken, he ordered a full-dress parade at 4 p.m. The men turned out in that dreadful heat and apparently executed various movements. They came in from parade about 6 p.m., and were rationed to about half a mug of tea. At sundown they came over to my lines in dozens, offering a 100 piastre note—£1—for a half-bottle of water. Of course, I had to be adamant, as my own men were in sorry plight ; but they loitered about the lines, as they knew very well there was water in my tank. By eight o'clock there were so many of these poor fellows hanging around that matters looked serious, and, about twenty minutes later, exactly what I thought would happen actually occurred. They attempted to rush the tank. I had previously arranged a signal with " Shorty," and at a sign he quietly moved over to the infantry camp. I stood on top of that tank and made the speech of my life to keep those fellows off, until the guard arrived and they were driven back to camp.

In about half an hour a shout arose ; there in the distance, by the starlight, a long line could be discerned moving across the horizon ; and, as the moon rose, the shape of the camel convoy could be seen. I have seldom seen a more welcome sight than that frieze of laden camels on the skyline. The relief to mouth and stomach after such privation cannot be described. One can stand the lack of water during the day, but at sundown thirst becomes abnormal, and when it cannot be quenched the consequent agonies are terrible indeed to bear.

It was whilst at this post, that on an evening patrol —against regulations, of course—I shot a flamingo and, proudly bringing him into camp, placed him in the stew-pot. Imagine how anxiously we sat around, anticipating this delicacy as a change from the eternal "bully." When boiled, the flesh looked a beautiful resida green, rather like a piece of Dri-ped leather, it was as tough as old boots, and of a similar flavour. It is a favourite habit of mine at dinner-parties when the conversation becomes gastronomically boring, to break in, "Have you ever tasted flamingo ? "

The gourmets pause and interestedly murmur : " No."

" Well, you haven't missed much," is my reply.

I had two notable instances of the wonderful homing instincts of the horse, whilst at this outpost. On one occasion I had ridden in eight miles or so to the main camp, to bathe in the Canal, to get the lads' mail, to have one or two in the mess, and to bring a bottle of Scotch back for " Shorty." There were regimental reasons for the journey, no doubt, but the items mentioned above were easily of chief importance. Riding by daylight there were a certain number of landmarks, slight indeed, but recognizable, by which one took direction, but I was foolish enough to stay longer at Shaluffa than I should have done, and consequently night came down like a blanket when I was but a mile from the main camp. I immediately took a compass bearing and began to march on a star, riding along in solitude with heavy nosebags containing the mail and two bottles of Scotch—to preserve balance—banging against old Dick's side, till he thought he carried John Gilpin himself. It was pitch-dark, but the stars seemed so near one could have plucked them out of the sky. Over the first three miles of sand-dunes I suddenly dipped into the Scrub Valley, about another two miles and then up the next range of sand-dunes, all just as it should be. I rode on and on, until time told me I should be near Wigan, but no sign of a light anywhere—another half an hour and still no sign ; something must be wrong. I was utterly lost. Those who have never tried night marching on a desert will fail to realize how extraordinarily difficult it is to keep direction. I have known a whole regiment led twice round in a circle before finally realizing their direction ; though perhaps on that occasion the C.O. was finding his way home by the pigeon stunt. I had apparently overshot the post, but whether to the left or right, or by how much, it was impossible for me to estimate. I was contemplating off-saddling, and lying out there on my lonesome till dawn, when Dick suddenly stopped dead. I tapped him with the spurs, but he almost reared and snorted. I tapped him forward again, he swung to the left. I dismounted and feeling down to the front of him, found he had stopped dead on the brink of a sheer drop into a " nullah." It had been impossible to see this mounted, but he had sensed it, and probably saved my life by his instinct. I guessed now that I must be somewhere on the banks of the Wadi Muksheib, and, walking carefully and leading Dick, I eventually found a way down into the wadi. Now this wadi had been patrolled every morning for a fortnight, but " which was up and which was down " ? I mounted, dropped the reins on Dick's neck, gave him a tap with the spur ; he turned half-left and started off at a quick walk. So certain did he seem, that I let him have his head, and in less than half an hour he brought me right dead into the post.

One day a young officer came over from the infantry lines with all the swank imaginable and ordered —mind you, ordered—the loan of a horse to take him to Shaluffa. Infantry one-pippers should always be fairly respectful to, or at least wary of, a Yeoman. To my mild enquiry of what kind of a ride he liked, he " spelled me a lot of hot air and did a song and a dance," about riding to hounds. I hadn't Floss with the troop at the time, or he could have had her. Anyhow, I gave him a nice quiet ride ; Charlie's horse, a chestnut with a white blaze, just a trifle hard on the mouth, and a rather awkward trot, who had been rested from patrol work since we had been at this post, on account of a slight sore back. By midnight he hadn't returned, and his C.O. sent over to the lines to know if we'd heard anything of him. We hadn't. He came back late the following afternoon leading the horse. From his somewhat incoherent description, it appears he had been taken at a fast pace to Shaluffa, and nearly had his bones shaken out of him. The horse had then started half-right straight across the open desert to a little patrol point six miles out, and then taken him back to Shaluffa and stood still in the regimental lines whilst he got off. The horse knew thoroughly well its old patrol, and thought that that trip was what was required of him ; the officer did some twenty miles of country he didn't know, and didn't want to know, because he couldn't stop the horse, and he couldn't get off at the trot. Nobody else ever borrowed a horse from our troop whilst we were there.

After three weeks or so, we were relieved and went back to the Canal camp. It was a weird sight from the camp to see a big liner passing down the Canal, as she towered high over the banks, and the water being invisible she appeared to be sailing straight across the desert.

The sand-storms here were terrible, but between whiles life was not too unpleasant; there was bathing in the Canal, and swimming alongside the liners in " the altogether," whilst passengers threw down tins of Gold Flake and Three Castles.

A curious coincidence happened here. I was sitting on the Canal bank with only a towel wrapped around me, when I saw a four-funnelled battle-cruiser coming down towards Suez. When she " hove " in sight— must be nautical—I saw she was the *Euralys*. I knew I had an old chum from the Belsize Boxing Club on board, and knew him to be an officer, but he had last written to me from the North Sea. As she came alongside, I recognized him on the aft deck and, standing up, took off my towel and waved it. What was more peculiar, was that he recognized me, and some days after wrote and obtained me three days' leave to sing at a concert in the Theatre Royal, Suez, and to stay with him at Port Tewfik.

There was fishing at nights on the Canal, but we seldom caught much. The natives had remarkable skill; they would take a boat out into the centre of the Canal, keep it moving slowly, whilst two or three stood up with a spear poised a foot above the water. As the fish swam within range they could be seen phosphorescent through the dark water; a rapid movement of the forearm and wrist, and a decent-sized fish would be brought out well and truly gaffed through the body.

Jim Bly, the farrier-major, was a great fisherman, though we never saw any of his catches. He invariably came in late to the mess with a yarn of " such a big 'un, just got away as I got him to the bank."

One pitch-dark night Mick and I went fishing, and took up a stand about eighty yards from Jim. We only had a line out, without hook or bait, and we repeatedly called to Jim: " Any luck, Jim ? "

" No, 'Appy, caught anything yourself ? "

" No."

" They don't seem biting. Now if you'd a come last night," etc., etc.

We kept up a desultory conversation with Jim for half an hour or so, when Nic came down to bathe. He undressed fifty yards away, slipped silently into the water, swam down to us, and coming in quietly took our line out to mid-stream. It was impossible to see more than ten yards from the bank, so when he was well out we started shouting and he started splashing. " Jim, Jim, we ain't half got one."

" What d'ye say ? "

" Quick, Jim, give us a hand."

" Pooll 'im up on the bank. Pooll him up on the bank."

" Give us a hand, Jim, God's truth, he's nearly had us in."

Jim came clambering along on the stones.

" He's lying quiet now, Jim, you'd better do this, you know more about it than we do."

" Yus, they always sulks. I'll pooll him up on the bank."

We gave the line to Jim, when Nic gave a h—— of a tug and made a dickens of a splash.

Jim says, " Crumbs, you ain't half got a beauty. Here, I'll go and fetch my knife—pooll him up on the bank."

Whilst Jim had gone we made a devil of a lot more splashing, and getting our imaginary fish almost in when we shouted :

" Hurry up, Jim, we've got him close in." Splash, splash, wallop.

" Oh, Jim, he's broken the line."

Nic dressed quickly and we all went into the mess to hear Jim's description of the wonderful fish we'd nearly caught. For nights afterwards Jim could be heard, buttonholing some unfortunate with :

" I shouts to them, ' Pooll him up on the bank.' "

Jim had a birthday about this time, and a day off to Suez to celebrate. It was customary on birthdays

to jump right into the sergeants' mess after guard-
posting, with a " Drinks all round the mess, boys,
my birthday to-day." Jim was not exactly famous
for his generosity, but he returned from Suez after tea,
and in a fairly good mood. He went into the mess,
and found only five sergeants present. He counted
them carefully, made a lengthy mental calculation
and then said tentatively : " My birthday, to-day,
drinks all round the mess, boys. Four of the five
made a bolt under the brailing, and before three of
the drinks were drawn, there were sergeants crowding
into the mess at the double. Nigh on thirty eventually
wished him " Jolly good health, Jim."

From Shaluffa, during the heat of May, the Regiment moved higher up the Canal to Geneffre and
camped on the margin of the little Bitter Lake. This
was a beautiful camp, with splendid bathing in shallow
water, and however hot and trying the day, a beautiful cool breeze from off the lake at night. There was
a small gunboat, the H.M.S. *Fox*, out in the lake,
and many delightful fraternizings in the way of
concerts, football matches, and swimming contests
were enjoyed with our brothers from the senior
service.

Dab and crab fishing were popular for a time here.
Several of us would go out paddling along the shallows
of the lake with lances poised above the water.
Moving slowly, we could see the dab lying on the
bottom and if—if, mark you—you were sufficiently
agile, you got the lance-head into the dab. Mick, on
so many occasions only just missed the sergeant-
major's foot by a fraction, that the sport was dis-
couraged.

The discovery of crabs in the lake led to the hire
of a native boat. Bert, the farrier-sergeant, made a
wonderful wire cage in the forge, and we went out
fishing with knobs of bacon tied on string. You
pulled the crabs to the surface, and Bert gathered
them in his cage. We caught so many, and behaved

so gluttonously, that we were all ill for two days, and another sport went by the board.

There were many long and very exhausting reconnaissances out to the limestone hills from Geneffre. It was said that underneath the limestone hills ran rivers of water, and I believe in places where engineers blasted the rock, water was found. This would make Moses out to be clever in native lore, when he struck the rock and water gushed out. I mention this, as one such expedition, known as the " Pumping of the Wells," had for its purpose the emptying of all wells to our front, so that enemy troops or Bedouins could come no further than the mountain foothills for lack of further supplies. We arrived at the wells, after several days, beat to the wide for water ourselves, and in this broiling heat, 125 degrees in the shade, if any. Water was found deep down in caverns in the cliff, and when pumped up from these limestone cisterns, seemed the finest drink we had ever had. It was clear as crystal and icy cold—it tasted like wine itself.

The return journey from this expedition necessitated the last lap of forty miles being done at a stretch, and the men were pretty far gone with thirst when we arrived back at camp. The mile after mile of monotonous riding in line of troop column was somewhat relieved by an impromptu competition, each troop trying to sing a fresh popular song against the other. We got right back to " After the ball was over " and " Daddy wouldn't buy me a bow-wow-wow." By the time we were nearing camp our tongues were badly swollen, our heads dizzy, and our legs stiff with the continuous riding. Some of the horses were fairly distressed, but on the whole I think it safe to say that at desert campaigning, on account of their mobility, the horse proved more effective than the camel.

I think it was on the return from this " stunt " that I entered our E.P. tent to find a fellow just out on a draft, who had been in the Yeomanry pre-War, and had so far seen no service. He looked very smart with spotless riding-breeches, polished boots and spurs, buttons fit to shave in, hair nicely brushed, altogether, " very pretty." Mick came straight in from the horse lines, covered in dust from head to foot, breeches soaked with his own perspiration and horse sweat, and looked at him in amazement. The fellow went forward and in a nice Oxford manner said :

" Hullo ! been out for a ride ? "

Mick was nearly speechless—controlling himself with an effort he looked him up and down again, and then said : " You done any riding lately ? "

" Oh, a little hacking on Hampstead Heath," was the reply. We nearly had to put Mick to bed from apoplexy.

During one of these long desert reconnaissances, A and B Squadrons, which had always been the firmest friends, lost touch with one another, and in consequence came under heavy fire from a Bedouin stronghold in the centre. Had the advance-guard action been better arranged this stronghold would have been discovered. " A " Squadron thought it was " B " Squadron's fault and vice versa. A little strained feeling existed for a day or two and then " A " Squadron decided to send Sergeant Munchausen, as we called him, or alternately, " Boer War Washington," on account of his exaggerated yarns, to Suez to buy supplies in order to heal all wounds with a banquet. A very notable feast it turned out to be ; Charlie the cook did his very best, and the mess waiter Milky dropped more perspiration in the beer than ever. Milky was, as you may guess, a milkman in civvy life, and at every meal, as he entered the sergeants' mess, the following chorus greeted him :

" Any milk to-day, lady ? "

"No, thank you," in falsetto voice. "Shut the gate."

" Blast the gate ! Gee-up, Ned."

A notable character in the Regiment who attended this repast, was the " B " Squadron farrier-sergeant, a man with a thirst for mighty big words, and a mighty big thirst. For this auspicious occasion I wrote a memorial, in Chaucerian style, mentioning every " B " Squadron sergeant with a word of greeting; I will quote the lines to Jack Dodd, this farrier, as it describes him rather well—and—I know he won't mind :

> Whilom a brawny knighte, MacDodd
> An oozying, boozing drunken Sod,
> Righte fulle of cheste, a hairy man,
> Of rugged features. Who could scan
> That heavy browe, that visage stern,
> For which ye flames of Hell did burn,
> With fearsome, fieryness withal.
> His voice when not in drunken brawl
> Like unto a thunderclape would sounde,
> An e'en hys fiste weighed nigh four pounde.
> " One punche, my boy " how oft saith he ?
> " One punche, my boye, and thou wilt be
> Five leagues from here, Shalluffa West.
> Thine abdomen beneathe thye veste
> I'll stryke, and straightways knock thee sheer
> From off the b——y hemisphere."
> Great whyskers twain hys lips bedeck
> Wound thrice four times aboute his neck
> With eke a yarde to spare, I trow.
> " A Soldier I, thou son of cow,"
> Eftsoones, he would exclaim.

Jack of the fiery countenance and ponderous threat was one of the dearest souls living, and really as gentle as a lamb. He marked his approval of this feast, by gently gliding under the brailing, and stopping there an hour before we broke up, needless to say with all differences settled.

Whilst we were at this camp we received a welcome visit from the Prince of Wales. The junior officers got very windy and there was a devil of a lot of saddle cleaning to be done, and the transport burnished its steel work till it shone like Bardolph's nose. His Royal Highness arrived at noon in terrific heat. The Colonel, Sir Mathew, greeted him affectionately and waltzed him off to the officers' mess for a drink. He had just to pass down the lines to get there—but we needn't have worried.

We had a very notable sports meeting with the R.H.A. in which we were fortunate to win all the events : I had the honour of captaining the wrestling on horseback team. The sergeants of the R.H.A. were invited back to our mess in the evening, and I think just one arrived home for early stables ; the track between the two camps was strewn with bodies like a battlefield.

There being little else to occupy the tremendous intelligences at Headquarters, the brass hats turned their attentions to the dress of the men. In the extreme heat the tendency of the troops was to cut more and more off the shirt-sleeve till it ceased to exist, and to curtail the length of the shorts till in many cases they were little more than bathing drawers. These practices invoked the wrath of H.Q. and many Regimental Orders as to the correct length of the shorts appeared. Colonel Sir Mathew started a new fashion by wearing them full and baggy and long enough to cover his knees.

The ridiculous repetition of these orders which usually started : " It is noticed that shorts are getting shorter . . ." prompted a poem from my pen intended for the *Regimental Magazine*. Such, however, was the talent that distinguished journal could command, that this little effort was rejected, and being somewhat of a pet of mine, now blushes into print for the first time :

We read with moral turpitude, the trend of Fashion's sway,
   And from photographs of ladies in Revue,
Weekly culled from *Sketch* or *Tatler*, consternation we betray,
   That the skirt should end " au-dessous du genou."
      But this tendency distressing,
      Inclination to undressing,
Through the Regiment must cease without delay,
     It's a fact that's quite depressing
     And by no means prepossessing
That " Shorts are getting shorter every day."

It incurs the greatest wrath from high and mighty at H.Q.
  Brigade Headquarters issue notes galore
And the Brigadier sends orderlies as " mannequins " on view,
  To show us how the breeches should be " wore."
      To escape the flames eternal,
      Learn prudence from this journal,
Suppress this vulgar corporeal display.
      Adopt a mien paternal,
      Try to emulate the Colonel,
Whose shorts are getting longer every day.

One little anecdote of our Squadron leader, Captain
Bullivant. If ever an officer was loved by his men,
Bully was, and he cared for us as if we were his very
own children. He was just a grand fellow, self-
lessness personified, kind and tender as a woman, yet
fearless and foolhardily brave in battle. A sheer
bundle of nerves withal, and as absentminded as a
Greek professor. Bully, we just loved you. You
were killed in action, as you meant to be ; but I for
one can never think of you without " my mother
coming to my eye."

We had a special concert and being rather stuck for
fresh imitations, I suddenly thought of a syce with
a melancholy character who always wanted to go
" Cairo-kismas day, bukra me, kidda, kidda, kidda,"
raising his hands to show the range in height of his
offspring.

I was giving an accurate representation of his
manner of clearing dung from the lines, and everyone
was in fits of laughter, when I saw at the end of the
marquee two shining bright eyes above a row of
flashing teeth : it was Abdul himself.

Bully was amused at this turn, and as I went off
the improvised stage he came and caught me by the
arm, telling me it was a damned good show : how
much he thought of all of us who had come out from
England with him. He asked me to go and have a
drink, and I stood in the little cookhouse just outside
the officers' mess whilst he called the mess waiter.

He muttered in his well-known drawl, " Bring Hatt

a double whisky and soda, and, oh! I'll have a lemonade," then turning to me he said sweetly : "You don't mind, do you, I never overdo it, you know." The drinks were brought and of course I waited for him to take his up first. I tasted mine— it was the lemonade.

CHAPTER V

SALONICA

" Come over to Macedonia and help us."

FROM the glare of the desert, from the burning
sands and blast-furnace "khamseens," to the
snow-capped mountains of the Balkans, the
icy winds of the Vardar ; frost-bite for ourselves
and unsheltered standings, knee-deep in freezing
snow and slush, for our horses ; such was to be our
portion. Tanned the deep brown of the Arab himself, finally acclimatized to the desert life and its
hardships, the Regiment moved from the Canal to
Alexandria and there embarked on the s.s. *Nitonian*
for Salonica Harbour.

My chief memory of this trip is that of a violent
Mediterranean thunderstorm. The ship was very
hot below decks and very lousy too, so that Nic,
Mick and I slung hammocks between the stays and
derrick chains on the fo'c'sle deck. On one particular night which was exceptionally hot, there was
hardly a ripple on the water or a breath of air above ;
we slung our hammocks near one another, and undressing to our shirts, dumped our clothes on the
deck, and finally covered ourselves in the hammock
with our waterproof sheets as a protection against
dew. Not allowed to smoke, no lights were shown
anywhere on the boat—on account of the submarine
menace—we lay beneath the star-spattered sky and
engaged in the usual bantering back-chat. We must
have fallen off to sleep when a wind of terrific velocity

suddenly sprang up, and our hammocks began to
swing furiously with the motion of the boat. Almost
immediately a torrential rain burst down from the
sky. We tucked our heads under the waterproof
sheets, but each concavity rapidly filled with a pool
of water, which, as one moved in the hammock,
washed all round one's back and sides. There was
nothing for it but to bolt, so grabbing our sopping
clothes from the deck and in drenched shirts, we
tore down the hatchway. Here we stood in complete
darkness, soaking and shivering till dawn, and next
morning spent several hours walking around in
blankets, whilst our clothes were dried at the boiler-
house.

There were many scenes of considerable beauty
during this journey, as the ship passed through the
Grecian Archipelago quite close to many of the
smaller islands ; but the crowning glory of the
voyage was witnessed as we advanced up the Gulf
of Salonica, with hills stretching away into mountains
on our right, the town of Salonica a little white spot
on the horizon before us, and the gigantic snow-
capped Mount Olympus towering in majesty above
us to our rear. As with slackened steam we rode
into the harbour, what a beautiful sight this ancient
town of the Thessalonians presented from the sea. A
long strand with a large white tower marking its
extreme right stretched along the margin of the deep
blue Mediterranean waters, a town white and glittering clustered behind it, and then the suburbs
stretching up in terrace-like formation on the hills
above. The sight of the green grass and trees of the
hills around the town was goodly indeed to eyes that
long had strained over arid desert lands ; the whole
city seemed dozing in the sunshine with the peaceful
serenity of a pussy-cat well fed. The romantic
beauty of this city, like many other things in life,
hardly bears investigation ; for on landing, the
streets were found to be narrow, ill-kempt and filthy

with all manner of muck and refuse. Bad sanitation
caused a perpetual fœtid odour which, mingling with
the ever-present smell of perfumes and spices in such
cities, always reminds me of a woman who has put
powder on over a dirty neck. The streets were filled
with a most cosmopolitan crowd—soldiers of all the
Allies and their Colonials mingled together in gaily-
coloured uniforms. French, Zouaves, Italians, Moroc-
cans, Greeks, Servians, and even Russian Cossacks,
jostled one another in the roadways or filled the
low-ceilinged little cafés on the front. Again it was
a musical-comedy scene; hence, we presumed to
complete the picture, they had sent for us—" Fred
Karno's Own."

We marched out through the town northward,
and high on the hill slopes overlooking the harbour
we pitched our camp at a place known as Summer
Hill. On the way up we had passed the camp of the
Cossacks, and here let me explode another myth.
To all fair ladies who, lushed with sights of Valentino
as the Sheikh, long to be carried off in strong brown
arms to desert fastnesses, let me tell you I have never
yet seen a sheikh who hadn't to scratch himself
every few minutes, nor a Cossack—a dashing Cossack
—who looked clean.

The Cossack camp appeared a disorderly rubbish
dump, and the horses standing in the lines, ill-kempt
and unclean. Throughout the whole of the War, I
have yet to see a body of men who looked after their
horses as well as the British Cavalry ; and for general
horsemanship and horse management, no one—these
Cossacks least of all—could hold a candle to them.

In this camp at Summer Hill they started the
" funny " business again, having everything just
straight, white stones at the tent doors and all that
comic aligning so dear to the heart of certain army
authorities. However, it was pleasant on these
slopes, for, although November, the sun was quite
warm at noon. There lay the town below, reflected

in certain lights in the cerulean waters of the harbour,
and way above the ridges to the right the rugged
peaks of Olympus seemed in that rare atmosphere
like some hugh iceberg bearing down across the
entrance to the gulf.

There were a tremendous number of lorry depots
in and around the town, and at night time it was a
wonderful sight to see the constant stream of head-
lights, as thousands and thousands of these transport
and hospital lorries made their journeys to and from
the various front-line dumps.   Hundreds would pass
in an hour, and the monotonous low rumble of their
wheels could he heard incessantly all through the
night.

We were now to be thoroughly equipped for the
rigours of a Balkan winter, and scarce a day passed
without a parade at the " Quarter Bloke's " stores to
draw something or other.   Extra blankets, warm
winter caps with ear-flaps, thicker underclothing,
leather jerkins, huge field-boots, waterproof capes and
ground-sheets in one, woodman's axes, bivouac
sheets and picketing pegs, chains, wire-cutters,
heavy mallets and gas helmets were drawn as gifts
from a grateful Government.   When paraded in full
marching order the saddle and its hanging accessories
weighed such a devil of a lot, that two men usually
worked together to sling their saddle into position
on their horses' backs.   I cannot imagine the weight
of the whole equipment ;   all I know is that if you
had a horse anything approaching sixteen hands or
so, it was a dickens of a job to mount, as the back
pack was so high and bulky ;   and I've seen many a
saddle pulled round in mounting a tubby-bellied
pony, simply by the weight of the rider attempting
to mount without someone holding the other side.

However, decked out like Nansen, and riding horses
with parcels hung about like Christmas-trees, we began
to trek up-country.   Up and up we went through a
pass in the great ring of hills above Salonica.   The

hills were highly fortified and were known as the Birdcage Lines ; they were to be the last line of re- sistance—and one imagined they would be almost impregnable—should the enemy drive down and attempt to capture Salonica for the purpose of establishing another submarine base on the Mediter- ranean Sea.

Through these rocky hills, down on to a plain across the wide mud-flats where the river Gailico widens into its estuary on its journey down to the sea. Here now was a beautiful open plain covered with thick coarse grasses, here and there bushes, and often clumps of trees. The plain was wide enough for the Regiment to ride in line, and the many rabbits and partridges that were disturbed, together with the long echeloned flights of wild duck at even, excited the officers with promise of game-shooting.

One evening we bivouacked outside of Saragol, and here a native after dark turned a dishonest penny by selling several bottles of " white whisky " to the troops. This vile stuff is sheer poison, quickly intoxicates, and leaves one with a most fearful head in the morning. Dear old Bert found some of this, and on his return to lines had such an argument with several " bivvies " that he decided his best course was to walk triumphant over all the lot. Mine was one of them, and rather than set about re-erection, I took my blanket into an empty barn near by. I had hardly settled down in the dark when rats in their thousands leapt all over the place and, they having no respect for my prostrate body, I deemed it better to sleep in the open, so shifted again.

The remainder of the trek passed without incident, and eventually we found ourselves climbing up into the foothills of the main Balkans, until we halted on the inner slope of the topmost ridge overlooking the plain of Lake Doiran. Here the squadrons separated, and moving across beautiful country intersected by many sharp ravines, each with its rapid little stream, we went into camps about two miles apart, and about three miles from the margin of the lake itself.

My own squadron set down its lines in a spot where two ravines almost met, known as Galliene. We took over from the Lothian and Border Horse, and so careful were they not to leave anything behind that, after they had ridden out two hours, a corporal came tearing back for his " bloudie hammer."

Ride with me up the grass-covered slope to the skyline from Gallieni, through the many little oak trees that flourished here, dismount under cover and crawl up carefully till the ridge is reached. A wonderful sight meets our eyes, and before using our field-glasses we take in at a glance bare brown hills and mountains to our left front, terminating in the craggy slopes of the Grand Couronne. The near side of the Grand Couronne drops down a sheer precipice almost into the lake, around the margin of which runs a white road into the town of Doiran nestled underneath the mountain slope. There is just a gap above Doiran through which runs the pass and then to our front, and ranging all around the lake the mighty snow-capped Bellshitza Group of the Balkans themselves. The Lake of Doiran is almost circular and some five miles in diameter, its water of a pale blue and an almost deathly stillness.

Now with the glasses, trenches can be picked out on the Petit Couronne and the Grand Couronne, the town of Doiran appears a mass of white stone houses, whilst down by the lake can be seen a large white house ruined with shell-fire, and then, amongst the dense bushes and the trees to our front and below us, glimpses of a railway track where the Salonica to Constantinope railway ran. Here and there a shellburst can be seen, but the firing is desultory and with little apparent object. To our extreme left and invisible from here is the Vardar Front, and to our extreme right and again invisible is the Struma Front.

Here, then, is this track of country between these

H

two bastions which is to be held by line of cavalry outpost. Should Mackensen drive through, the Yeomanry are to fight a rear-guard action back to the Birdcage Lines at Salonica. Several outposts were immediately established on our front at suitable vantage-points, with a strong picquet down by the lake near the ruined house which was known as Doiran Station. It was as well to keep well under cover, as any movement here immediately attracted the attention of " Doiran Annie," and of course the range was known almost to an inch.

Although the lake formed a natural barrier, there was just this stretch of open country to be held, and there were insufficient troops to hold it more firmly than by outposts and patrols.

Away over to the right of the lake was the village of Akenjali, where the Bulgars kept a picquet. About once a week this picquet was wiped out by British troops and eventually it became a " Box and Cox " post ; the Bulgars rode out as we rode in and came back as we rode out. We immediately commenced the task of wiring in some seven or eight miles of our front, this being done during the night. I well remember my first night of wiring here. The importance of silence had been so impressed on us, that we rode out with muffled bits and used mauls muffled with blankets to drive in the long stake pickets. We had been wiring as silently as we could for some hours when there was a h—— of a noise to our flank. It sounded like a division of cavalry with guns on the move. The rattle and jangle came nearer and nearer, and as they approached it proved to be a train of A.S.C. limbers bringing up more wire. What struck me as so ludicrous was the contrast between our silence and the noise and rattle of this convoy. The Bulgars, however, left us alone, and provided no open movement was seen in the daytime the shelling was little and usually passed right over our outposts and camps on to the dumps in the plain behind.

The winter now set in thoroughly, and torrential rain-storms and extreme cold were our chief enemies. The little streams in the ravine turned to flooded rivers, and the horses in open standing were often almost up to their bellies in mud and icy slush.

At the camp we set about achieving what comfort we could, and most of us managed to procure sufficient wood from the ruined village of Pateriche to build some sort of hut to provide better shelter, as the "bivvy" sheets proved to be useless against the incessant downpours. I was fortunate in securing a little hut already made. A cave had been dug out from the side of a ravine, the top extended with wood—two old pews from Pateriche church helped to make the front—and there was a door. The wooden part of the roof was tiled with red tiles so that the hut really looked very like "the house we built for Wendy." This illusion was maintained as the fireplace was a hole cut in the cliff and the chimney-pot, a tube constructed of old fruit-tins, came out at the side. The water unfortunately came in a bit where the wood joined the cliff, and there were rats, but nevertheless through this terrible winter it formed some sort of a house for Nibby, my second sergeant, and myself.

Nibby was a dear kind fellow and we struck up a great friendship here. I took over the husbandly duties of the shack, and Nibby the wifely. For instance, it was my job to go out with a couple of sacks tied across a saddle and a pickaxe, to cut out the decaying roots of the trees. These we found made excellent fuel and burnt much longer than ordinary wood, which was scarce, whereas it was Nibby's to see the fire was kept alight and to tell me when more fuel was wanted. Whatever the hour I came in off patrol, Nibby always managed to have either porridge or cocoa hot for me in a mess-tin. He was a real gem ; although he used to get thoroughly fed-up with me on mail days, as I insisted on reading through the whole of the *Observer* to him, especially Mr. Garvin's

articles on the " possibilities "—" on the one hand
the Germans might break through Roumania, on the
other hand they might not. There were these two
distinct possibilities—should the former occur it must
follow the second cannot maintain and conversely,
etc., etc."

Anyhow, the *Observer* was a great comfort to me—
I could read about all the books I should never handle
and the critiques of all the concerts I could never hear.

As the winter advanced the weather became very
severe, and heavy snowstorms and blizzards were
frequent. There was an icy cold wind (we called it the
Vardar wind) that came off the mountains, and I can
sometimes imagine it on my back now. Sickness and
frost-bite from exposure took ready toll of the men,
and, as always happens in the Army, those who could
stick it longest had double work to do. We eventually reached saturation point when practically every
man was on duty every night. The cry of the orderly
sergeant at dusk would ring out like a cathedral
cantoris—" Fall in the night guard, Doiran patrol—
and wiring party "—in fact, it became the standing
joke to intone this phrase, curling the voice on " and
wiring."

The night guard would parade dismounted, but the
patrol and wiring party mounted—numbers having
been checked the patrol and wiring party would " half
sections left," and move off in the pitch-dark and icy
cold. At the head of the first ravine the wiring party
would ride off to the right and continue the task of
wiring up the lake until just before dawn, when with
a couple of wooden wiring stakes apiece under their
arms, " to keep the home fires burning," they would
ride back to camp.

The patrol made its way through the bushwood to
the Doiran Station and there relieved the twenty-four
hour outpost and picquet. This was a very cold job,
and sleeping in the open in the snow every other night
or so is a memory that lingers yet. The men suffered

agonies from frost-bite, though the best remedy for this I found to be soaking the socks in whale-oil. It made the feet clog with mud, but it seemed to keep the cold out. As we often went as much as a week without undressing, except to slip the top-boots off, lice became our constant companions in ever-increasing numbers.

The plight of the horses during this time was cruel ; as I have mentioned before, they were just in open standings, and could get little protection from the wind and rain. Moreover, we now became faced with another serious problem. It was never an easy task to get supplies up to us, and as the hill-side and mountain roads became impassable, the last mile or so for the transport of all supplies had to be made by pack-mule.

Food-ship after food-ship was being sunk in the Mediterranean, and through most of December we were on one-third rations for men and horses. As we had suffered from thirst in the heat of Sinai, so we now suffered from hunger in the icy cold of the Balkans. There was a mere handful of corn for the horses daily, so we adopted the expedient of letting them loose during the day, to wander on the inner slopes of the hills, and scrounge what they could for themselves. At about four o'clock in the afternoon they would be brought in for their daily feed. At first we had to ride them out bareback, leave them, and then round them up to come in, but in a few days they learnt what was required of them, so that after breakfast—theirs was a scrunch of tibbin—we just released them and they cantered off. If was a curious sight in the evenings, a sergeant would blow heartily three blasts on a whistle, and from all corners of the hills they would come cantering in and stand exactly in their right places in their lines.

The shortage of rations became so acute for the men that squadron leaders scoured the countryside to purchase flocks of native sheep to give the men fresh

meat. My own squadron leader sent me right down
country to the town of Salonica itself to buy up what
supplies I could. I rode down to Janus, which was
now the railhead, and thus received considerable
attention from enemy aircraft, and then entrained
to Salonica. Here I bought up supplies of meat,
tabloid soups and things, and packed them into small
boxes, so that they could be readily taken from the
railhead by mules. Incidentally I was enabled in
these two days to see something of the city, and I
found my first impressions thoroughly justified. The
White Strand along the front and Venizelos Square
were the only streets of any pretentions to dignity
of architecture, the remainder were grey, drab and
shabby. I strolled through the covered-in street, the
bazaar rather like the Mouski in Cairo, but in all the
back streets of the city was the same filth and mucki-
ness, and the same nauseating stench. Many of the
houses in the centre of the city were built of wood,
and report had it that they were so badly infested
with bugs and lice that the terrible fire of Salonica,
which burnt out the greater part of the old city in
1917, was really a blessing in disguise.

I experienced, however, a brief moment of beauty
as I entered the austere Christian church, built of grey
and white stone. The interior was very simple and
dignified, and has been built around the original
church of St. Paul. I confess to a feeling of wonderment as I stood before the very stone pulpit from
which that patrician traveller and missionary had
preached his mighty sermons to the Thessalonians.

About this time there was considerable political
trouble in Greece and, with a section of the people, the
Allies were by no means popular ; in fact, the London
Scottish and other troops were sent south to guard the
passes near Olympus, to prevent Southern Greeks, in
the event of a rising, from coming into Macedonia and
threatening the rear of our positions. In Salonica
itself, two battalions of Greek troops were quartered,

known as the Venizelos Army. These paraded about
10 a.m. near the White Tower, and led by a gaily
bedecked officer riding on a pony so small, that his—
the officer's, of course—feet nearly touched the ground.
With resounding flourishes of trumpets and rattling of
loose equipment, they marched along the entire front
to Venizelos Square, where they were dismissed, and
rapidly disappeared into the cafés for the remainder
of the day. We called ourselves " Karno's Own "—
but these fellows—soldiers ? 'Nuff said.

There was a shortage of foodstuffs in the city itself,
especially of certain commodities. They say that at
this time the virtue of many a respectable matron was
sorely taxed by the sight of a pound of sugar. I don't
know—I had no sugar. I reckon soap must have been
dreadfully dear.

However, the three days' change from the excep-
tional cold of the outpost work was as welcome to me
as the sight of the stores was to the rest of the squadron
when I arrived back at the head of a team of pack-
mules with the much-coveted " mungaree."

On an exposed part of the road to Pateriche were
three old oxen waggons that had apparently stopped
a shell in full flight. By dint of much hauling we
fetched these in under cover of night, and made two
of the weirdest carts imaginable for moving sacks of
corn and tibbin about the lines. They were made
entirely of oak, which abounds in these parts ; and
the wheels, solid oak also, were most beautifully cut
and jointed. They were a lesson to anyone, for the
craftsmanship and the patience that must have been
called upon in their making. Nibby and I also
" borrowed," with the aid of one of these carts, two
pews from the ruined Pateriche Church, out of which
we made an excellent two-decker bunk with the aid
of some sacks, and an officer, newly arrived, whom we
kidded to do the sawing for us.

Our little shack in the sheltered ravine was comfort
itself compared with the rigours of the elements outside,

and by having a good supply of "oak roots" we managed to "keep the home fires burning," unless the wind was in an awkward direction, when it would blow clean down our improvised chimney and smoke us out.

One evening Nibby and I were sitting on the floor before a brightly burning fire, playing cribbage, when the fire began to smoke terribly. We continued as long as we could with our "fifteen two—fifteen four—blast the smoke."

"Whuff whuff—two for a pair, a run of three—crimes, it's getting awful."

"Your crib, Nibby—damn it, you can't see for the blasted stuff."

"Fifteen two only, perhaps that rat has got in the chimney."

We stuck it as long as we could, and finally barking like a walrus and with eyes watering, we had to fling open the door, stand in the open and let the fire clean out.

In the morning I found a wet shirt of mine, which I had hung over a bush to dry, well and truly stuffed down the chimney, and as we passed the forge we heard Farrier Bert chuckling : " Fifteen two, one for his nob—blast the b——y smoke. Perhaps there's a rat in the chimney," and thus learnt whom we had to thank for the evening's discomfort.

Just before Christmas we experienced several terrible snowstorms and blizzards. Outpost duty under these conditions called for all the endurance a man with an empty stomach could muster. Rations were still dreadfully short, and to go out hungry and attempt to get snatches of sleep, lying on the snow with one blanket wrapped around you, holding your horse's rein with one hand at the same time, during a long and icy cold night, was a great tax on one's stamina and disposition. It was not an unusual thing for even the strongest of men to faint from cold and lack of nourishment at this time.

The London Scottish who came through our wire

on such a night had had several days' forced marching
from Olympus through blizzard, and had accomplished
a remarkable achievement. Though I believe they
lost several men from exhaustion, they proved what
" hardiness and cheerfulness " can conquer when
called upon to make supreme efforts.

One great comfort was the rum issue. Many nights
we were allowed a double issue, and good strong blood-
reviving rum it was, too. They say that Store Quarter-
masters at the base became a little worried about the
number of bottles which were returned as broken in
transit for replacement. It certainly was rumoured
that our Quarter bloke had found a way of getting the
bottom off the bottle without spilling the contents—
and, of course, bottles can so easily get broken when
bumped about by mules. Anyone with a teetotaller
for a pal—if any—was a lucky fellow. Nibby and I
were very conscientious about the issue of rum to the
troops—they saw to that—but if anyone failed to turn
up at the cry : " Roll up for rum," we put his issue in
a bottle and kept it a fortnight for him. If he hadn't
drawn his issue by that time, we wished him good
health. " If the sergeants pinch your rum, never
mind."

I shall never forget that Christmas in the Balkans.
After a week or two of the severest weather, Christmas
dawn broke with brilliant sunshine and a sharp dry
frost, but it was an invigorating morning. Full
rations were issued, a mail was up bringing welcome
news from home, and parcels of " goodies." Nic,
Mick, Nibby and I arranged to ride over the three
miles to Gola where the Padre was holding Christmas
service in the open. We had a most wonderful man
for a Padre ; there will be much more told of him later.
He was a true " Christian "—no pride. He understood the rough natures of the men, and yet could
inspire the men to go to service for the service's sake.
Soldiers often feel shy at worship—but the Christian
spirit of the Padre somehow spread itself over all the

men when he had them gathered together, and his services were scenes of real enthusiasm.

With tummies well lined with rich fat bacon—which we hadn't tasted for weeks—we rode over the hill-slopes, our horses' hoofs ringing on the frost-bound turf, till we came to a little hollow half-way up the hill-side. Here the Padre had erected a little altar out of old boxes, neatly covered with a white cloth, with a simple wooden cross standing on it, with the communion vessels either side. All around the sun shone sparkling and glittering on the snow-capped mountains, the sky was as blue as periwinkles, and the air like wine. What a cathedral for the Christmas festival, and with what joy we sang the old hymns—"Hark, the herald angels sing," and "Christians, awake, salute the happy morn." The whole regiment was gathered round that little home-made altar in the hills, singing with heartiness and fervour ; a little given to chokiness of throat and mistiness of eye, as scenes of former Christmases, with beloved families in dear old England far away, floated through our memories. The Padre's sermon was brief, joyous and hopeful as always, and then he gave communion to all of us who could stay. It was a morning of spiritual beauty, and every man felt something of God's spirit in his veins, and happiness and peace in his soul as we rode away.

To-day they spend Christmas dancing to jazz bands in hotels.

The men were too isolated for general Christmas rejoicings so we spent our evening at a party in Nic's shack. Everyone had brought something to the feast—if it were only his goodwill. Real coal was burnt, a gift from the forge from Bert, but the *chef-d'œuvre* were the pancakes made by Nic, who had bartered bully beef for flour at one of the villages. There was plenty of rum—several bottles had arrived broken—plenty to eat—plenty of kindly talk of folks at home—plenty of singing, and " Good King Wenceslas " could have heard his generosity proclaimed well on into the morning.

New Year's Eve was as crisp, cold and clear as Christmas Day. I was out on patrol by the lake, and as I looked at my watch to make sure of the hour, to give a silent wish to herald-in the new-born child of Time, every gun along our front broke out with a salvo of greetings to the Bulgars.

Both food and weather conditions improved rapidly after Christmas, and with a better supply of rations for men and horses the constant patrol and heavy fatigue work were easier to bear. The cold was still intense—" Oh, for the hobs of hell," I heard one trooper apostrophize, as he shifted bales of tibbin with frozen fingers—but it was drier, and what snow remained was now frozen hard into the ground.

Through the foresight of our versatile Quarter bloke, the sergeants were able to lay in a good supply of whisky about this time. As he had to go down to Janus to draw stores, the Squadron Commander gave him a chit for a case of whisky—half to go to the officers and half to the sergeants. Whisky was about 4s. a bottle, and a rapid whip round provided Quarter with the necessary " verluse." In transit the chit somehow changed from one to ten, and consequently Quarter drew ten cases of " Scotch "—nine and a half for the sergeants and half a case for the officers. These cases we fetched on pack-mules which were covered with brushwood as they entered camp.

Some brands of whisky were very much better than others, and, curiously enough, the lesser known brands were often the more mellow and matured. Amongst the sergeants we gave them rank : R.S.M. Antiquary, S.S.M. Crawford, Sergeant King George, Corporal Christopher, and so on ; I will not disclose what popular brand was known as Sanitary Wallah.

We all seemed to have bags of money in Salonica. Miles from anywhere where it could be spent, and the exchange being goodness knows how many

drachmas to the pound—everyone carried a wad of
drachma notes the size of a bookmaker's roll. In fact,
at poker and pontoon the smallest stake at one time
was a five drachma note—five shillings.

There was a sergeant who had been away from the
Regiment on gas services and one thing or another—
you know the kind of officer or sergeant who is always
being sent on duties away from the Regiment, R.T.O.'s,
A.P.M.'s, etc. This fellow was a jolly chap, with a
big red face beaming with smiles, a knack of telling
a story, and a most infectious laugh, but—if he could
do a damn silly thing instead of a reasonable one, he
somehow managed to do it. He will long be remembered by two little incidents.

Having to take his turn with the others, he was sent
out in charge of the Doiran patrol to relieve the
twenty-four hour post. He started at half-past five
and by seven o'clock frantic telephone messages were
coming from the outpost as to when the h—— their
relief was coming. Eight o'clock, nine o'clock and
ten o'clock, and then a small party rode off in search
of him. They found the patrol only half a mile from
camp riding in the home direction. Heaven alone
knows where he had led them—they'd been round in
wide circles several times, and to all requests from
corporals to be allowed to show him the way, he had
replied : " Hi ! mind your own b——y business, I'm
in charge of this patrol ! " It was the last one he
ever was in charge of, I can tell you.

Anyhow, a few days later a message arrived that
sheets of corrugated iron could be drawn from the
railhead for covering in dug-outs, cookhouses and so
forth. Our jolly friend was thought well capable of
this little expedition. Accordingly he was given six
pack-mules and half a dozen men, just to go down
through the pass and draw the corrugated iron. He
was allowed, I believed, twenty-four hours for the
journey ; anyhow, at the end of a day and a half he
arrived back with his six men, but devil a mule and

devil a sheet of corrugated iron had he with him.
It appears that he had loaded up the iron sheets just
before dusk. Now, I have before stated, that if he
could possibly find a silly thing to do—his name was
Grock. In spite of protest, he would have his own
way, and instead of loading up the sheets lengthways
and sideways on either side of the pack-saddle, he
had insisted on their being strapped on across the top
of the saddle. The sheets were some nine feet long,
and what happened was easy to imagine. All went
well across the plain in the half-light, but soon they
started climbing up the narrow and loose-stoned hill
tracks. A mule slipped, as he recovered—wallop—
a bang on the head from the corrugated iron above.
Up goes his head, a corresponding wallop on his behind.
Up goes his heels, wallop on his head again. Now,
docile as a mule can be, he won't stand that sort of
see-saw trick for long. It only required one to turn
and knock aside the lad who was leading him, to get
himself thoroughly tangled up with those coming
behind. Such a scene there was in the pitch-dark in
a narrow ravine, mules kicking, iron bending and
banging, in fact it was one glorious shimmozzle, until
eventually the whole convoy broke away.

Shortly afterwards Mules No. 9207, 6402, etc., were
struck off the strength, having left the Regiment,
and Sergeant X. was posted to Brigade Headquarters
as gas sergeant.

Not only were sergeants occasionally slow in the
uptake. There was an officer posted to us, obviously
from somebody who wanted to "drop him." The
Colonel stood him a week and then he went as railway
officer to railhead.

Old Charlie had been taken to cook for the officers'
mess, and many a delicate dish came my way. On one
occasion a squadron leader had shot a few partridges,
and at Charlie's invitation I had gone round " to 'ave
a bit of partridge." We managed one apiece whilst
Charlie told me of his woes.

" I says to 'em, I can't cook and chop the wood for
the fire too ; these great logs 'ere. They says, ' We'll
chop the wood,' but they soon get tired. So I says,
' No b——y wood, no b——y dinner ' ; that's what
I says to 'em. And I mean it.

"He says to me : ' Cook,' says he, ' the rum don't
seem to last as long as it should, and what there is
seems very weak.' Nasty like, as if I'd touch his rum.
' I puts a little in the soup,' I says, and it ain't half a
little I may tell you. ' Yus,' says he, ' and what happened to those partridges I shot the other day ? '
' Well,' says I, ' I left 'em hanging in the cookhouse
to get a bit 'igh, and I don't know, perhaps the
wolves had 'em—plenty of wolves in Salonica,' says I.
Yes, that's what I tells 'em, if they don't chop the
b——y wood, they gets no b——y dinner."

This squadron leader always carried a sporting gun
with him and made many a bag of partridge, hare and
wild duck. The wild duck could be seen nightly flying
towards the lake in their long echelon "follow my
leader " flight. He once rode out to the Doiran post
by the lake and interrogated a picquet thus :

" Seen anything ? "

" Well, sir, there seems to be a bit of movement on
that big hill there ; a couple of shells dropped about
a mile half-right, less than an hour ago, the connecting
foot patrol reported at eleven and . . ."

" I don't mean that ! I mean, seen any duck ? "

" Seen any duck ! " became the squadron catch-
word.

The same Major certainly "took the mike out of
me " on one occasion.

Having surveyed the lake carefully from a sheltered
position he said : "Damn, there ought to be some
good fish there. We'll bring a few Mills' bombs down
to-morrow evening, and bomb a few." Laugh ! I
went back with "What do you think the damned old
fool's up to now ! Bombing fish, that's his latest."

So we went bombing, and I wondered how on earth

he expected the flying pieces of bomb to hit fish. He was right, however, a bomb was thrown about ten yards from the bank and in a second there were dozens of bodies of dead fish floating on the surface. He explained to me that the explosion caused such a sudden change of pressure in the water that the gills of the fish couldn't stand it, and they died immediately. Laughs, laughs, last.

Spring broke rapidly in the Balkans, and the warmth of the sunshine and the drying of the red brown earth was indeed a welcome change from the snow and its consequent mud and slush. Just as in England, it seemed to come down suddenly; one particular morning, and everyone was singing and cleaning his rifle and saddlery in the open. The earth quickly clothed itself in fresh green grasses, the trees sprouted forth so freely one could almost watch them grow. The hill-side became alive with all manner of living creature, snakes and tortoises abounded in the long coarse grasses, and the bush and woodland echoed with the song and chatter of myriads of birds bustling over domestic duties newly developed upon them.

It was glorious to be alive—it all seemed so much like dear old England. One could get clean, too. I well remember the first bath after that winter. A spring afternoon, I stripped by a translucent rock-pool of water harvested from a swiftly running stream. The water was icy cold, but it was sheer joy to plunge in after having soaped oneself on the bank. The afterglow of the flesh atingling, and the act of dressing again, feeling clean, were sheer delights.

With the renaissance of the animal and bird life— the sporting Major mentioned previously was in his element and made many a handsome bag.

On one occasion I shot a large golden eagle that was perching on a crag. I took its wings and pinioned them up over the dug-out as a mascot. The next evening I began to think I had " shot the albatross," for in our absence the dug-out had fallen in ; had we been sleeping there we should have been buried under a couple of tons of earth.

There was a very large wild bird that could be seen occasionally known as a bustard. He was quite the size of a large turkey and, rumour had it, very good to eat. Crossing a narrow plain one day with my batman, we thought we saw one of these birds a good mile away. My batman dismounted and took a couple of pots at it, but it somehow disappeared. I only mention the incident because for days after we kidded the batman " that he'd better lie low—there was a h—— of a stink abroad—someone had shot the Brigadier of the artillery, and two Yeomen had been seen riding away." The poor fellow made himself so miserable that we had " to blow the gaff " to ease his mind. Pranks played upon one another with dead nine-foot-long snakes were common, but the greatest fun of all was the tortoise-racing. There were regular meetings every Sunday afternoon for this exciting and exhilarating sport, and large sums of money changed hands over the results. A soldier, as is well known, will make anything the medium of a wager— who'll get tight first, who'll expectorate the further, and a thousand other less civilized points of comparison. Tortoise-racing was great fun indeed. The procedure was as follows :

A stake about a foot high was driven into the ground and around it a circle was drawn of from six to eight feet in diameter. You brought your tortoise, who had been stabled outside your dug-out in a water bucket, and numbered him by sticking a piece of stamp paper on his back. Someone was elected stakeholder, and all owners deposited a five-drachma note with this worthy. The tortoises were then placed in the centre with their heads close to the stake and their backs to the circular line. First tortoise completely over the line won the race and brought the fifty or sixty bob to the owner. No one was allowed to touch the tortoises, and the fun, of course,

was that some wouldn't move at all, some would only
move an inch or two, others would back out and start
for the line only to stop dead and ruminate, an inch
or two from it. Others would just reach the line and
then turn back and continue in zigzag directions, but
never over it; sometimes two long-separated lovers
would meet at the post and forgetting the purpose of
their presence, indulge in amorous combat in the lists
of love. Some races lasted but a few minutes, others
nearly an hour, but they were always the occasion
of great laughter and merriment. In addition to the
stakes there were side bets, and usually someone or
other would make a book on the runners. Nic and I
possessed in half-shares a lusty young tortoise known
as Little Sidney. He was a really good runner;
we rather fancied from various observations that he
was of a wanton disposition, much given to Ovidian
delights, and we attributed his general sprightliness,
vagrancy, and purposefulness of movement, to his
constant search for some long-lost Sophia. Be that as
it may, he was nearly always one of the first to move,
and generally made fairly rapid progress with his
little head stretched well out in front of him. He just
could cover the ground all right, and Nic and I bought
many a gallon of " pig's ear " with the stakes provided
by his prowess.

One Saturday afternoon he won no fewer than
four times, and we had badly hit a " bookie " who after
each successive win increased his odds against " Little
Sidney winning again." This " bookie " was an
officer's servant, very proud of the fact that he was
a member of " Ladbrook's " or some other firm of
commission agents, and consequently felt that his
knowledge of pedigree horses entitled him to " shout
the odds " about tortoises. He made a book at many
of these little gatherings and this particular afternoon
Nic and I had given him a real good " caning." When
Little Sidney had won twice, he apparently consulted
his law of averages and laid eight to one instead of

I

four to one. Nic and I had been doing well, so that we, increasing our stakes in proportion as the odds lengthened, sadly diminished his wad. He came to us in the evening and asked if he could buy Little Sidney for the Sunday afternoon, and would we not let on he'd bought it, but let it race in our names—we to collect the stakes—and hand them over to him afterwards ? He paid us handsomely and on the following afternoon we took Little Sidney down to the Chester Rodeo. We met him brimming over with coarse enthusiasm at the prospect of getting his money back and Nic said :

" You know, this tortoise knows us, he'll only race for us—I always make a low hissing noise outside the circle and he comes to me."

His reply was gobular.

" Straight away," says Nic.

More spheres, only larger.

" What'll you bet he doesn't win in the first four ? " queries Nic.

Only his gross egotism led him into it. " I'll lay you six to one he does."

We took him heavily and for the first four races backed something else. Strangely enough, Little Sidney actually did not move from the post in the first race, nor the second. When he still remained a non-starter in the third, our friend the bookie became redder and redder in the face and extremely expostulate as to Little Sidney winning the fourth. Little Sidney seemed to be in a meditative frame of mind, for he refused to move in the fourth race also. We drew our money, and Nic said : " If you hadn't been so cocky and not believed me, you wouldn't have lost all that. I'll hiss at him at the next race and you'll be all right."

Before the race Nic stepped into the ring to give Little Sidney a shaking up. Would you believe it—truth is ever stranger than fiction—Alas, alack´! Little Sidney was dead.

Nic exclaimed : " After all that winning yesterday. The excitement of waiting for the race must have been too much for him."

The advance of spring brought with it an increased activity along the front. When concert parties come up the line to amuse the troops, you can bet there is going to be a big push shortly. News of it was constantly in the air and after many smaller raids the infantry made two gallant attempts to capture the heights of Petite Couronne and Grand Couronne—as previously mentioned the keys of the position on this part of the Doiran front.

We as cavalry were massed in rear, standing-to for days at a time waiting to burst through. The P.B.I. had a dreadful time attempting the impossible in the storming of these heights, and after a fortnight's bombardment and engagement there was a temporary lull.

This front was badly served by English aeroplanes and consequently we received considerable attention from enemy aircraft. There was a famous squadron of nineteen planes which came over every other day or so, and wrought a deal of damage behind the line. On one of their visits they reached as far as the Summer Hill Camp, where a large number of men were waiting to go on leave, and the casualties were said to have been over a thousand.

I am neither more plucky nor less brave than the average; I certainly am blessed by not suffering from nerves, but this air squadron really made me feel very much afraid on one occasion.

After the frustrated attempt to break through the enemy lines, a little home leave to England was going, and one was allowed from our squadron. The troop sergeants tossed up and luckily the lot fell to me. I had not been home for two years, and was naturally very bucked indeed. Now I was quite accustomed to being bombed by this famous air squadron, as it was often our lot, and usually one waited under cover till they had passed, but circumstances alter cases. I was due to go down the line to catch the boat for England on Easter Monday, and early on Easter Sunday morning, we heard the familiar and ominous drone of the enemy planes. Looking out, they could be seen coming up through the gap in the mountains like giant flamingoes flying into the rosy dawn. Nearer and nearer they came until it was evident they would soon be right overhead. I was going to England, home and beauty the next day—if I didn't " cop " it right now. My God, I was windy. I could see the line of explosions coming nearer and nearer, the next one only a quarter of a mile ahead. Breaking out into a cold perspiration I rushed for a dug-out, buried myself with my head in my hands, as deeply as possible, and almost quivered with fear, until two bombs dropped quite close and I judged they were well over. Usually in a battle there is too much to do and think about to get the wind up properly—but on this occasion I had it badly. On their return flight we managed to bring one of these planes down by machine-gun fire ; a rather notable achievement.

It was my lucky day all right, as in the evening I rode over to say good-bye to " B " Squadron sergeants. I hadn't drawn my pay as I knew if I did I should be treating half the Regiment, and I arrived at their dug-out with about five drachmas. By the light of two candles stuck in bottles, eight of them were playing " Slippery Sam," mugs well filled with whisky and water by their sides. At their invitation to join in I had three lucky turns, then " went the lot " and got it. I finally left the table with a huge wad of notes which, when I changed into English " dough " at the base were worth nearly thirty pounds. A good gamble starting with five " bob."

I enjoyed the journey home immensely, although we had to go cautiously on account of the activity of the submarines in the Mediterranean. On their account we put into a most beautiful harbour in

Crete and stayed two days there. Similarly we bolted for the harbour of Palermo on hearing of the tragic fate of the *Transylvania*, which was sunk with four hundred nurses on board within twenty miles of us.

A little picture of the trip is impinged on my memory. One evening I went up late on deck and marvelled at the magnificent red glow on a patch of the sky which was almost overhead. Later as the moon came up, one caught the great outline of Mount Etna, and wonderful indeed the sight seemed to me. Next morning we rode into Messina Harbour and it struck me as awesome to think of the power of that mighty volcano, that it could hurl tons of rock such a distance.

The harbour of Palermo is one of the most beautiful sights I have ever seen ; and as very few troopships ever called there, our ship was surrounded by small craft out sight-seeing on the Sunday evening. Thousands of the inhabitants gathered around the ship, whilst we gave them an impromptu concert with an improvised band. The National Anthems of the Allies were very popular—but they repeatedly called for the Italian Anthem. This we didn't know, so we did our best with a rendering of

> " Oh, oh, Antonio, he's gone away,
> Left me all aloneio,
> All on my owneo "

We sang to them for hours, and if they didn't enjoy themselves, we did.

The very day I landed in London they had a very celebrated daylight raid over the city. It didn't seem anything like so bad or so intimate as those we had been subjected to on many occasions.

The happy days of leave flitted away and I eventually found myself boarding the well-known and ill-fated *Aragon*, at Marseilles. She was a beautifully equipped boat, well-known to us by name, as she had

been a kind of Staff rest-boat off the Dardanelles.
Weird and wonderful stories were told of life on board
the *Aragon*, and rumour had it that when they wanted
to raise steam and leave Gallipoli, they couldn't
move her at first for the empty champagne bottles
floating in the water around her! That's a tall
one.

However, I had only been on board a few hours
when an important-looking officer sent for me and
made me ship's quartermaster for the trip. We took
on board a lot of poor young rookies, whose physique
so infuriated old Farrier-Sergeant Dodd that he could
only walk up and down the deck all day, twisting his
gigantic moustaches and shouting, "Blimy! what's
the b——y Army coming to ? One punch, boy—I'd
kill the lot of 'em."

Ship's quartermaster proved a good job; I had
special officer's food in the purser's cabin and "buck-
shee " rum from the storekeeper nightly.

I was almost sorry when Salonica Harbour was
reached, and my surprise can well be imagined when,
as embarkation was in full swing, I received the order,
" Yeomanry ranks, remain on board." There were
only six of us and we then learnt that whilst on leave
our regiments had been shifted back to Egypt.

We looked out over the city of Salonica and somehow most of us felt very glad we were not landing
there again. In two days' time the headquarters of
the 60th Division with several Generals came on
board, and also a battalion of the London Scottish.
Amongst these good fellows I found three old school
chums, an officer, a sergeant and a private. The
officer was a great chum and treated me well—the
sergeant also—so I did what I could with the rations
for the private.

The *Aragon* after many rumours of attack sailed
safely into Alexandria Harbour, and with two large
bottles of ship's rum as a parting gift I went ashore
and entrained for Ismailia. The night was very cold,

and so three of us shifted the two bottles neat before
morning. When morning arrived it brought a lovely
fat head as well as the tropical sun ; so we all kipped
under a railway truck in Ismailia station for a good
twelve hours, before attempting to find the Regiment.

CHAPTER VI

THE ADVANCE TO GAZA

" In the morning and at the going down of the sun,
We will remember them."

I FOUND my Regiment once again camped on loose drifting sand, sweltering beneath the rays of a July sun, on the desert at El Ferdan. The joys of leave had been sweet, but it was also grand to be back with one's pals, to wander in the horse-lines and see how this and that " longed-faced friend " had fared.

In exchange for news of their friends in England whom I had visited, they gave me all the doings of the Regiment after my departure. The manner in which they left Salonica was both interesting and illuminating. The Higher Command did not wish the Allies to realize that large bodies of troops were leaving Salonica, so the final embarkation took place very stealthily at night. After trekking down country to within four miles of the harbour, all kit was taken away and packed, including saddles and rifles. The entire " clobber " of the Regiment was thus driven off in transport waggons, and one evening the Regiment rode down to the harbour, barebacked and with no equipment, just as if out for exercise ; but the horses after standing in the dock yards were loaded up surreptitiously after dark, and thus the Regiment crept away from Salonica.

The horses looked very fit now, and three or four days' concentration on saddle fitting and blanket folding presaged a long trek in front of us. Indeed, on July 1st, we rode out of El Ferdan for the long

desert journey up to Palestine, an adventure that did
not really end until the Regiment entered Damascus
some eighteen months later.

Our first halting-place was Kantara, and those who
had seen it two years previously, when it was a derelict
native village, with but a few mud huts, and an old
mosque hiding among some fifty date palms, were
amazed to find it had grown into a base camp of large
proportions. It was now a great canvas city with
well-marked roads, huge dumps of stores and ammunition, connected by the other bank of the Canal
and, incidentally, direct with Cairo, Alexandria and
Port Said, by a gigantic swing railway bridge. It had
a station with many sidings, and it was indeed curious
to see the engines and rolling stock marked L.S.W.R.
and L.C. & D.

We did not enter this town, which was to become the
real base of the Palestine operations, but after bivou-
acking the night on its outskirts, we started off next
morning across the old desert caravan route running
parallel with the coast, the ancient pilgrim way from
Egypt to Palestine.

This was the track along which the armies of
Biblical times had passed ; the road that Joseph trod,
when he fled from the persecution of Herod, with the
young Christ into Egypt ; and again the route taken
by Napoleon after the sacking of Cairo, in his ill-fated
attempt to conquer Europe from the rear. The Turks
themselves had advanced this way for their early
attack in 1915 on the defences of the Suez Canal. It
was a route pregnant with history. Oft-times when
the horses' hooves sank deeper than ever into the loose
shifting sand-dunes, one fell to musing and marvelling
how Napoleon could so have inspired his men, that,
dressed in the heavy and cumbersome uniforms of
their times, and with such primitive commissariat
and medical services, they managed the long and
tedious trek to the Holy Land, and dragged their
field-pieces with them.

We halted the first evening at Pelusium. Here, at
one time, one of the many delta mouths of the Nile
had emptied its waters into the sea, but the heap of
old ruins by the shore was all that remained of a once
flourishing Roman port. The next day a short trek on
to Romani, where the Gloucesters and Warwicks had
so successfully avenged themselves on the Turk for
his surprise attack, and the loss of so many of their
comrades at Katia in April, 1916.

Thence by daily stages through Khirba, Bir el Abd,
Tilul, Bir el Mazar, Badaweel to El Arish. These
places, though named, were isolated and uninhabited,
usually small clusters of palm trees around a few
brackish pools. In some cases we had to depend on
our water from these pools, but it was very salt and
horrible to the palate.

A native explained to me that if you cut down palm
trees and threw small logs into the water it sweetened
the taste; and I couldn't help thinking of Moses at
Marah; when the Israelites had murmured that they
could not drink of the waters for they were bitter.
" And he cried unto the Lord; and the Lord showed
him a tree, which, when he had cast it into the waters,
the waters were made sweet." Again the native
saying in Sinai had been, " where you find limestone
you'll find water "—Moses had struck the rock and
the water had gushed out for the people to drink.
Mostly, however, we drew from " the pipe."

Three masterpieces of engineering ran almost
parallel from Kantara to El Arish. A single-line
railway, which had been laid by the Royal Engineers
at the rate of a mile a day, was the first wonder. It
must have been extremely difficult to get sufficient
hardness of surface on which to lay the sleepers, and
the constant shifting sand had given them much
trouble.

The second was the pipe. There was an old Arab
saying, " When the waters of the Nile flow into Palestine then shall the land be freed from the infidel."

BRITISH GRAVES AT GAZA. SAMSON'S RIDGE

WATERING BEFORE BEERSHEBA

This prophecy was " being brought to pass," for a large pipe was being laid across this desert, sometimes open to view, sometimes covered with sand, but carrying Nile water further and further up the line. At various stopping-places this pipe was tapped, so that water could be drawn off for men and horses. It received spasmodic attention from enemy aircraft, but I never heard that it was ever hit.

The third feature had been laid down to facilitate the movement of infantry when required. It is dreadfully tiring marching dismounted in the heat over sand into which your boot sinks up to the top at every step you take, and again one had to pity the P.B.I. A brainy idea, however, had struck someone, and whole lengths of fairly fine meshed wire—like tennis-court surround—were being stretched down upon the sand to form a wire road. The wire was kept down by means of roping it at intervals to small sand-bags filled and buried in the sand ; in some places pegging had proved sufficient, but the tying down was the more secure. This road was in course of construction as we trekked up, and must have proved a great benefit to the infantry who followed after.

We had a complete day's rest at El Arish, and I for one could do with it. Here was a native village and groves and groves of fig trees. The sand was so tick-ridden that it was impossible to sleep for long. Being July, the sun had been intensely hot throughout the trek, the dust and sand raised by a column of cavalry had become grimed in with the perspiration. We were able to wash at El Arish, but I foolishly lay down to rest in the heat of the day beneath a heavily foliaged fig tree without my pith helmet. With the shifting of the sun, a direct ray through the trees had focussed on a spot on my head and gave me severe sunstroke. A really bad touch of sun is quite lowering, a splitting head—worse than after a couple of bottles of bad port—and constant vomiting was my portion, but

I woke up fairly fresh the following morning to move on to Rafa.

Rafa was one huge camel camp ; it was obvious that camels for transport were being massed here from all parts of Egypt and Sinai. Wherever one looked the face of the desert seemed pimpled by rows of these squatting, meditative quadrupeds. Horses as a rule dislike camels, and many will refuse to go anywhere near them. In large quantities they smell strongly, and their fur and skin are usually so alive with ticks and fleas that wherever they have camped the sand is left unclean for months. Certainly no other troops could camp on the sand at Rafa.

A further day's trek took us to Abasan, where we relieved a brigade of Australian Light Horse, and now found ourselves in reserve to the line. We had been continuously trekking for a fortnight and, although it had been always " hot and unwholesome, dusty and dry," in·the main I had enjoyed the constant move-ment and change from place to place.

An examination of the horses after this trek proved that at last we could reckon ourselves A1 for horse-management. There was hardly a sore back in the Regiment and not one in our squadron at all.

Abasan, though still on the desert, was a far worse place to camp than any we had yet encountered. It wasn't even decent clean sand, but a loose and coloured dust on top of a harder surface. There was a perpetual wind, and a dust storm blowing every day. We spent an unholy month here, practising full kit alarm parades at all hours of the day and night. We certainly became proficient at packing a saddle in the minimum time, and galloping out to alarm posts.

I hope we pleased the authorities ; we used to say that the Brigadier looked out of his tent in the morn-ing, rubbed his hands and said to the Brigade Major : " Fine day, this morning, Major, let's get off and mess the troops about a bit."

About five miles from Abasan, riding towards the

THE ADVANCE TO GAZA

coast was a wonderful old Arab village called Khan
Yunis. Here the prickly pear hedges, those giant
cacti, grew to a great height, enclosing fertile fields
and compounds. We enjoyed many a feast of this
fruit, cutting the ripe pear off the ear of cactus with a
bayonet, and rolling it thoroughly in the sand with the
foot to rub off the outer prickles. By careful slicing
with a jack-knife, the pomegranate-like interior could
be extracted, and the sweet juicy core thoroughly
enjoyed. There were small wooden burrs in this,
however, which stuck in the tongue and palate,
hardly revealing their presence until the fruit had been
swallowed.

There was a narrow native bazaar that was one
continuous babble of bartering and cacophony of
street cries. Just outside this village was a wonderful old ruin, a church built by the Crusaders, with
Norman pillars and arches, on which a dome had been
superimposed, in an attempt to convert the building
into a mosque at some later period. There stood this
ancient pile, rising above the jumbled mud huts of
the villagers in austere grandeur, recalling romantic
days of Saladin and Cœur-de-Lion.

In the middle of August we moved up to the line
at Shellal on the desert side of the Wadi Ghuzzie.
The Wadi Ghuzzie has to be seen to be believed.
Shellal was just a dirty spot upon a dust-laden wind-
swept filthy plain. It was grit, grit everywhere—grit
and chlorine in the tea, grit and chlorine in the stew ;
but grit without chlorine on the bread and jam. Water
was very scarce as this was the dry season, and a wash
twice a week was a luxury ; but by saving a little tea
one could shave every day. On the right of this plain
of Shellal was a huge and solitary hill, known as Tel el
Fara, which looked as if a monstrous baked potato
had been cut in two, and a half stuck upon the plain.
The Wadi Ghuzzie was a deep ravine, so sudden that
one could almost fall over it from Shellal, before being
aware of its existence. It was sixty feet deep and in

places dropped sheer from the plain ; it was about
eighty yards across and was a partially dried-up
watercourse in summer. Like many of these wadis
it was so clear cut that, standing two hundred yards
away, it could not be seen, and the desert appeared
continuous. There were, of course, several narrow
tracks leading down from either side, in fact we daily
took our horses down to water at the pools still left
at intervals along the bed. During the rainy season it
became a raging torrent to the sea.

I must now explain roughly the military situation.
The wadi really marked the line between ourselves
and the Turks, and ran from Beersheba in a semi-
circle right across the whole front to the sea. This
was the last sign of water before one reached the
Turks, who held a strongly fortified position from
Gaza to Beersheba, with special fortifications and
trench systems at Gaza, Es Sheria, and Beersheba. At
Gaza the wadi ran into the sea some five miles from
the town ; our troops holding a position on the Gaza
side. At Shellal, roughly the centre of the line, the
wadi was ten miles from the Turkish line, and the
ground in between being waterless, was No Man's
Land. It was therefore our duty as Cavalry to keep
it constantly patrolled. Across the wadi for a considerable distance the whole front was wired, and
infantry posts from the 60th Division—all London
boys—occupied these scanty battlements. We were
responsible, in addition to the constant patrolling,
for outpost duty at night well outside the wire, and
during the month we spent here, many little brushes
occurred between ourselves and the Turkish cavalry.

The ground was so undulating some way out to the
front, that it was not uncommon to come round the
bend of a sand-dune and on to scouts of the enemy,
quite suddenly.

There was always sufficient " doing " to keep one
alert and interested. Usually they fled and we chased
as far as we dared without getting on to their main

positions. Several longer desert reconnaissances in force, lasting three or four days, were undertaken towards Beersheba and around the enemy's left flank. On one occasion we chased back several groups of enemy cavalry, and remained holding a position from which we could plainly see the city of Beersheba and the people moving about in it, whilst artillery officers made a full survey of the ground behind us.

We became proper campaigners, each section of four and, indeed, each man, being entirely able to shift for himself for days at a time. Dust-stained and tanned a dark mahogany, we rode without tunics, shirts cut short to the sleeves (new tennis fashion), each man carrying spare feeds and two water-bottles, and an old fruit tin or billy can. Wood was very scarce and so were matches, so that we learnt to scrounge every bit of wood that we could. At an hour's halt on such a reconnaissance, you would see a whole regiment break up into little groups, each two or three men bringing their quota of wood to make a fire. Water was poured into the billy-can, and when boiling a good pinch of mixed tea and sugar was thrown into the can. We all carried our own tea and sugar rations separately in little screws of paper, and, dirty though these became, after parching all day, the brew tasted just grand in the cool of the evening.

We were under constant surveillance from enemy aircraft, all German planes, and on more than one occasion were very heavily bombed, although we marched in small irregular groups by day known as aeroplane formation.

I remember, on the chief reconnaissance in force to Beersheba, watching a most thrilling fight between three large enemy bombing planes and three small scouts of our own flying corps. The German planes had only just commenced to drop bombs, and were circling, when the scouts seemed to appear from no-where. The circling, swerving and nose-diving, with the accompanying rattle-rattle of their machine-guns, up in the clear cerulean sky, with the sun throwing off glints and sharp reflections as they twirled and wheeled, was a fascinating sight. The scouts, of course, drove off the bombers. Just as it should be.

We were often bombed in camp, but little damage was done.

This life with its constant patrolling and scouting was hard work, and called for long periods of endurance in the matter of spells without food and water, but on the whole, truth be told—it was rather fun.

The country in front of the wire was so uniform in all features, and the gaps in the wire so similar, that it was easy to lose oneself after dark. A squadron leader left to lead the Regiment home after a long reconnaissance, once took us round in a circle three times to my knowledge and all within a mile or two of the required opening. Tel el Fara looked so much alike from all sides one could never quite take direction from it.

A chum of mine, an officer in the London Scottish, who were near us at this time, tells the following story:

He was on duty in a small dug-out with a post guarding a gap in the wire one night, when another officer knocked at the " bivy " sheet.

" Excuse me, could you tell me where the ' London Irish ' are ? "

" Yes, come in. Have a swig out of the bottle ; half and half, you know, then I'll put you right."

He took him to the opening of the " bivy," and pointed to some lights which appeared to be at the base of the Tel el Fara.

" Yes, there you are, you can't go wrong. Back half a mile, and then turn along a path to the left, along the top of the Ghuzzie."

About an hour afterwards an anxious voice knocked at the " bivy " :

" Excuse me, but could you tell me where the London Irish—— Oh ! I've been here before."

" Yes, you have, cully. I know it's very difficult—
but I'll show you another way. Have a spot before
you go ! "

" This time, go down the same way as before, but
go right down into the Ghuzzie, up the next opening
and then back to your left about a quarter of a mile."

" Thanks old man, sorry to be such a b——y
nuisance."

Two hours later my chum had well and truly
kipped down, leaving a light on in case the picket
should want to call him hurriedly, when he was
awakened by a scrambling of feet near by—a bang on
the "bivy" sheet and

" Is this the London Irish ? "

At sight of each other they were too overcome to
do anything but roar with laughter, and the wanderer
finally decided to spend the night with the Thistle,
and find the Shamrock in the morning.

The two previous battles of Gaza, in both of which
the Turk, when almost beaten, had managed to drive
us back on the desert for lack of reserves, water
and rations, had been directed by Headquarters at
The Savoy Hotel, Cairo. There was now a new
General in charge, and Headquarters was moved on
to the desert itself, just behind the line. Rumour had
it that many a muddler had been sent back to London.
This new General rode about among the troops with
only an orderly, instead of a retinue of thirty, and
spoke to the men themselves, asking after their
comfort, if rations were good, and when they last had
leave. Our new chief was none other than General
Allenby himself, and it is stating nothing but the
truth to say that his coming bred a new confidence
amongst the troops, especially the Yeomanry. He
understood horses, their capabilities and limitations,
and we soon felt that we could trust him to look after
the interests of all ranks, and see that those behind
the line did their job as well as those in it.

There's nothing a soldier dislikes so much as being

K

unnecessarily messed about—you know his term for
it—and, mark you, he usually gets a bellyful. But
under Allenby nothing was done without a purpose.
At his advent, our rations and water almost immediately became more regular, more to proper
quantity, and better in condition. There were not so
many having a picking.

The whole of the Yeomanry and the Australian
Light Horse were now organized into the Desert
Mounted Corps under the able leadership of Major-
General H. G. Chauvel.

One peculiar sight that was always noticeable on
these reconnaissances out in front of the wire, was
that there seemed to be a clear line of demarcation
as to where the desert ended and the fertile land—the
land flowing with milk and honey—of Palestine began.

" And he went down to Gaza, which is on the edge
of the desert," accurately describes it. It was possible
to stand on our side of the Ghuzzie and, looking behind and away to the right, to see the great unending
stretches of the Sinai desert rolling on to the horizon ;
but across the Ghuzzie and to the north-east one
could see green fields and an occasional tree of the
Promised Land.

Our patrol reconnaissance work was taken over by
the Light Horse, and we rode back through the coastal
sand-dunes, through the great cactus hedges of prickly
pear around Khan Yunis, to a spot right on the beach
known as Marakeb. Here the sand was beautiful
and clean, our horse-lines were within two hundred
yards of the dashing breakers of the Mediterranean,
and life was joyous indeed.

There was a sand-shelf a short distance from the
shore which caused a peculiar current close in and
very high breakers ; but after the dust and grit, the
constant bathing and swimming was glorious. The
delights of getting clean are unknown to those who
have all their lives been able to turn the tap on.

We frequently bathed the horses as well. It was

great fun riding barebacked and naked into the foam,
being knocked clean off and swimming back alongside
your own daily mount. How devoted you can become to a particular horse when he is your constant
care and companion ; when you are both more or less
interdependent for your very existence.

We had mounted sports here, many concerts, a
gramophone, with only four records—" La Bohême,"
" You great big wonderful baby," " If you were the
only girl in the world," " From the trenches the boys
are calling." I can remember them to this day, and—
wait for it—a canteen. Beer again—some of it was
Bomonti, that ghastly wishy-washy stuff—but it was
beer. How dreadful that men should think that so
important, but when you're fond of a pint of God's
good ale and it's two months since you tasted it—it
does remain rather an event in the memory.

All this " keeping the men cheerful " always pre-
sages " something doing," and after a month of this
luxurious life on this " Lido " beach, we rode back
again to the line at grit-swept dusty Shellal.

Great activities during our absence were evident,
as huge dumps had grown up everywhere, and a
branch of the railway from Kantara now ran right
across the Ghuzzie itself. Water bases had also been
developed well out into the desert so that troops could
be supplied when operating at a considerable distance
from the ordinary water supply. Moreover, there was
a constant bombardment of Gaza in progress on our
left ; the land batteries being assisted by the Navy.
Lying off Gaza were four monitors, two gunboats, a
cruiser and several small craft, all harassing the
enemy's strong posts on the right of his line.

Although this line extended from Gaza to Beersheba, and he had good lateral communications, so
that troops could rapidly be transported to any
threatened part, Gaza was his great stronghold. Here
he was fairly entrenched along a high and almost
impregnable ridge known as Samson's Pillar, and

with good water supplies behind him, he was certainly going to take some shifting. The continuous heavy bombardment warned us that a general attack was about to take place, although the men knew nothing of the date or the scheme.

There was a good spy scare about this time, and it was as well not to travel far from your regiment alone, or some over-zealous person would place you under arrest.

Moreover, whilst down at the beach we had had Turkish lessons and had been taught to say very precisely:

Tesleem olonooz !	Surrender !
Nerdadir Ferrik ?	Where is the General ?
Ablooka olondenoz !	You are surrounded !

and various other phrases.

I don't suppose that is anything like the original Turkish, but that's how I took them down in a note-book, very phonetically.

Now, every regiment has its great battle, its own big show, and though we were to go through many battles and operations on a much greater scale, our big " do " was to come almost immediately.

In the general scheme of things it was perhaps little indeed, but it was great to us and, although we lost heavily of the dearest and best of our comrades, we covered ourselves with glory, and brought honour and renown to the Regiment.

It is just a typical outpost story. The official despatch of General Allenby says :

" On the morning of October 27th the Turks made strong reconnaissance towards Karm, two regiments of cavalry and two or three thousand infantry with guns being employed. They attacked a line of out-posts near El Girheir, held by some Yeomanry, cover-ing railway construction. One small post was rushed and cut up, but not before inflicting heavy loss on the enemy ; another post, though surrounded, held out all day, and also caused enemy loss. The gallant resistance made by the Yeomanry enabled the 53rd (Welsh) Division to come up, and on their advance the Turks withdrew . . ."

I can only tell you how it all appeared to me.

The railway had now been pushed forward well beyond the wire to Karm, in preparation, as we afterwards understood, for an attack on Beersheba.

Our regiment, with the Sharpshooters supporting on our left flank, and the Roughriders on our right, were to take up a line of cavalry outposts covering this railhead. This outpost duty, was, of course, no new thing to us. We had done this scores of times, and when they read out in orders the usual gaff about green flares being sent up for danger and red flares for artillery, we just yawned heavily and prepared to move off.

In the dusk we rode out some five miles from Goz el Gelieb, a post well in advance of the wire, to take up a position of outpost covering the railway along the El Buggar Ridge. This high ridge of loose sand and sandstone overlooked the enemy positions by day, and we had held this as observation post many times before. The key positions on the ridge were two rising hills known as Points 630 and 720. These two posts were allotted to C and B Squadrons, my own Squadron " A " was to patrol the ground between during the night. The regimental Headquarters were three miles behind at Karm, and the reserves at least six miles back. But we had so often done "this turn" and seen not a vestige of the enemy, that no one worried very much about that, or the fact that the only means of communication with Headquarters was by signalling, lamp by night or helio by day.

Point 630 on the left was in command of Captain McDougall, a very fine soldier, known to many of us as " one eye quaiss, one eye mush quaiss." You see, he always wore a monocle, and an Arab syce in trying to describe him to me had used that phrase meaning —" one eye good, one eye not good."

He found some sort of cover for his led horses, and occupied two shallow cruciform trenches just on the reverse slope of the hill with three of his troops; sending out picquets over the crest. With his remaining troop he occupied a small post on his right flank. The garrison on the hill itself with Hotchkiss gunners, signallers, etc., numbered about fifty.

Point 720, on the right, allotted to B Squadron, was in command of Major Lafone—" dear old Laffy " as he was affectionately known by all his men. This was a cone-shaped hill having a small ruined stone house on the summit. There were two shallow rifle pits on the right of the house, a small trench on the left flank and a slightly deeper cruciform trench some hundred yards in the rear. About three hundred yards to the right flank was another small hill across a hollow which would give flank protection. Major Lafone occupied the trenches on the hill with two troops with a strong picquet on the smaller hill to the flank and placed one troop as a standing patrol about one mile to the rear.

In the centre, our Squadron, " A," under Captain Bullivant—" absent-minded Bully "—formed a series of patrols and standing patrol. Mick and Nic's troops did the actual mounted patrolling, whilst " Bart's " and my own took up standing patrol positions to the rear.

One incident during this night will ever remain clear in my memory. We were rather short of water and a " packal "—a goatskin filled with water—had been placed upon the sand, and I had given strict orders that it was not to be touched on any account. I was half asleep during the night when I distinctly saw one of my troop coming away from this packal with a water-bottle. I woke up and challenged several, but I never found out who it was—the incident annoyed me very considerably at the time as I placed such implicit trust in the lads under my command.

We " stood to " about 3 a.m., and shortly afterwards from the direction of 630 I saw green and white flares going up into the greying dawn, and heard a muffled rattle of rifle fire. This went on for some time, and still we were under the impression that it was just a desultory engagement with a passing Turkish patrol.

I mounted my troop and rode in to join " Bart's," the other standing patrol.

Shortly afterwards Captain Bullivant rode up and said :

" I don't know what's happened as I can't get into touch with either " C " or " B " Squadrons, but there seems a devil of a lot of Jackos out there. Bartlett, you take your troop up to support 2 and 3 troops, and Hatton, you make a detour and see if you can reach Captain McDougall, I rather fear he's surrounded."

In the growing light I led my troop rapidly under cover of a ridge, and galloped away to the south intending to wheel again straight for the rear of 630. In extended order we wheeled out into the open plain and galloped with heads " remarkable close to the horse's neck," towards the hill. We were met with a murderous rifle and machine-gun fire. They had got the range, the bullets spattering amongst the horses' hooves like hailstones. Several saddles were quickly emptied, but it was mainly the horses that had been hit. I wheeled them again to the right under cover and then out into the open about half a mile further round. The light was now good and, although I could see nothing of the enemy, they had us severely " taped." We again rode clean into a rain of bullets, and realizing it was useless to go on, as I shouldn't have had a man left, I wheeled again into cover, and brought my men into action dismounted.

Luckily, I found myself in some sort of formation with the rest of the squadron and some Roughriders, who came up and did gallant work in reinforcing us ; but many quickly became casualties. It was difficult indeed to get any cover and we seemed to be under

an enfilading fire from all quarters. There being no
proper communication we had no idea what was
happening to either " B " or " C " Squadrons ; all
we knew was that there was nobody behind and a
devil of a lot in front. Unfortunately the Hotchkiss
gun in my troop jammed with the sand—rather a fail-
ing of these guns, I'm afraid—and we were dependent
on rifle fire ; but we could not get a target and could
really only let off rounds vaguely in the direction we
judged the bullets to be coming from. We were
absolutely at a loss as to affairs even in our own
squadron.

No. 1 Troop somewhere on my right had the whole
of their Hotchkiss team wiped out, all six being killed
or wounded ; as one man was hit, immediately another
had taken his place ; in fact, of this troop only three
came out unscathed.

The action went on all through the day and, without a bite or any further water, we fought on till late
in the afternoon. We had managed to get our
wounded back except one, a new lad named Puncher,
and I was rather worried about him. He had been
shot down during the first attempt to reach 630 in the
early morning, and his exact whereabouts from where
we were was difficult to calculate. Towards the end
of the afternoon the firing seemed to have lifted a
little, and I discussed the possibility of getting to him.
His pal, Jim Carroll, and Hazelton, a Lancashire lad,
volunteered to go out and find him.

Just before Puncher was hit he called out to me
under a shower of shrapnel : " Is this a scheme, sergeant, or the real thing ? " and as he fell, Jim Carroll had
shouted in his rich Irish brogue : " Jack, I'll have four
or five of they bastards for you." I think he did, too.

Carroll and Hazelton went to the rear and, making
a circuitous route, found him, and got him back so
that he could receive medical attention, and he was
taken down the line to hospital.

About 5 p.m., after continuous engagement since

TURKISH GUNS AFTER THE FAMOUS CHARGE OF THE WARWICK AND
WORCESTER YEOMANRY

BRINGING IN THE WOUNDED BY CAMEL CACHOLET

3 a.m., we saw infantry reinforcements marching across the plain. The Turk apparently saw them too, and withdrew his forces.

It was only on a reassembly of the Regiment that one could get any idea of what had actually ,aken place. It appeared that our outpost of little over two hundred effective rifles had been attacked by a Turkish force of nearly 5000 troops ; several battalions of infantry, two regiments of cavalry and guns. This was a powerful raiding expedition, whose object had been to destroy the railhead, and so delay any projected advance of Allenby's troops. We had held them successfully throughout the day, and whilst our losses had been heavy indeed, theirs had been very much greater. Most important thing of all—they had failed in their objective, and General Allenby's plans were not delayed a single day.

As my own squadron collected it was pitiful to notice the number of led horses. Mick, who had had charge of one of the patrolling troops, had been dreadfully wounded in the stomach and his life despaired of—our squadron had lost a third of its men, but what of " C " and " B " ?

The story of the resistance put up by these two posts is an epic, and I will endeavour to give you a brief outline of the doings at Points 630 and 720.

As the dawn broke over 630, Captain McDougall saw large numbers of enemy troops marching to his front, attempting to establish themselves on the crest of the hill. A heavy fire was opened by the little garrison of fifty. The Turks retired and attempted to work round the flank. Here the machine-guns played havoc with them, and the Hotchkiss from the outlying picquet also took terrible toll of the enemy. Corporal H. Jeacocke, now well known as the famous Surrey cricketer, did devastating work with his Hotchkiss team, lying in an exposed position himself on the parapet, to get a better view of his objectives.

Soon, however, the gun teams were put out of

action, all six at one gun being dead or wounded, and at another the gun jammed as the last man of the team began to work it.

Captain McDougall with his dead and wounded was faced with the extreme difficulty of getting a message through, and also of getting ammunition up from the rear. I have it on good authority, that about this time a Turk approached near enough to shout "Ablooka! Ablooka!"—Surrender—to which McDougall in the Yeoman language replied: "Ablooka be b——d," and with a dead man's rifle fulfilled the Mosaic law with the body of the challenger.

Trooper Finlay, a bluff jovial cove, jumped from the trench and, under heavy fire, dashed to the rear, commandeered a horse, and still under heavy shell and machine-gun fire galloped back to Headquarters. Captain Carus Wilson, in charge of the led horses, dashed through heavy fire, loaded with the horse holders' bandoliers of ammunition, up to the firing trench. His perilous journey accomplished, he ran back and again attempted to reach Captain McDougall with two heavy boxes of Hotchkiss ammunition. He dropped one into the part of the trench held by Lieutenant Matthews, and as he went to reach his squadron leader, fell into the trench at Captain McDougall's feet, badly wounded through the thigh at point-blank range.

Had the Turks found sufficient resolution to rush the trench nothing could have saved the post, but Captain McDougall with his handful of men, surrounded by dead and wounded, managed to bluff the Turk off, and so hang on. Towards noon Sergeant Randall attempted the dangerous task of getting a message back to Headquarters, and jumped from the trench with bullets spattering all around him. He ran like an Olympic champion and, safely reaching Headquarters, he was able to give such accurate information, that our artillery began to shell the Turk and kept him down throughout the terrible afternoon.

At the end of the day Captain McDougall brought the remnant of his gallant little garrison out as the reinforcements arrived; there were less than a dozen survivors; but in front of their trench were over two hundred Turkish dead. For the heroic defence of 630 Captain McDougall gained the D.S.O., and, mark you, he richly deserved it; Captain Carus Wilson, Mr. Matthews and Mr. Abrahams the M.C., whilst amongst the decorations for the rankers were a D.C.M. for Sergeant Randall and an M.M. for cheery Trooper Finlay.

And now to 720—the post held by " B " Squadron under Major Lafone; but a word first of the Major himself.

" Laffy " always had that peculiar mannerism, possessed, I believe, in common with the Prince of Wales, of fidgeting with his tie. He was exceptionally fond of his men and withal possessed a rather dry sense of humour. I remember on one occasion a new officer rather fancying " his weight " had gone into " B " Squadron mess-hut at Geneffa and in a high-falutin modern-mannered voice had called, " Any complaey-ents." The tone of his voice struck the troopers as so affected, that they promptly gave him the " bird," " blew him out one," " cut him off a slice of cake," or " gave him a raspberry "—whichever expression you prefer. " Laffy " had ordered two or three offending ones before him and, after remonstrating fairly mildly, had finished up by saying : " You know, I really can't have my junior officers presented with the Order of the Royal Richard."

The post of 720 had no sooner expressed amazement at the appearance of the flares on 630, than they could discern in the half-light large bodies of horsemen riding towards them. They rapidly opened fire and caused them to turn about, whilst further Turkish cavalry, who had somehow ridden round to the rear of the post, were given an equally hot reception until, realizing their mistake, they also retired in disorder.

As it grew lighter, the little post saw a large body of Turkish infantry massing for an attack. Heedless of losses, on they came, attempting to carry the hill with the bayonet ; they formed an easy target and dropped in dozens. " Laffy " with a rifle was calling his score : " Eight, nine, ten—missed him—eleven." Their assault was held up, so a squadron of Turkish Lancers came through to the attack. They charged, but their saddles were emptied like knocking down nine-pins. Corporal Rangecroft—a prominent member of the Catford Bridge Rugger Club—(How are you, Rangy ? —I have often scragged you in a tackle since then) with his Hotchkiss swept off a line of about thirty, shouting, " That's the stuff to give the b——s." Twice more they came, infantry and cavalry together, but still the little post beat them off. Then they brought up their artillery and started heavily shelling the trenches and the stone house. Sergeant Broster who, at great risk, had got back with a message to Headquarters, arrived back at the trench at 7.30, with a verbal message that Major Lafone was to hang on. The right flank was driven in, so that the main garrison was now unprotected on its flank, and as the firing line developed, the whole of that hill was so swept with rifle and machine-gun fire from about two thousand troops, that all the garrison who could not find shelter in the shallow trenches, became casualties.

Lieutenant Van den Bergh, in face of increasingly desperate odds, and with nearly all his men killed or wounded, showed invincible courage and lightheartedness in his defence of the stone house, but he was soon mortally wounded, his last words with a wistful wan smile being, " Give my love to my mother." Lieutenant Stuart rushed across to take his place, he was soon wounded also, and Major Lafone on hearing this rushed to the rifle pits by the stone house. " Laffy " now sent his last message : " My casualties are heavy, six stretchers required. I shall hold on to the last, as

I cannot get my wounded away." He constantly cheered on his survivors, remarking : " The infantry will soon be up," but a glance behind showed not a vestige of movement on the desert plain. The wounded had drunk all the garrison water, and as the sun rose higher thirst became intense.

A body of enemy cavalry creeping round the flank attacked the waiting led horses ; they had come badly under fire earlier in the day and every horse holder had about ten horses apiece. Squadron Sergeant-Major Dixon, in charge, managed to get a Hotchkiss into action and successfully beat them off. Alas ! the horses were waiting for riders who would never return ; for about eleven o'clock, under cover of machine-gun and artillery fire, the Turks launched a final attempt against the stone house. There were only wounded here, but under " Laffy's " enthusiasm they fought till they were killed. As the enemy came on and on, Major Lafone marched out into the open firing point-blank from the shoulder, and at twenty yards beat back this last attack, only to fall desperately wounded. His last words to Sergeant Broster were : " I wonder if there is any chance of the infantry getting up in time ? "

Thus died a hero and a gentleman.

The little garrison fought on until there were only three survivors, and these, helping as many wounded as possible, made a dash for Karm. Looking back, they saw the Turkish cavalry sweep over the hill, but the post had been held to the bitter end, and long enough to render its capture useless to the enemy.

The following morning two hundred and eight dead Turks were counted in and around the position.

It would be impossible to mention all the heroic deeds that were done that day—October 27th—two days after the Feast of Crispian, nor can I append a list of those who received decorations for their services. The total honours received by the Regiment for its gallant defence were one V.C., one D.S.O., six

M.C.'s for the officers, and for the men, two D.C.M.'s and seven M.M's. I was happy to see my own squadron leader, Captain Bullivant, awarded the M.C., as he tried most gallantly to reach two posts most heavily attacked.

Major Lafone was granted a posthumous V.C., and the following is an extract from the *London Gazette*:

Major A. M. LAFONE, V.C.

"For most conspicuous bravery, leadership and self-sacrifice, when holding a position for over seven hours against vastly superior enemy forces. All this time the enemy were shelling his position heavily, making it very difficult to see. In one attack, when the enemy cavalry charged his flank, he drove them back with heavy losses. In another charge they left fifteen casualties within twenty yards of his trench, one man, who reached the trench, being bayoneted by Major Lafone himself.

When all his men with the exception of three had been hit, and the trench which he was holding was so full of wounded that it was difficult to move and fire, he ordered all those who could walk, to move to a trench slightly in the rear, and from his own position maintained a most heroic resistance. When finally surrounded and charged by the enemy, he stepped into the open and continued the fight until he was mortally wounded and fell unconscious. His cheerfulness and courage were a splendid inspiration to his men, and by his leadership and devotion he was enabled to maintain his position, which he had been ordered to hold at all costs."

We were a sad and sorry regiment when we re-assembled to ride back under a starlight night. Many, many were the led horses, and heavy were our hearts at loss of so many fine companions who had laughed, joked, and sworn with us but yesterday.

The next morning we were paraded dismounted in a square; General Allenby came and thanked us personally for what he termed "a very gallant show."

One curious coincidence arose out of this engagement. Sergeant Tommy Broster, who was known to have been badly wounded near Major Lafone, was reported as " missing, believed killed ; " and everyone gave him up as lost.   Months afterwards, Captain Bullivant was looking in a shop in Jerusalem, at some picture postcards which depicted life in the Turkish Army, and had obviously been for sale among the enemy troops when they had occupied the city.   He was particularly attracted to one—called " Scene in a Turkish hospital," for sitting up in bed was a fellow greatly resembling Tommy Broster.   He bought the card and, becoming more certain, instituted enquiries, which after a time proved that it was indeed Broster ; and that instead of being dead, he had been taken a prisoner by the Turks and, after his wounds had healed, sent to a prison camp near Tarsar.   The story of his exploits make good reading, but I will bring this chapter to a close by giving you the narrative of Corporal Meering, for the reprinting of which I am indebted to the editors of the *Middlesex Yeomanry Magazine*.   Corporal Meering's own words appear *in italics* :

Corporal Meering was with the outpost on Hill 720. Early in the action he was wounded through the arm and chest. Later he received a wound in the leg, but he worked his Hotch-kiss gun until the end when a high-explosive put it out of action and wounded him in the back. Finally a piece of shrapnel passed through his back and stomach so that he lay absolutely helpless when the Turkish lancers charged over the hill, sticking the living and the dead.

" *Luckily for me, I missed being in the way of this charge, having cover from view behind some scrub and seeing all but remaining unseen. I was congratulating myself on my luck when up from the rear came three Turks and a German officer. He ordered them to take me prisoner and then went away. They dismounted, one holding the horses, the other two commencing to search and strip me. After divesting me of everything, they kicked me and tried to get me up on the horse ; naturally I could not move, having six wounds. At last they threw me on the saddle, and the memory of that ride makes me shudder even now— riding stark naked, swathed in gory bandages (the remains of my shirt), through the rear of the Turkish lines. Eventually the*

*Turk holding me on the Arab pony became tired and let me go ;
being weak, I fell off, and the next thing I remember was an
Armenian doctor bending over me and telling me in English that
I should probably live another hour, with luck, and asking if he
could write home for me—which he did. He did not trouble to
bandage me, thinking I was too far gone."*

Corporal Meering remembers being questioned by German
officers, and then being put in a sort of dog-cart bound for Esh
Sheria Hospital, where boiling-hot stimulant was given him,
and then—oblivion.

On the morning of the 29th he regained consciousness to find
that he had been operated upon—a portion of his intestines
having been replaced. He awoke in an ordinary field tent
with straw mattresses on the ground, mostly occupied by
Turks by no means goodly to gaze upon.

In the hospital there was an utter disregard for sanitary
conditions. The Turks never washed.

*" I was only able to get the Turkish orderly to wipe my face
round with a damp towel. . . . The beds were never changed,
one dead Turk would go and another wounded one take his place.
The flies were a black swarm, and the lice . . ."*

The diet was barley water and Ideal milk (captured British
stores from Gallipoli). The pro-British sentiments of the
Armenian staff did much to keep up Corporal Meering's spirits.

The Armenian doctor, although told by the Turks to leave
Corporal Meering, continued to attend him, occasionally in-
jecting welcome doses of morphia to deaden the very great
pain.

One or other of these Armenians would steal round to
Corporal Meering's bed for a brief conversation, especially to
discuss the possibility of their giving themselves up to the
British. One day the Armenian doctor came into the tent and
whispered the good news of the fall of Beersheba.

*" Following the capture of Beersheba the days were full of
excitement. Turkish reinforcements were being rushed up, and
as these had to pass the hospital I had a good view of the troops,
which caused me some diversion. For the most part they were
of splendid physique . . . some of the men wore ankle boots,
but the majority wore sandals—these consisted of leather soles
with string for uppers, and made one wonder how on earth they
could march. The cavalry were very poor in saddlery and
horses."*

The hospital stood on a high plateau east of Esh Sheria, and Corporal Meering witnessed from his bed the bombing and destruction of the five-arched railway bridge, and later the gradual approach of the artillery.

" *The Turks immediately set about evacuating the patients. That I was left behind was entirely due to the good offices of the Armenian doctor who, learning that I would prefer to stay, told the Turkish doctors that I was too ill to travel. Had I known what I was to go through I should have asked to be moved, for the subsequent days were simply hell itself. British shells began to fall in and around the hospital. Two Turkish soldiers came into the tent for loot. Seeing me on the floor, they tried to drag me out of danger, probably not knowing I was English. On my yelling ' Suya es mich ' (bread and water) they laid me down, and returned later with some bread, barley and a French ewer full of water.*"

For two days and three nights Corporal Meering was left alone in the hospital with a dead Greek. Artillery and machine-gun fire grew more and more intense as the battle developed round the region of the hospital tent, and Corporal Meering prayed for one to put him out of suspense, but the " only hurt " he received was a broken leg.

" *This last wound luckily came with the advance of the British. They stormed the high ground on which the hospital lay, and my feelings can better be imagined than described when I saw a thin line of khaki advancing.*"

Unwashed and with his growing beard, Corporal Meering had great difficulty in assuring British soldiers that he was English.

At last—

" *A kindly old padre, who was following close behind the storming troops, bandaged my leg and stopped the bleeding, which up to now I had been unable to do.*"

Corporal Meering was eventually evacuated to U.K.

CHAPTER VII

THROUGH PHILISTIA

"Tell it not in Gath ; publish it not in the streets of Askelon."

AFTER our heavy engagement we moved back to Shellal to refit and the great bombardment of Gaza commenced the next day. The incessant mumble and grunt of the guns could be heard all day, and at night the "phits" and "flashes" told what a rough time the enemy was undergoing.

It was General Allenby's plan to deceive the Turk that the main attack would be made against the Gaza positions, whereas he intended by frontal attack by infantry, and flank attack by cavalry, to capture Beersheba first, and put himself thus on the flank of the Turkish main positions.

Both sides knew that the "big show" was coming and there was tremendous aircraft activity, including considerable bombing from German planes.

During the days of October 28th and 30th the infantry were massing for their attack on Beersheba, and the Desert Mounted Corps were making a long thirty miles' detour to arrive on the flank of Beersheba and within striking distance.

The attack on the outworks of Beersheba was carried out on the night of October 30th by the 60th Division and the 74th Division.

The 60th Division was a famous division comprised of all the 2nd lines of the well-known London Territorial Regiments. All London lads, they formed a very cheery crowd, the Hackney Ghurkas and the Mile Enders mingling with the London Scottish,

Civil Service, Queen's Westminsters and Kensingtons in friendly rivalry.

The 74th Division, another magnificent fighting Division, was comprised of many regiments of dismounted Yeomanry. This Division, with their pathetic yet aptly chosen divisional sign, " A Broken Spur," always had the especial sympathy of the Mounted Troops. To have trained hard in peace days and in the early days of the war as cavalry, and then to have had your horses taken away, and an infantry pack given to you instead, was the hardest of luck. It might have been our portion, and we should have loathed it.

In this Division were the Devon, Somerset, Fife and Forfar, Ayr and Lanark Yeomanry in one Brigade ; the East and West Kents, Sussex, Suffolk and Norfolk Yeomanry in another ; whilst the 3rd Brigade consisted of Shropshire, Cheshire, Derbyshire, Pembroke, Montgomeryshire Yeomanry and the the Welsh Horse.

To you, fellow-Yeomanry, who fought with us on Gallipoli—greeting—yours was a hard task, but you bore it manfully and well.

The strong outworks of Beersheba were gallantly carried at the point of the bayonet, and the artillery now coming up, heavy fire was concentrated on the main Beersheba positions, doing much damage to the wire and entrenchments. At dawn on October 31st 1917, the great battle for Beersheba really began ; and after a brief but heavy bombardment by the guns of the 60th and 74th Divisions, heavy infantry frontal attacks were launched on the main positions, the London lads and the Yeomanry taking and consolidating position after position throughout the day.

Meanwhile mounted troops, chiefly Australians, had deployed round the flank and were attacking in force from the east, north-east, and north of the city. The main body of the Aussies reached the plain to the north-east of Beersheba, and detached a force to capture the Hebron–Beersheba road to protect their own flank and to render it impossible for further reinforcements to reach Beersheba. This road in the hills was stubbornly held by Turkish cavalry, and a long and desperate fight was made before the Light Horsemen eventually captured the required positions.

The flank now secured, the mounted attack developed on the plain, and with the Londoners and Yeomanry attacking from the front, and the Aussies from the flank and rear, the Beersheba defences were having an exceptionally bad time. Meanwhile the continuous and insistent bombardment of Gaza still led the Turkish Higher Command to anticipate that the main attack was coming from that direction.

I have the greatest admiration for the Australian Light Horsemen and, having seen and fought with them mounted in Palestine and dismounted on Gallipoli, I say unhesitatingly that the Australian is one of the grandest, bravest, and best-tempered fighters in the world. Their discipline was often the despair of our own " red-tabs," but when it came to getting on with the job, you could depend upon them through thick and thin. They would attack and take a position without first filling in a form to say they were about to do so.

In this attack on Beersheba, finding their dismounted action held up badly, as there was no vestige of cover on the plain, they decided to capture the city mounted.

I should like to see a painting of this action : eye-witnesses say it was perfect. It must be remembered that the Light Horsemen were only trained for dismounted action, and it had been a source of great soreness with them that the Yeomanry used the sword, whereas they were equipped with rifle and bayonet only.

Not to be deterred by that, however, they mounted and formed into line ; then fixing their bayonets and holding their rifles down under the right armpit, they galloped across the plain and charged at the remaining Turkish trenches, using the rifle and bayonet as a lance. It was a magnificent sight to see these fellows setting their horses to jump the trenches, and at the same time lunging and thrusting with this cumbersome weapon. To my knowledge, this is the only mounted bayonet attack in history ; it was completely successful and, laughing and cheering heartily at their own impudence, the Wallabies occupied the whole town of Beersheba about 7 p.m. The remnants of the garrison fled westward and the 60th and 74th Divisions consolidated positions north-west of the town.

Thus fell the ancient city of Beersheba, two thousand prisoners and thirteen Turkish guns were captured, and the battlefields around lay strewn with nigh upon a thousand Turkish dead.

The 53rd Division, composed of Welsh Territorial Regiments, now came through and established outpost contact with the Turkish flank, some five miles to the north and west of Beersheba. Throughout the 1st and 2nd of November, General Allenby was concentrating further troops for an attack on the Turkish centre at Sheria, and at the same time the bombardment of Gaza by land and sea was still more intensified, whilst several storming attacks on the outworks of Samson's City were carried by the 52nd Division, the Highland boys, and the 54th, the East Anglians. Meanwhile, the 7th Mounted Brigade of Yeomanry, the Derbys, South Notts Hussars and the Sherwood Rangers had marched north of the town, had positioned themselves firmly across the road to Hebron at Dhahariyah (the troops had no need to alter that name), and by fighting a strong holding engagement, prevented reinforcements from Jerusalem attacking the flank.

From November 3rd to November 6th, John Turk managed successfully to hold a line around the Kheuweilfeh wells and fighting now being in arid hilly country, the 53rd Division, though making a little progress in the centre, were held up on the flank.

Now to our own doings. After refitting and receiving small drafts, we trekked on November 5th to Beersheba, arriving at the town just before dusk. We had been bombed during this trek, but the hostile plane was rapidly beaten off. We rode past the scene of our outpost action on the El Buggar ridge, and we soon approached Beersheba. It was a wonderful sight to witness the havoc that had been caused by our guns and assaulting troops. There was little enough water in the town, although it had been thought that would be sufficient to supply the needs of the whole Yeomanry Mounted Division, and thus our horses had to go rather shorter than we should have wished. The water was pumped from wells known as Abraham's well, possibly a name it had held since the time that patriarch thousands of years before had gone to Beersheba to dwell.

After a hurried sleep we moved off in the dark, under a starlit sky, along a track bordered by high sand-dunes. As the day broke the whole column was heavily bombed, but we rode on, and early in the morning we were thrown into the attack on Kheuweilfeh wells, that the Welsh troops had been so gallantly pursuing for several days. This Division had had heavy casualties and many a poor lad from the land of the leek was seen stretched out stiff in death, or dying of wounds in agony on the hard and stony desert land, but they fought on bravely and Kheuweilfeh fell into our hands on the night of November 6th. We took up a line of outposts, and our horses having had no water since before dawn, the horse holders had the task of riding them back nine miles to Beersheba. Eighteen miles during the night for a drink.

Early in the morning of the 8th we moved forward with no water for the men and very little rations. We soon came under fairly heavy shell-fire, but we rode on. Everywhere showed evidence of the hurried movements of the Turk. We saw many of his dead lying around in stiff and strange attitudes, and there were signs of camps broken up very hurriedly ; one curious object passed was an open landau, in which it was said that the Commander of Beersheba had made a hurried escape as the Aussies entered the town.

The enemy continued to worry us with shrapnel— " pip-squeaks " we called the guns—but our chief personal concern was the fact that we had had to move off without water, and thirst was rapidly becoming a trial. News came whilst trekking that Gàza, that impregnable city of Samson, had fallen to the infantry the night before, November 7th, and this was received by a cheer that ran from troop to troop.

Deploying from a ravine which held many Turkish dead and dying, on to an open undulating plain, we came under heavy shell and rifle fire from our right flank. Captain Bullivant wheeled our Squadron to the right, and in extended order we galloped over a crest and came into dismounted action up a precipitous stony hill well marked by the Turks. We suffered several casualties, but we reached the crest and could see our enemy retiring and fighting a rearguard action on a still higher summit. There was a little stone house on this hill with a broken wall at right-angles. We naturally attempted to occupy this house as shelter for machine-guns, so took the cover of the wall to reach it. A Turkish sniper had a gap in this wall beautifully ranged, and it cost us six, including the second in command, Captain Broderick—" Bully and Brod " the pair were affectionately named—before we realized it were better to make it in the open. Jerry. O——, a corporal and one of my best section leaders, received a funny wound. We were just crawling over the steepest part of this hill when I saw him turn a complete somersault and curse.

" What's up, Jerry ? " I called.

" Damned if I know ; something hit me, but I can't
b——y well find where."

Blood soon began to trickle, and we found that a
bullet had gone clean through the lobe of his ear and
failed to touch him elsewhere. One fellow received
three nasty head wounds just as he reached the hut
to bring his Hotchkiss into position, but as we got him
away he remarked, " He knew he'd cop it one day for
poking his nose into other people's business."

Soon we saw behind the guns of the Hampshires
galloping up and getting into action, and they relieved
the pressure on us considerably. We maintained a
holding action all day, and at night began to march
due west. A little water had reached us for the men,
but the horses had had none that day. This night
march was over chalky sandy country, and one could
see nothing, for the great dust cloud raised by the
column. It was like riding blindfolded ; now and
then your horse would rush off at a canter to catch up
with the column, and then halt abruptly in a bunch.
Presently the going became harder, the dust less, and
the moon came up slowly as we reached the central
position of the Turkish line, Esh Sheria, which after
a stubborn fight and many a gallant bayonet attack
by the London Scottish, had fallen the day before.

We could see the shattered ruins of the great white
railway bridge across the wadi. Now blown to pieces,
it had once been a famous landmark to us from the
other side, and we had lain out on the desert for hours
watching movement around it, when on scout patrols
and outposts.

A cloud of dust covered us as we rode into the wadi
to water from improvised troughs. I vaguely discerned little mounds and pyramids at intervals of
fifty yards all along this river-bed ; the stench was
overpowering and enough to make one vomit if one
had had any food in the stomach at all.

On closer inspection of these mounds, I soon
ascertained the cause of the stench ; there were heaps

of Turkish dead thrown carelessly together, each
mound consisting of some thirty to forty corpses all
beginning to swell and blacken.

The water had been severely taxed and only came
through in a trickle : the horses got a little, but barely
enough ; in fact, the rear of the Regiment had hardly
started to water when the order was given for the
Brigade to move off again before dawn.

When daylight came we found ourselves in the
open rolling plains of Philistia, and we continued to
trek all day. It was dreadfully hot and we were without water. Many horses were very weak for want of
water, and at every halt the men automatically fell
asleep, as we had now had no sleep for five nights. In
fact, we rocked in the saddles as we rode, and we were
heavily laden with equipment, one of the irksome
articles of which was the gas respirator, which with
the bandolier, haversack, water-bottle, etc., fitted
tightly round the neck and nearly choked one.

I heard this conversation in my troop behind me :

" There won't be no b——y gas—I can't stick this
bastard thing any longer." A faint thud on the sand.

" Same as you, chum "—another thud.

" Old So-and-so's dumped his "—another one.

In a few moments, looking around, I found I was
the only one carrying the respirator, and so mine went
too. I believe the whole Regiment's gas protectors
were dumped on that desert between Sheria and the
coast.

Everywhere now we encountered dead Turks, dead
horses and dead camels. A dead Turk smells dreadful
after a couple of days in the sun, and those we passed
were turning black and green, and their bellies were
swollen like barrels. There is one thing that stinks
worse than anything on earth and that is a dead
camel; we came upon these in profusion, and what
with the smells, the lack of water and, worse still, the
dog-tiredness, this trek will long remain in my
memory.

Towards dusk we reached Huj, and here a memor
able sight met our eyes. We came upon the captured
batteries of guns which had been taken, at the point
of the sword, by the Worcester and Warwick Yeomanry the previous day.

The Londoners of the 60th Division had been held
up by two batteries of Austrian gunners occupying a
fine position on a ridge ; another battery and machine-
guns operating at right-angles provided enfilading
fire. General O'Shea sent for assistance, and two and
a half squadrons of the Worcester and Warwick Yeomanry coming up on the flank, the order was given
for the position to be cleared by them. Dismounted
action was useless, and so, dividing into two groups,
under Captain Valentine and Lieutenant Albright,
the Yeomen charged across an open half-mile of plain
clean into the teeth of the guns which were firing at
zero.

Through a perfect tornado of shot, shell and
machine-gun fire, as the Turks redoubled their efforts
to stop the oncoming wave of horsemen, those Mid-
land Yeomen rode, till, with full-throated cheers they
reached the guns, and, though the Austrian gunners
stuck to their task to the last, they were sabred where
they stood. In any other war than this, this superb
charge would have received more due commendation :
those who saw, say it was magnificent indeed and
should rank with Balaclava.

So long did the gunners remain firing, that shells
in some cases went clean through the horses without
exploding. Twelve field-guns, four machine-guns and
large quantities of ammunition were captured in this
desperate rearguard action.

The Worcesters and Warwicks lost fairly heavily,
at least a quarter of their effective rifles, and many
horses were killed. The Warwicks chiefly mourned
the loss of Captain Valentine, who was killed at the
head of his squadron. Well-known in the hunting-
field, he was a popular soldier and a great sportsman.

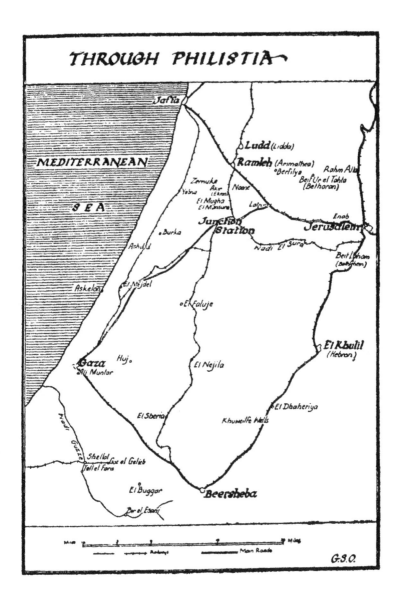

A quotation from Robert Graves forms an appropriate requiem :

> " For those who live uprightly and die true
>   Heaven has no bars or locks,
> And serves all taste . . . Or what's for him to do
>   Up there but hunt the fox ?
> Angelic choirs ? No, justice must provide
> For one who rode straight and at hunting died.
>
> So if Heaven had no Hunt before he came,
>   Why it must find one now :
> If any shirk and doubt they know the game,
>   There's one to teach them how :
> And the whole host of Seraphim complete
> Must joy in scarlet to his opening Meet."

From the records of the Worcester Yeomanry I beg leave to steal also this little cameo :

" The gallant little Sergeant Allen, whose service with the Yeomanry dated back to 1896, was found dead by the guns, still grasping his sword thrust up to the hilt through the body of the Austrian gunner who had killed him."

Huj had evidently been a base, for it was littered with equipment strewn all over the place.

The one thing we desperately wanted was not there —there was no water—and many of our horses had now been fifty-six hours without, in this broiling hot and dusty land. They were weak and ill, and the men themselves were dropping from hard riding and lack of sleep.

However, the Turk was apparently on the run, and we'd just got to keep him at it. Some of us were thrown into a rearguard action on the right, but it lasted only a very short time as the Turk again gave way.

Allenby's plan had been to capture Beersheba, roll up the flank, capture Gaza, and then send the cavalry through up the coast. This had all worked out splendidly, but it had meant very hard riding to get across from Beersheba to the coast in time to carry on this pursuit. In fact, we seemed " done " for want of sleep before the genuine pursuit began.

Amongst the various dumps at Huj we found two welcome articles of food : circular cakes of Turkish bread and sacks of compressed dates. We devoured these slabs of dates with avidity, and thankfully enough late at night we received a small ration of water for the men, but none for our mounts.

At last, however, we could " kipp down." Go five days and nights without sleep, fight an engagement or two as well, be without water and with very little food, ride your twenty miles a day, and believe me— insomnia won't trouble you overmuch.

We dropped down by our horses and slept solidly till dawn.

The question of water for the horses was so serious that it simply had to be found ; so we started off and marched inland in search of pools of some kind. Some of the horses had been sixty-eight to seventy hours without water, and we couldn't ride them, so we marched dismounted, leading them.

To add to our trials a terrible khamsin wind, in- sufferably hot, blowing like a blast furnace, arose, which scorched our dust-encrusted skins into sores, and dried our parched and thirsting throats most painfully.

Men and horses continually stumbled from weak- ness, but we eventually arrived at Nedjeli, where were three or four pools of stinking, stagnant water. It was filthy and villainous to look at, full of black and yellow leeches, but we gave the horses what we could and stumbled on. We found a little better watering towards evening, but it was really aptly put by the trooper who described it as " One whole b——y day spent in getting half a b——y drink." Most of this day I felt so " done " and my horse was so weak that I've little recollection of it except stumbling on, find- ing myself dropping asleep as I walked and catching myself up before I fell. I find, on consulting the map, that this morning march from Huj to Nedjeli was not much over five miles ; it seemed like fifty-five.

However, bad as was the water in the wadi, it revived the horses a little and, drinking it ourselves with two chlorine tablets, it somewhat allayed our thirst, although it tasted like the " stink cupboard " in a " chemmy lab."

In the afternoon we passed through a native village, really the first sign of habitation we had seen since leaving Beersheba, and then halted in a field of cut maize on the outskirts. The halt was short, there were a few dumps of corn and horse fodder, and we proceeded to refill our two nosebags.

With a rattle like the artillery going into action, A.S.C. limbers in line galloped up and supplied us with the two days' rations for the men we were already in arrears. We crammed our bellies with bread, jam, and bully and felt much better. After a good feed the horses picked up visibly. We rode on over a plain of red loam where stubble showed that the crop had been harvested, and managed to get some sleep, as réveillé was not until 2.30 a.m.

Through most of the next day we rode and walked alternately. The khamsin was still blowing and many had now thrown away their great-coats and tunics, a foolish procedure as they were afterwards very badly needed.

We still suffered greatly from thirst and had to carefully husband every drop of water in our bottles. But we had food and had had a few hours' sleep, so there was " not so much merit in being cheery " as on the previous day.

By night we had reached El Faluje and had caught up with the Australians, who held the front outposts against the Turkish rearguards. We were to take over the main pursuit in the morning.

During the night a heavy thunderstorm arose and just lying down in the open as we were, it was really a treat to be drenched. We had not seen rain since leaving Salonica, and I remember yet the joy of the renewed sweet coolness in the air, and the rich smell of the wet earth, after the protracted heat and dust, and that terrible khamsin wind. I awoke, cold, soaked, and found the earth slippery with mud, but it was good to have a change of discomfort.

Meanwhile Askelon and Ashdod, on the coast, famous cities of the Bible, had fallen to the Light Horsemen, so that once again " the daughters of the Philistines could rejoice and be exceeding glad."

We moved off before dawn, and at about 10 a.m., having gone through the Australian lines, were actually in touch with the Turk again. We rode through the cactus hedges of a village and found it full. of Royal Scots from the 52nd Division. They moved out to an attack on the enemy's position across the Wadi Sukereir, and we supported them on the flank. I well remember during this morning action, seeing several batteries of artillery come galloping up as at the Military Tournament, and getting their guns into action in fine style just behind us.

We met with a fairly determined resistance from the Turks that day, but another attack on Burkah during the early evening dislodged them with a few casualties to ourselves. We had been able to see them again—that meant something ; it is simply wretched loosing off shot after shot aimlessly, without real sight of the enemy.

We held a line of cavalry outpost all night on the ground taken. During this night a rattling and noisy movement on our right was at first taken to be another counter-attack, but it proved to be our old friends the A.S.C. making a dash up to us with jam and cigarettes.

Our water troubles were over, as we were now well into the land of Palestine and the rain had filled the pools and wadies to some extent. The men were in good fettle, it was quite exciting this driving "Johnny" on before he had time to settle. At him and after him,

that was the game. Off again before dawn we rode
some eight miles before getting into contact with
James T. He was now establishing himself along a
high ridge, Yebna, Zenouka, El Mughar, El Mansara,
and was bringing fresh troops up to make a determined
stand to save his railhead communications at Junction
Station, an important link with Jerusalem.

We rode through the outskirts of a beautiful Jewish
colony, a Rothschild settlement, and it was a delightful
sight to see the little white villas, like an English
garden city, surrounded by olive and orange groves.
As we rode on, troops who had captured this village
threw up rich ripe juicy Jaffa oranges to us in the
saddle. They were like wine after the days of our
water shortage. The little groups of our own dead
covered over with waggon-sheets or blankets told that
the early engagement had been a hot one. We were
halted in olive groves and, as usual, lay heavily sleeping until about four o'clock the order came down
sharply, " Get mounted." We moved off in line of
troop column, and the word was passed on, " Look to
your sword-straps." We deployed out into the open
across a plain some two miles wide, and a wonderful
sight met the eye. Our brigade and regiment were
riding on the coastal flank, but way across to the
right could be seen three whole brigades moving in
perfect order across the plain. We immediately came
under very heavy shell-fire and the shrapnel rattled
on our tin hats like rain, but the whole Division
moved steadily on.

As the shell-fire increased Captain Bullivant, leading our squadron, increased the pace, and we were
riding at a canter and expecting to form line and
charge the position at any moment, when we found
ourselves well and truly in a trap.

The long grass completely hid from view an open
ravine some twelve feet deep and perhaps fifteen feet
across. At the pace we were going it was impossible
to check ; moreover, as we reached it, the Turk having

accurately ranged the spot, opened up a deadly fire with machine-guns and rifles. Over we went ; some horses leapt it, some stumbled down it, others turned a complete somersault and threw their riders headlong. It was a wretched business ; we received heavy casualties in the space of a few seconds, but once down the gully we sorted ourselves out and came into dismounted action on the other bank. A furious engagement ensued, and our cursed Hotchkiss jammed just as we'd spotted a small group of snipers who were working great damage upon our flank. We kept it up until our rifles were too hot to hold, and by dusk the enemy fire died down somewhat. A very dear friend, Sergeant Self, who had won the D.C.M. at the 720 engagement, was badly hit in the head and lay in dreadful agony just at the bottom of the gully, but we could do nothing for him except to give him what few drops of water we had left in our own bottles. Dear old Farrier-Sergeant Dodd remained holding his hand half into the night, but he died before the horse ambulances—sand carts—could get up to take him away. A gallant soldier, a lovable, charming disposition, a dear fellow in every way.

We had not had time to watch events on our right, but a magnificent charge of the Dorsets had captured El Mughar with about five hundred prisoners, and a dismounted action of the Berks had taken El Mansara with the same number of captures.

Yebna had fallen, so it was up to us to straighten out the line by getting Zenouka, our objective.

After night had fallen we mounted and galloped to a hedge just near to the village. Here we halted, and Captain Bullivant, taking a couple of men with him, moved out to scout—he came back with two natives, but we could get little out of them.

About 10 p.m. he came up to me.

" Hatton, the men must have water. We'd better try a raid on the village and see how things are ; but I believe the Turk is leaving."

M

We took seven men, with all the water-bottles of
two troops and with bayonets fixed—"Bully" carrying
his share of bottles, with a sword in one hand and
revolver in the other—we crawled through the
cactus hedge and moved on our bellies till we came
to a mud wall of the village. We skirted this and
stealthily crept up a little lane, high mud walls on
either side. All seemed very quiet, and we continued
on till we reached the corner where the lane led, as all
such native streets do, to the square in the centre of
the village. Peering round the corner, we just caught
a glimpse of some twenty Turks making their final
preparations for leaving, who, at sight of us, thinking
possibly there were many more, bolted before a shot
could be fired. We thus finally took Zenouka with
seven men. Joy of joys, there was a large well in the
centre of the village, and we quickly sent back word
for the troops to come in. Another squadron formed
the outpost for us that night, and "Bully" having
awakened the inhabitants, we soon had flare-lights
around the well, and the horses and men enjoying the
best drink they had had for weeks. It was a strange
scene to watch the natives standing silently gazing at
us from the outskirts of the square, and wondering
whether we should subject them to the same tyranny
and robbery as the Turks. I lay on the stones,
propped against a mud wall, and fell into the dead
sleep that only those wearied by extreme physical
endurance can enjoy.

Early in the morning, about 4 o'clock to be precise,
I took a section out for reconnaissance in front of
Zenouka. We rode up to a ridge over cultivated but
garnered fields, and entered an olive grove. Here a
curious thing happened. I rode through the grove
alone, my pointers being some fifty yards to the front,
and suddenly came face to face with a richly apparelled
and caparisoned Turkish cavalry officer on a white
Arab charger. I was but four feet from him, and,
although holding my rifle across the saddle at "the

carry," the meeting was so sudden I didn't know
what to do. He smiled a broad grin and rode off. I
followed him, putting my rifle into the bucket and
thinking to throw him in the manner of wrestling on
horseback, but his pony had the legs of me and I lost
him in the distance. I came back to the centre of my
outlying pointers as mine was only a reconnaissance
patrol. Down in the valley in front of us, I could see
thousands of the Turks all making preparations to
move. They were some five hundred feet below me,
and they looked like ants as they bustled to and fro,
loading stores and ammunition very rapidly. It was
evident that they had preserved a base in front of this
last line of resistance, and that they were making
every effort to get away as much as they could.

I rode back and reported, taking in a native Jewish
boy whom I had found taking more than ordinary
interest in our movements, and was not surprised to
hear that the Colonel had impounded the sheik of the
village for making apparent signals from his roof.
Heavy shelling killed several that day, but by eleven
o'clock we were riding out on to the open again
through beautiful country full of vineyards and
orange groves, towards the towered and minareted
city of Ramleh. Ramleh, known as Arimathea in the
Bible, lay two miles before us, in a hollow on the
plain. A beautiful city it looked in the distance, and
before us we saw waves of Australian Light Horsemen,
galloping over the plain in an attempt to take the
city by storm. We were in dismounted action during
the early afternoon, attacking Turkish troops to the
right of the town, but apparently during the night
the Turks after putting up a stubborn resistance
evacuated the city.

The city was of some considerable beauty, for as
dusk had fallen the sun shone on several mosques,
on a white church steeple, and on a tall square tower
of what proved to be a Catholic hospice. The whole
city was surrounded by olive groves and orange

orchards, and looked magnificent to those of us who had spent months in the open desert.

We rode into Ramleh about 10 o'clock the following morning, after doing cavalry outpost all night on a hill overlooking the town. As we paraded for our triumphal march through a newly captured city, it was with a thrill of pride that we received the order : " Draw swords," " Carry swords." With as much ceremony as we could muster we marched through the streets. A large crowd of the inhabitants were out cheering, and as we came to the centre of the town a carillon rang out from the bells of the church steeple. I turned in the saddle to my own men and shouted : " Come on, lads, this is fine, look your own height and chuck a chest, boys ; hark to the bells a-pealing." Rounding the church where the bells were welkin ringing, I looked upwards where the sun struck the turret, and was somewhat surprised to see that the ding and jangle of the " bells—bells—bells," was accounted for by the presence of a couple of Aussies in the balcony, who had climbed up, determined to give us the welcome that the inhabitants might have denied us. I laughed like fury, but the next minute my laughter was turned to concern as a couple of German aeroplanes circled over the city and worked havoc among us, as they swooped low, using their machine-guns with deadly effect. They were, however, quickly pursued by four of our own planes and we rode round the beautiful white buildings of the Catholic hospital to halt in the olive groves of Ramleh.

On the same day to Ludd, the Lydda of Biblical fame, and here apparently the horses of many of the Turkish cavalry had shot their last bolt. The city of Ludd was centred in olive groves, but the whole place stenched vilely with the hundreds of horses, mules and donkeys that had been left to die by the roadside.

We rode down sandy olive groves, and corpses of men and animals lay on either side of the roadway, men and beasts who had lain down and died, not

from wounds, but from sheer exhaustion. Stopping
to think, we knew the time we had been through had
been bad enough, but the plight of the Turk, continually harassed, badgered from pillar to post,
without decent rations, time to water or sleep, had
been far worse. Ludd marked the total collapse of an
army, and the putrid stink from the rotting bodies
was simply terrible. The smell of swollen and rotting
flesh always makes me vomit, and this march through
Ludd was one of the most trying afternoons to me in
the whole campaign.

We found good watering here from several wells
in the centre of the town and, as the limbers came up
with the stores, a dump was formed in the near
vicinity of the well. I mention this as, in the early
dusk, a box was dumped there, labelled " General
——" and marked in the well-known words " White
Horse." It was too good to believe, but a couple
of troopers went out to investigate and found it to be
true. Far from containing maps, reports and orderly-
room charts, it contained " White Horse." I am
sorry, General, if you didn't enjoy it, but I assure you
a good many of us didn't require any rocking that
night. " Knocking it off," that's called, a loathsome
practice, but it's " an ill wind that blows no one any
good."

Soon after the fall of Ramleh, Jaffa the seaport had
been captured, so that we now held a line well across
the main Jerusalem–Jaffa road The troops were very
tired with the constant riding, the hurried snatching
of meals, the frequent fighting and, worst of all, the
lack of sleep.

We camped in an olive grove just by the Catholic
hospital, my troop being sent for a few days' duty as
escort to Divisional Headquarters. A complete rest
was promised, and we set about putting ourselves in
order. Boots and puttees which had not been off for
a fortnight were cast, and cramped and dirt-encrusted
toes cleaned and stretched out to the glorious sun-

shine. Little by little and bit by bit off came those
crisp curly beards, and our mothers would have known
us once again. Then determined attacks and on-
slaughts on the brigades of lice in breeches and shirt.
Weary overworked limbs soothed by soap and water,
stretched out in slumber through long afternoons in
the warm shade of olive trees. Good water for man
and beast, and food enough to spare. Life was
" bon." I met here a big cheery-faced Quarter bloke
of the Stafford Yeomanry, whose plum-pudding
features were always breaking into a grin. We
became firm pals, but for the " love of Mike " I cannot
remember his name, though we met several times
afterwards and promised each other hundreds of
drinks " when we get our civvy clothes on." " Quarter
bloke, I'd like to meet you again."

The luxury of our sweet rest and leisure came to an
abrupt ending, for on the third morning the early watering parties on their return to camp found " bivies "
struck, horse lines up, and a mild panic to be on the
move prevailing everywhere. Before noon, carrying
two days' rations, the columns mounted, swung to
the right, and up into the stony hills of Judæa. As a
wit perfectly described it, it was " Gallipoli on horseback."

CHAPTER VIII

THE HILLS OF JUDÆA—TO JERUSALEM

" When the waters of the Nile flow into Palestine, then shall the prophet from the West drive the Turk from Jerusalem."—*Arab Prophecy.*

THE town of Ramleh is some fifteen miles north-west of Jerusalem and so our movement up into the hills of Judæa due east, was really an attempt to reach the main Jerusalem–Nablus (Shecham) road north of the Holy City and thus complete an enveloping movement, and at the same time cut off the retreat of the Turk to the north.

General Allenby had given orders to his Divisional Commanders that if it were humanly possible to capture it otherwise, neither shot nor shell should fall into the Holy City itself. This city, wherein were the shrines of so many religions, and which held the most sacred stones in all Christendom, was to be spared from the scenes of battle, but the position of the Turk was to be rendered so precarious that he would have to evacuate and leave the city in the hands of the New Crusaders.

Eastward then from Ramleh we left the fertile coastal plain and started up a rocky pathway heavily strewn with loose stones and boulders, into the barren stony hills of Judæa. Through Annabe and Berfilya over the hills and down into the stony course of a dried-up river bed, with terraced hills on either side.

These Judæan hills deserve a word of description. They are for the most part in general outline steep convexly-curved hills, rising, in places, to a height of from five to six hundred feet, barren, ugly and bare.

The narrow valleys are strewn with limestone rocks and boulders of all shapes and sizes, so that progress even on foot is a difficult proposition.

The most remarkable feature of these, however, is that they are terraced all round, the terraces being usually from twelve to twenty feet wide according to the slope of the hill-side, and anything from four to eight feet above one another. The perpendicular drop from terrace to terrace is bound in with stones and boulders, many of which have been dislodged and have rolled either on to the terraces below, or continued their course down to the valley to render more confusion there. These hills thus presented the appearance of curved sloping downland cut into irregular steps at irregular distances and heights. In the historic past, probably before the time of Christ, the peasants had laboriously built these terraces for purposes of agriculture, but they were now barren in every respect, and difficult for the traveller to negotiate either upward or around on account of the huge boulders everywhere, and the stone slides which had occurred in the course of ages, and which had in places almost obliterated the original structures. One could well imagine that for the sower on such a Judæan terrace, much of the seed would fall on stony ground.

Into this forbidding rocky country—hill-sides without sign of habitation as yet—we now advanced. My impression of the ride up to Annabe is that of riding up an inclined plain of red sandstone strewn with loose stones and pock-marked with pit-holes. Then the steep descent by Berfilya—Annabe and Berfilya were names only ; there was no sign of any village—down to the winding stony watercourse below, horses constantly slipping even on to their haunches and every foot or so striking sparks from their hoofs against the sliding stones.

We halted that night in the valley and took what brief snatches of sleep we could, the horses, of course, remaining saddled, and each man lying down just as he was on the wadi bed, either holding his own bridle, or, if the horses were linked in threes and fours, taking his turn at guard.

Most of the advance up to now had taken place in tremendous heat, with a khamsin wind blowing daily, but this night it was bitterly cold ; and in thin drill, without top-coats or blankets, we felt it chill right into our bones.

Throughout the next day the advance continued, we for the most part leading our horses, but owing to the nature of the ground our rate of progress was rather less than a mile an hour. Towards nightfall the constant rattle of musketry and machine-guns, the ricochets from the hill-sides and the " ping-ping " of the bullets overhead showed a distant enemy trying to get our range. We took what cover we could and just before dusk climbed a stony hill-side towards the village of Beit ur el Tahta. Under Captain Bullivant we went into dismounted action and, driving the enemy from the topmost pinnacles of three hills, consolidated our position around this village—the ancient Beth-horon of Biblical times. It was but a collection of about a hundred mud and stone huts in which dwelt a simple peasant folk scratching a precarious living from grazing their emaciated sheep on the barren hill-sides.

During this night it rained a gentle drizzle and, without cover of any kind, we were soon soaked, a condition which, added to the cold, rendered sleep impossible and life in general thoroughly wretched and miserable. Moreover, now out of touch with any transport we were on half-rations of " bully " and biscuits ; meagre fare to tired, cold and hungry men.

I think it was during this night that, huddled up to Nic and two or three others on a boulder, I tried to cheer them.

" Well, boys, just imagine we are back in old London town and I'm just going to stand you anything you like to eat and drink. Here we go down Old

Compton Street to the Petit Riche. We fling wide the door and enter. What a confused smell of good food cooking greets our eager nostrils! Young Madame in scarlet and black, her dark eyes flashing 'neath the waves of her jet-black hair greets us with a beaming smile from pearly teeth. She knows what warriors we are. (Grunt from Nic). Yes, Nic, old boy, I like you, you shall have the very best that money can buy. Madame, we'll have a dozen oysters each to start with (this didn't appeal to all). Then Madame, some tomato soup, very hot—and a bottle of Amontillado— yes—best sherry.

Now, Nic, *sole à la bonne femme* for you. Yes, Madame, the growling gentlemen will take sole with the rest of us."

As graphically as I could I led them, course by course, through a splendid dinner, till their mouths were really watering and they hovered between amusement and anger. I must have overdrawn the description of the tenderness of " *chicken en casserole* " with shallots, as Nic broke in dourly : " Yes, 'Appy, and if you don't b——y well shut up, the punch'll be served without the rum."

I mentioned this incident, one of many, to show that whatever wretched and miserable conditions maintained we tried to raise a laugh somehow. Many war books lately, especially German ones, have portrayed a tendency of the private soldier to psychoanalyse the emotions of his misery and to dwell introspectively upon his misfortunes. The outstanding feature of the whole war, to my mind, was the way in which Tommy's humour and comradeship on every occasion rose to the required heights to conquer his misfortunes.

We continued our march next morning, but the road now ceased to exist, and it became a mere goat tract across which at intervals lay huge boulders often four and five feet in diameter. We attempted to lead our horses in single file, but progress was dreadfully slow. Our boots were cut to pieces on the rough stones, but with aching and bleeding feet we blundered on up the goat track to Beit el Fokka—Upper Beth-horon.

One memory of this journey from Tahta to Fokka is embedded deeply on my memory. The Regiment in front of us had gone into action around Fokka and suffered rather heavy casualties. A gallant section of the Australian Field Ambulance operating in the hills on our left had managed to reach them, and were attempting to get the very badly wounded back down through the hills. Their only form of ambulance was the "camel cachelot." This was an arrangement of two flat baskets, gruesomely enough rather like coffins strapped on either side of a camel. Half-way up this goat track we met a half-dozen Aussies leading down these cachelots. It was a pitiful sight. Imagine the agonies endured by a fellow, say, with a couple of legs broken, strapped in one of these cachelots on such a journey. At every step the cachelot swung and swayed violently, and every yard or so the camel stumbled, often on to its knees. The cries and moans of these wounded men as we scrambled up the hill-side to let them pass are something I shall never forget, but the Aussies were determined to get them back alive if it were humanly possible.

Fine fellows these Aussies, they made light of everything, and grander troops to fight with on such a stunt as this could not be found the world over.

The track became a little better near the summit and we soon reached Fokka. We passed the flank of this village, similar to Tahta, perched on a hill-side and surrounded by a stone wall in formation somewhat like a hill-side village in the Cotswolds ; and then around the terraces of a perfect natural amphitheatre on the grand scale.

Soon, sheltered from the enemy, groups of men and horses could be seen clustered at intervals on every tier above and below. There must have been some sixty tiers of terraces around that amphitheatre, and I well remember the sight of these little groups. We were in reserve here and sufficiently under cover to be allowed to light little fires and make tea, the first we had had for three days. The tea was crude, of course ; each man emptied part of his water-bottle into his billycan—an old peach tin—and, when boiling, threw in a pinch of the mixture of tea and sugar we all dearly cherished and carried in screws of paper in our tunic pockets. No milk, of course, but it tasted " good-o."

Night fell and with it came terribly heavy rain. It simply teemed down all night, and in less than half an hour we were soaked to the skin. It poured on to us and through until we dripped from every angle as we stamped up and down to keep a little heat in our drenched and half-frozen bodies. My diary, written at the time, writes this down as " most wretched night of the War." It probably was.

Dawn came, I can see the streams of light stealing over the hill-side now, and with it welcome sunshine. As old Sol rose higher so we thawed and began to steam as we dried.

We were still in reserve, but the Sharps and Roughs, with another brigade, had gone forward over the ridge to attack Beitunia, a village on a height, within a mile of, and actually commanding, the main Jerusalem–Shechem road.

News came to us that the attack south of Jerusalem was proceeding successfully with the capture of Enab, and that the Australians on our flank had also made considerable ground. A terrible day's fighting ensued to our front The Turks realizing that once across the main road, Jerusalem must fall, put up a terrific resistance, so that groups of six and seven Yeomen scaling a hill-side and dragging their machine-gun and ammunition with them were often engaged by half a regiment of enemy. Heroic were the battles throughout this day, the twenty-first of November, and many were the casualties which found their way back to the Fokka amphitheatre. My troop was not actively engaged, but the Turk had managed to get his heavy artillery along the road, whereas we were without artillery support at all except camel guns.

Towards the early afternoon a battery of camel guns wandered casually across the skyline of this amphitheatre, and this just did the trick. Johnny, realizing where the main bodies of reserves were, set up a terrific shelling, which we suffered for some four hours on end. There was no cover, and we could only crouch close to the wall-sides of the terraces and hope for the best. A hateful sight we had to endure was to watch these shells falling among our linked horses and taking terrible toll of these our mounts and friends. Into one group of some eight horses near me a shell fell direct ; it must have killed a number outright,but the remainder, panic-stricken, careered backwards and fell a mass of dead, dying and maddened life over a terrace. It was a difficult job to stop panic spreading throughout the horses during this afternoon.

An equally gruesome scene was enacted before my eyes. Right in the pit of the amphitheatre lay a group of very badly wounded men on stretchers and saddle-blankets taken from dead horses. Some dozen of these poor fellows had been placed a little to the left, as their chances of survival were small indeed. They formed a little group, and a padre, I think a Catholic priest, was trying to ease their death-pangs with comforting words of " Our Saviour Jesus Christ." I watched them from above, when to my horror a shell burst right in the centre of the group. I turned away sickened and hid my face in my hands, but summoning courage to look in a moment or two, saw that by some miraculous chance the padre was unhurt, and was sitting up in a dazed fashion gazing around him. Many of the dying were now dead, having been literally blown to pieces, limbs and parts of limbs with the flesh exposed lay around, stretchers were smashed to fragments and the whole sight was a holocaust of slaughter. The padre soon collected himself, and calmly moved about among those still alive, turning them over, gathering the remnants of this his flock about him and continuing his message of peace and absolution.

Towards evening the action ceased, firing became more desultory, and it fell to the lot of our Regiment to cover the retirement of the rest of the Brigade to the lower slopes of Fokka.

In contrast to the torrential rain of the night before, it was a beautiful moonlight night with the stars seeming to rest on the hill-tops themselves, but it was bitterly cold and we were all desperately hungry. We had come into the hills with three days' rations and none had reached us since. The keen mountain air had sharpened our appetites, but as the ravens had not yet come to feed us, we tightened our belts and attempted to forget our hunger by snatches of sleep on the cold stones. Added to the shortage of food, nearly everyone was out of tobacco, and such was the scarcity of matches that a man would walk half a mile for a light. Most of us smoked tea-leaves at intervals, but found them far from satisfying.

The next day we rested and, water being fairly plentiful in the earthern cisterns in the village, we washed well and some even attempted a shave. A small ration was got up to us late in the day, but a spare tin of " bully " would still find plenty of bidders at well over ten shillings.

I seem to remember this day was a Sunday, and in the evening I sat around a brushwood fire under cover of a huge boulder with a few lads of my troop when we were joined by a padre. He was not our own padre, but he was handsome and bearded like one of Christ's Apostles, and as he sat and talked to us simply and honestly, a kind of hush and peace of spirit fell over us all. It was difficult to believe, as he tried to bring life to the old simple stories, that we were sitting at Beth-horon, within a day's walk of Jerusalem itself, and that the very Christ had walked the narrow alley-ways between those silent stone houses just above. The life and habits of the people had not changed one single jot from Christ's day to this, and hardened old sinners and sceptics as we were, it all seemed strange, wonderful, and more than beautiful as dusk enveloped us chatting there of the stories we had heard at our mothers' knees, and in village schools in green old England so many miles away.

Throughout most of the next day we rested also, some taking turn at picquet and outpost duty.

Lying dozing lizard-like upon a stone in the direct rays of the warm sunshine, a body of men tugging, hauling and lifting came into view down the valley below. This proved to be a battery of the Leicester artillery who by sheer naked determination and super-human efforts of strength and endurance, were man-handling their guns up through this dreadful country. With a cheer we gathered a group of lads off duty and scrambled down the hills to give them a hand. Clad in shorts and shirts only, the sweat dripping all over them from under their pith helmets, covered in dust, scratched, bleeding and bruised, their boots cut to ribbons on the sharp stones, these lads had somehow got their guns thus far. We set to work on the gun wheels and the ammunition limbers with a will, and in an hour's time had the pleasure of seeing them in action and working havoc on direct targets of Turks holding the hills covering the Jerusalem–Nablus road. Climbing to the ridge, through our glasses we watched with glee the hurried scuttle into cover of groups of the enemy who had not believed it possible for us to get artillery up so far, as shell after shell fell among them.

The next morning, November 24th, the whole Brigade went forward dismounted, whilst a party took most of the horses back to Ramleh. A few troops were kept mounted, my own being one of them, being detailed as escort to General Barrow's Divisional Head-quarters. The Brigade took up a line along those mountain-tops and a curious line it seemed. Not attempting to hold the valleys, little groups of half a dozen to a dozen men with a Hotchkiss gun scaled those craggy hill-tops facing the enemy. Little isolated groups on pinnacle after pinnacle they could be seen stretching away to right and left. It was a dreadful task carrying boxes of spare ammunition for rifle and machine-gun up these slopes, and what with the hard work, the lack of food—rations were still short—and the cold of the nights, all our reserves of endurance were called upon. It was easy to maintain touch during the day as we could see those on our left and right, but it was a jumpy business at night, as a determined attack on any one post must have succeeded had the Turks been bold enough to attempt it.

They themselves, however, were in a very bad way, as in captured enemy despatches, written by Major Von Papen to Count Bernstorff and dated November 21st, the following passage occurs :

" We have had a very bad time."

" The breakdown of the Army, after having had to relinquish good positions in which it had remained for so long, is so complete that I could never have dreamed of such a thing. But for this complete dissolution we should still be able to make a stand south of Jerusalem, even to-day. But now the Seventh Army bolts from every cavalry patrol.

" Many reasons have contributed to this sorrowful result, chiefly incapacity on the part of the troops and their leaders. Single men fight pluckily, but the good officers have fallen and the remainder have bolted ; in Jerusalem alone we arrested two hundred officers and five to six thousand men deserters.

" Naturally Enver presses very strongly to hold on to Jerusalem with all possible means, on account of the political effect. From a military point of view it is a mistake, for this shattered Army can only be put together again if entirely removed from contact with the enemy and fitted out with new Divisions. This, however, can only take place after the lapse of months. Now is it just a toss-up."

So much for the condition of the Turkish Army that had been hammered and battered daily during the long pursuit from the Beersheba–Gaza line into these hills. Johnny was not, however, going to surrender Jerusalem without one last final effort, and bringing what reserves he could muster down from Nablus, he gave us one complete day of quiet in the solemn grandeur of these Judæan mountains, and then launched a determined counter-attack on our little force the very next day.

Imagine our little force extended over some five miles of these rocky barren terraced hills, each crest garrisoned with some six to a dozen men according to its size and significance, no reserves behind, the nearest support of any kind being way back on the plains, with the Turk in front massing for an attack to drive us back from our threat to the Jerusalem road.

This little force had been under constant fire by day, and fully exposed to the rigours of the cold by night, with little reserves of ammunition (only such as had been brought up on the pack-horses), had been short of rations for days, and now had absolutely none left.

Many Turkish patrols were seen deploying from the valleys, but by accurate gun-fire these were always beaten back into cover, but towards evening the attack developed in full, sometimes as many as a hundred enemy engaging one little post of seven or eight. The Turks could have had no idea how few we were or they would simply have rushed the positions. By clever sniping, reserving of rifle and machine-gun fire until good targets presented themselves, the attack was kept under and every post held throughout the day, but it was realized that under cover of the dark the Turk was bound to overwhelm us. At night, therefore, we scrambled down those boulder-strewn slopes and wearily lugged our machine-guns up others to the rear, to hold a line by Fokka.

N

Our transport had worked wonders to get rations up to us here. The ration column of another Brigade had been ambushed and captured completely, but the limbers containing our "mungy" had somehow galloped through the closing pincers of the Turks upon the road, and reached us. They deposited their precious burden and galloped out of the village of Fokka just as the Turks entered from the other side.

The Turks had now cut right across the main road to our rear and we were surrounded on three sides and practically cut off from Headquarters. There were some two thousand Turks around our little chain of posts and in addition to rifle-fire we were heavily shelled from time to time. For the whole of the 28th and 29th of November we were cut off and without rations except such as we had saved from the day before. It was a weird situation and holding all the vantage-points we could often see the enemy advancing to attack one of the other hills and yet be powerless to help or give warning. We just kept our heads down, refraining to fire unless certain of the target and that our fire would be effective, and thus in some strange manner managed to deceive the Turk that our forces were vastly superior to what they actually were. It was impossible to get any of the wounded away, we just tendered what slight first-aid we could. For our dead, we scratched away the surface of the soil and built small cairns of stones around them, and many a dear lad of ours lies just below the ridge of a Judæan hill with a small cross of stones to mark the resting-place of a young Crusader who died so near to the Holy City itself.

It is a curious fact, however, that considering the force against us outnumbered us by more than ten to one, our casualties were remarkably light during this time, and one can only attribute it to our holding the key positions and the difficulty of the enemy in actually hitting us, so good was the cover we could improvise, by holding positions just under the top-most ridge.

A Staff officer, when the attack had seriously de-veloped and it looked as if we should be surrounded, had managed to get back seven dreadful miles through those strong hills to the nearest means of communica-tion in the plains with Headquarters ; and in response to his appeals the 7th Mounted Brigade—The Sher-woods, Derby Yeomanry and South Notts Hussars—made a forced mounted march into the hills, and reached us on the 28th. This brigade fought gallantly and managed to recapture the road, and straightening out the line, they then came into it themselves on our left and helped greatly to hold up the attack until stronger reinforcements could arrive.

Several incidents occur to me that recall these anxious days without cover, food or sleep. My chief memory is the unfailing cheerfulness of the men, their confidence in themselves and their implicit faith in the Higher Command. Never for one moment did they feel but what the Turk would be beaten off, and that reinforcements would reach us in time. Though utterly tired out with the labours of fighting in that dreadful terrain, the lack of food and worse still the lack of sleep, their spirit and kindness one to another shone like a flame at the shrine of comradeship. Was a fellow dead-beat, someone gave his rest-hour for him, and many gave away water or biscuits they needed as badly themselves.

A source of courage and inspiration in these hills, as at all other times, was the padre. Our padre, the Rev. Young, was the "goods," he was a man first and a parson afterwards. He was beloved by every man in the regi-ment. He understood the men. He knew that under their blasphemous oaths and hardened outlooks the Christian spirit shone in their deeds if not their words, and he knew how to reach it. He never preached, he never nagged ; he just moved throughout the regi-ment, helping with his kindly presence and his cheerful

steadfast nature. We prided ourselves that nothing
" got us down," and I believe that were it possible to
imagine anything that could have " got us down,"
there would have been one man standing still and
that would have been " our padre." In these hills
the tirelessness of his spirit gave added strength to
his body. Throughout these days and nights he
clambered from hill to hill, constantly visiting and
cheering the men, thinking nothing of a two-mile
scramble over those terraces to give a word of en-
couragement to a hard-pressed post, to attempt to
help a wounded fellow back, or to hold the hand and
talk of England to the dying. You would be cursing
like hell when you would find him climbing up from
the terrace below towards you.

" Sorry, Padre," you'd shout.

" That's all right, laddie ; words don't mean much,
and if they make you feel better, then they're all right."

He would lie just behind the post and talk of a
thousand and one things, always beaming a " Brother
Cheeryble " smile through his glasses. I have seen
him when his limbs must have ached worse than ours,
dragging heavy boxes of ammunition up to the top of
one of those terrible hills, because it was as near an
act of fighting as he dared to go.

One evening as dusk was falling over these hills
and the stars were rushing down the darkness, I
remember his form looming up as he scrambled over
the boulders below.

We sat and talked for a time fairly cheerily. I
remember telling him it was no use his trying to
console me by telling me I was in the Holy Land. He
laughed at this, and I told him the old *Punch* story
of the two troopers riding through the pouring rain in
Mespot. Their padre rode up alongside.

" My men," he said, " do you know you are now
riding through the Garden of Eden ? "

" Yus," was the reply, " and it'd need no flaming
sword to keep me out of it, neither."

He laughed again, and then said, " Is there anything I can do to help—what's the chief worry now ? "

" Boots," I said, half jokingly, looking down at my
feet. The uppers of my boots had been cut and
slashed about on the sharp stones. One boot had the
sole off and my bruised and aching foot was bound
round with a piece of puttee, and two toes protruded
from the other as the upper flapped about when I
moved. Some of the men's boots were in a dreadful
condition, and with feet that had not been washed or
tended for over a month except for the brief day's
rest at Ramleh it was an agony for most of us to move
about. Those who had had an issue of boots just
before the advance were, of course, all right, but
those who had started with an old pair were now in
great distress.

The padre smiled, and left to visit another post.
I thought not to see him any more that day. Imagine
my surprise when some two hours later, on challeng-
ing a climbing figure, it was found to be the padre,
with a bundle over his shoulders.

" What have you got there, sir ? "

" Boots," was the short reply.

On questioning him, he told me he had unlaced
every good pair from the dead.

I somehow felt this was a little gruesome, and he
must have noticed the hesitancy in my face.

" Find a pair to fit you," he said softly. " In such
a fight as this, God would have the dead to help the
living to carry on." Then softer still, " And they
would wish it, too."

A thousand times since have I thought of that
remark of the padre's and wished its message could
be preached to others. When I see those around me
who have no thought of their fellow-men, who only
worship themselves and the great God Greed ; who
shelve their responsibility to create " a new Jerusalem " for the sons of those who died for them, I
would blazen it from the housetops that these men

died " to help the living to carry on." Dear padre,
when I visit your church occasionally, and see you
surrounded by the rather high ritual your church has
adopted, I often wonder if one-tenth of your present
flock know you for the man you are. We do.

The night of the 28th November, although the 7th
Brigade had recaptured the road, it was deemed
advisable to shorten the line, and the main force of
our Brigade withdrew from the Fokka-Zeitoun ridge
and occupied the high hills, wooded with olive trees,
between Tahta and Fokka.

My small troop occupied a hill slightly to the rear
of the main line, as personal escort to General Barrow
himself.

The General had a small bivouac made of a couple
of ' bivy ' sheets between two boulders near a tree. I
remember him pacing up and down anxiously towards
evening as the Turkish attack continued strongly.
He was a short genial little man, but he wore a rather
worried look. His servant, I think, named Pyle,
rushed up to him excitedly. " Sir, sir, shall I move
your " bivy " ? A bullet's just gone clean through, sir."
He smiled calmly as if half reproving an over-excited
child, " No, that'll be all right, Pyle ; there'll be
plenty more through, I expect, before nightfall."

That night the fighting died down considerably,
but there was a deal of desultory firing and the
familiar " ping-ping " often sounded close to one's
ear. Being now out of the front line it seemed an
opportunity to snatch some sleep, and so arranging
my guard on the General's " bivy " and my picquet on
the side of the hill with arrangements for relief, I
moved several huge stones to make a pillow and a
protection for my head, thinking as I did so these
were the type of stones of which it was spoken,
" the Son of man hath not where to lay his head,"
banking them well up for cover in case the firing grew
more intense. I fell asleep with that deep sleep of
physical exhaustion, but in the middle of the night

awoke with a start at a roar as if the whole earth were enveloped in an earthquake. I lay still and waited, wondering whatever was the cause. In a few seconds there was another roar, seeming to come from just below my feet, tremendous, deafening percussion which rumbled away through the whole hill-side. The definite intervals told me it was guns, and in the morning I discovered that by manhandling them they had brought about ten batteries of howitzers up, and that wheel to wheel these stood at the base of the hill on which I slept and had been sending their devastating salvoes over my head, accurately ranged on the masses of the Turks.

How these gunners must have worked to get these guns up to support and cheer us, as our powers of resistance were becoming weaker!

Apparently sensing stronger resistance, the Turkish attack the next day grew weaker and weaker, and during the small hours of November 30th the infantry of the 74th Dismounted Yeomanry and the 52nd, the Scotties, came into the hills and relieved us.

Major McDougall, with about ten men around him, was relieved by an officer of the 74th, who said, " If you will bring out your troops—er—sections, I will bring my men in."

" Troops," was his laconic reply. " This is my squadron."

We moved down the hills to several dumps in the valleys where we drew four days' rations owing to us at about 2 o'clock in the morning. Ravenous as we were, we tucked in, foolishly eating heavily of the dried fruit, raisins, etc., sent up to over-hungry troops. We over-ate badly and, drawing over a week's rum at the same time—a new issue to us here—within a few hours I was badly ill and vomiting. The stomach had been empty or on short rations for so long that a sudden cramming, together with the potency of the rum, was more than it could stand. Most of us were sick, and in poor fettle to move off next morning out of the hills

towards the plains again. However, we had had a
few hours' sleep in comfort, and a breakfast, mark you,
before my troop, still having its horses, moved off as
escort to Divisional Headquarters.

It was a glorious sunny morning as we rode down
out of those hills by a much easier route than we had
entered. With " tummies " lined after days of semi-
starvation, tobacco after a week without the weed,
and the prospect of a rest, life was good and the beauty
of colour in the hills contrasting with the blue of the
sky was given due appreciation for the first time.

We rode along a gully which gradually narrowed
to a small gap, from either side of which as we approached shell-bursts could be seen. The Turk had
accurately ranged this strategic point and meant to
worry us if possible. We were almost level with the
gap when a very young Staff officer, who should have
known better, turned to old Pyle, who was astride
one of the mules drawing the General's private half-
limber.

" What's that smoke just there ? Is that somebody blasting ? "

" Yus," answered Pyle with a grin, as he stuck his
spurs in and galloped hell for leather through the gap,
" and if I don't look out, they'll blast this b——y
waggon."

The shells were bursting simultaneously, as if the
batteries were firing at definite intervals, so riding in
close to the gap we waited for a series of bursts and
then galloped through in groups of eights or dozens,
and hardly anyone was hit.

Down to Annabe, where we camped in some olive
groves on a hill-side, had a whole night's rest, and
towards midday next morning the rest of the lads
from the Regiment came stumbling along the narrow
road dismounted.

I have seldom seen men so utterly fatigued and leg
weary as those poor fellows who, after the desperate
hill fighting, had had a long and painful two days'

march to get back. I have mentioned the bad state
of their boots, which for the most were now torn to
shreds, as covered in white dust they lurched along.
The Staffs and Lincolns came first, many of them
hanging on to the sides and tails of pack-mules to
keep themselves from falling ; then the Roughriders,
and then our own boys. They dropped down on the
stones in the olive grove dead beat. There was an
interval, and then round the corner came the
" Sharps."

One of the most popular squadron sergeant-majors
in the whole Yeomanry was Bowie Lawford of the
" Sharps." He was a big man, getting on to middle
age ; a deep pleasing voice, and a hearty smile. He
was a demon for fighting, a real good soldier who
couldn't see enough service to please him. He was
now in a most distressed condition, with his boots
practically off his feet. As he appeared round the
corner he was limping badly and leaning heavily on
the shoulder of one of his troopers. Absolutely spon-
taneously, those who could, stood up to give the
" Sharps " a cheer, and at sound of it, Bowie pulled
himself up, nearly knocked the trooper backwards,
and with head erect, and a smile almost from ear to
ear, swinging his limping leg, he led his boys past us
with a glorious attempt at a swagger. Bowie wouldn't
show himself beaten by anyone or anything, that was
Bowie all over, and we cheered and laughed and
cheered again.

To quote from Official Despatches, that night :

" At a Corps conference held near Yalo, in the
valley of Ajalon, it was decided, on account of the
absence of roads and shortage of water in the country
to the north-west, to attack the Turkish positions
covering Jerusalem from the south-west and west
instead of from the north-west."

After a day's rest, the regiment again mounted,
moved back to Akir, the " Ekron " of the Bible,
where the Ark of the Lord had rested after its sojourn

in the temple of Dagon at Ashdod, where its presence
had brought such disaster to the God of the Philistines.
" And when they of Ashdod arose early on the morrow,
behold, Dagon was fallen upon his face to the earth
before the Ark of the Lord. And they took Dagon,
and set him in his place again.

" And when they arose early on the morrow
morning, behold, Dagon was fallen upon his face to
the ground before the Ark of the Lord ; and the head
of Dagon and both the palms of his hands were cut
upon the threshold ; only the stump of Dagon was
left to him.

" Therefore, they sent the Ark of God to Ekron
. . . but ' there was a deadly destruction throughout
all the city ; the hand of God was heavy there. And
the men that died not were smitten with the emerods
and the cry of the city went up to Heaven '."

My own troop camped in an open field just by new
Akir, but it rained heavily from dusk onwards, and
thus by the time we " kipped " down it was decent
thick mud on which we laid our waterproof-cum-
mackintosh sheet.

New Akir was one long village, on either side of
which were little villas hiding away behind hedge-
rows and trees. It was a small Jewish colony of some
hundred houses, and I suppose about three to four
hundred inhabitants. The villagers were quite
amicably disposed towards us, although acting up to
the character of their race they charged us plenty for
oranges, eggs and tomatoes. I'm afraid we helped
ourselves rather liberally to wood for our fires, and
the lady who caught Charlie lifting her front gate off
its hinges had a definite right to protest.

The second night we were there we established a
sergeants' mess in a room under the synagogue, and
clubbing together bought ourselves a couple of huge
butts of Palestine wine. This was thick, of the colour
of port, rather sweet to the taste, and as we drank it
in pint mugs—five piastres, about a shilling, a mugful

—we soon found it a very potent drink indeed. It was warming, tongue loosening, and (so the doctor said) " good for the blood."

I remember several nights on which the strains of the prayer recital and hand-clapping in the synagogue above must have reached Heaven mingled with " Another little drink wouldn't do us any harm," and " The great big wonderful baby " being told that " She was the only girl in the world as I was the only boy."

On moonlight nights we were often visited by enemy aeroplanes which, spotting a row of horse-lines, would swoop down and open machine-gun fire, as they flew low over the lines. It was unpleasant, but they didn't hit much, and shortly after our own air supremacy became so marked that we were no longer troubled by this arm at all.

The peace and restfulness of these few days at Akir were much appreciated by all troops, who after the strenuous fighting in the hills, found it delightful to laze or stroll and smoke with nothing particular to do but get clean and write home.

At about eleven o'clock on Sunday morning, December 9th, a warm and sunny morning withal, a rumour spread through the village that brought troops and inhabitants into the street buzzing with excitement : Jerusalem had fallen.

The news was received with tremendous joy ; the mayor and one or two local dignitaries in their black robes and round beaver hats staged a kind of official welcome to General Barrow and his staff, on the verandah of the little schoolroom, and in the evening the " locals " entertained some of the troops to a kind of unofficial banquet.

Tables were set up in the village street and were spread with cakes and pastries ; butts of wine appeared, and wine was frugally handed around. They could not speak our lingo nor we theirs, so we made signs of thanks and lit a few bonfires with their wood, to show how much we appreciated their hospitality. It was a joyous night indeed, but long before midnight we repaired to the mess beneath the synagogue, as there the wine could be had more freely, as the inhabitants, with due regard to the dictates of sobriety, had been very careful that no one should have " looked too long upon the wine when it was red."

So many different stories have been told of the fall of Jerusalem, that at one time you could hardly enter a saloon bar in London without being introduced to the very man to whom the keys of the city were surrendered, so I intend to set down here the story as culled from the official despatches.

After our withdrawal from the hills north-west of the Holy City, and during the days of December 5th, 6th and 7th, General Allenby had massed the 60th Division (London lads), the 74th Division (the Dismounted Yeomanry), and the 53rd Division (the Welsh laddies) for an attack on the defences covering the south, south-west and west.

In heavy rain and mist the main attack was launched at dawn on December 8th, and after considerable resistance the 60th Division carried at the point of bayonet the carefully-prepared positions known as the Heart Redoubt, the Liver Redoubt, and the defence works at Deir Yesin. The 74th Division had captured hills overlooking the city to the west, and the 53rd Division, having driven the enemy from Bethlehem, were now close on to the outskirts of Jerusalem to the south.

At nightfall on the 8th the city was thus hemmed in on the south, south-west and west, and the hills to the north-west were securely held by the troops who had taken over from ourselves. After dark the Westminster Dragoons made an enveloping movement across the right flank of the 53rd Division and got partly astride the Jerusalem–Jericho road, thus cutting off the enemy's retreat to the east.

RIDING INTO THE JUDEAN HILLS

TYPICAL TURKISH PRISONERS

What was happening inside the city that had seen Turkish rule for over four centuries ?

On the morning of December 8th large numbers of the inhabitants had been warned by the police to prepare to evacuate. There was everywhere an intense latent excitement, and towards dusk news came that the British troops had passed Enab and Lifta, villages just outside the city walls.

I shall now quote from the record of the Egyptian Expeditionary Force :

" A sudden panic fell on the Turks west and south-west of the town, and at 5 p.m., civilians were surprised to see a Turkish transport column galloping furiously cityward along the Jaffa road. In passing they alarmed all units within sight or hearing, and the wearied infantry arose and fled, bootless and without rifles, never pausing to think or to fight. Some were flogged back by their officers, and were compelled to pick up their arms ; others staggered on through the mud, augmenting the confusion of the retreat."

After four centuries of conquest the Turk was ridding the land of his presence in the bitterness of defeat, and a great enthusiasm arose among the Jews. There was a running to and fro ; daughters called to their fathers and brothers concealed in outhouses, cellars and attics from the police, who sought them for arrest and deportation. " The Turks are running," they called ; " the day of deliverance has come." The nightmare was fast passing away, but the Turk still lingered. In the evening he fired his guns continuously, perhaps heartening himself with the loud noise that comforts the soul of a barbarian, perhaps to cover the sound of his own retreat. Whatever the intention was, the roar of the gunfire persuaded most citizens to remain indoors, and there were few to witness the last act of Osmanli authority.

Towards midnight the Governor, Izmet Bey, went personally to the telegraph office, discharged the staff, and himself smashed the instruments with a hammer.

At 2.a.m. on Sunday tired Turks began to troop through the Jaffa gate from the west and south-west, and anxious watchers, peering out through the windows of the Grand New Hotel to learn the meaning of the tramping, were cheered by the sullen remark of an officer, 'Gitmaya mejburuz' (' We've got to go '), and from 2. a.m. till 7. a.m. that morning the Turks streamed through and out of the city, which echoed for the last time their shuffling tramp. On this same day 2082 years before, another race of conquerors, equally detested, were looking their last on the city which they could not hold, and inasmuch as the liberation of Jerusalem in 1917 will probably ameliorate the lot of the Jews more than that of any other community in Palestine, it was fitting that the flight of the Turks should have coincided with the national festival of the Hanukah, which commemorates the recapture of the Temple from the heathen Seleucids by Judas Maccabæus in 165 B.C.

The Governor was the last civil official to depart. He left in a cart belonging to Mr. Vester, an American resident, from whom he had ' borrowed ' an hitherto unrequisitioned cart and team. Before the dawn he hastened down the Jericho road, leaving behind him a letter of surrender, which the Mayor as the sun rose set forth to deliver to the British Commander, accompanied by a few frightened policemen holding two tremulous white flags. He walked towards the Lifta Hill and met the first representatives of the British Army on a spot which may be marked in the future with a white stone as the site of an historic episode."

Patrols had noticed the movement of crowds early in the morning of December 9th, but the first definite news of the impending surrender was received by Private H. E. Church and Private R. W. J. Andrews, both of the 20th London Regiment (Blackheath and Woolwich). They had walked into the outskirts of the city to get water and were told the glad tidings by civilians.

About eight o'clock, however, the Mayor, accompanied by a few councillors and carrying a flag of truce and the keys of the city in his hand, rode in an open carriage from Jerusalem along the Jaffa road. About a quarter of a mile along the road, they left the carriage and on foot approached the first British soldiers they could see. These happened to be Sergeants Harcourt and Sedgwick of the 19th Londons, and it was to these rather bewildered London laddies that the keys of the city were offered and surrender made. They, of course, immediately informed their officers, who hardly seemed to know what to do about it all. The Major informed the Colonel, the Colonel informed the Brigadier, the Brigadier reported to Major-General Shea, who in turn communicated with Lt.-General Sir Philip Chetwode. Sir Philip Chetwode instructed Major-General Shea to accept the surrender of the city, which he did formally, by riding into Jerusalem and holding converse with the Mayor and Chief of the Police at about 11 a.m.

Actually the first British soldier to set foot in Jerusalem was Brigadier-General Watson, commanding the 180th Brigade, comprised of 17th, 19th and 20th Londons, who after he had passed news of the surrender on to Major-General Shea, rode with a small escort back to the city with the Mayor to reassure the inhabitants and to discipline the town.

Surely there is something in keeping with the history of this city of " the Christ " who came to plead the cause of " the meek and lowly," that on this crystal-clear December morning, the keys of the citadel of Christendom should have been brought out on foot to two wondering and bewildered Cockney sergeants from Camden Town.

Two days later, General Allenby, at the head of representatives of the Allies, made his formal entry into Jerusalem. After years of disuse the historic Jaffa Gate was opened for the occasion, and in all solemnity, without show or military pomp of any kind, the General marched simply into the city on foot. A large crowd of the priests and the people assembled to witness this simple ceremony. They seemed almost amazed at themselves, for during the Turkish regime it had been an offence for more than three people to foregather in the streets for any purpose whatsoever. The scenes were more of welcome relief and silent prayerful joy than of turbulent enthusiasm, as the Commander-in-Chief marched to the terrace below the Tower of David to read his historic proclamation.

The proclamation was read in English, French, Arabic, Hebrew, Greek, Russian and Italian, and declared that order would be maintained in the city ; that all the hallowed rites of the three great religions would be equally guarded and respected ; and that there would be perfect religious freedom of worship for all.

After having received the chief civic and ecclesiastical dignitaries of the various communities within the city, the conqueror left on foot as simply as he had entered.

Thus was fulfilled the ancient Arab prophecy, " When the waters of the Nile flow into Palestine, then shall the prophet (Al Nebi) from the west, drive the Turk from Jerusalem."

CHAPTER IX

BEHIND THE LINES

" Alas ! regardless of their doom,
The little victims play."

AFTER the fall of Jerusalem, and the Turk
had been driven from the whole of Philistia
and Judæa, General Allenby consolidated
his line some ten miles north of the Jerusalem–Jaffa
road, and it ran for a long way along the banks of the
Auja.

The troops now settled down to a period of rest and
recuperation. The winter rains had set in as we rode
back along the main coast road to the Arab village of
Medjel, and then turned toward the beach to spend
our fourth wartime Christmas, at Askelon.

Askelon, a citadel of the Philistines, was nothing
but a mass of almost buried ruins covered with
hummocks of coarse grass which appeared at intervals
along the sand-dunes. Drinking-water was plentiful,
rations were good and could be easily augmented
by purchases of oranges, tomatoes and tiny little
Egyptian eggs, from the villagers at Medjel. The
rapacity of the natives, and the careless generosity
of the men, rendered it necessary for the A.P.M. to
fix the price of these commodities. There were a
good many chickens in Medjel at one time, so the
troops had a rare chance of getting things back on the
" roundabouts."

The officers bought some fowls, and kept them in an
improvised wire cage, near Charlie's cookhouse, to
fatten for Christmas. Strange to say, even some of

these disappeared. As Charlie said : " Though I sit up 'arf the night a-watching 'em, some'ow they seems to go, blimy I knew there was wolves in Salonica, but what 'as 'em 'ere, it must be those b——y lizards."

In many respects it was a most wretched Christmas ; a torrential downpour began two days before, and lasted well over a week. We were not in tents, our only cover being single sheets, and thus by the time the " Happy Morn " arrived, our blankets, kit, and the clothes we stood up in were saturated. A couple of native sheep had been bought for the feast, but it rained so heavily, that it was impossible to get a fire going to roast them, so that dinner had to be postponed till the evening, and even then all Charlie's resource could produce nothing better than an undercooked watery stew. So we made up with bully and wet bread, and consoled ourselves with frequent " swigs " from the whisky mug. Whisky was plentiful, and there were barrels of Palestine wine, but no " pig's ear." The main trouble, however, was that the rain was so terrific that it was impossible for the men to foregather anywhere, and thus we had to celebrate, by twos and threes, cramped in dripping " bivies " and much of the joyousness of the Festival was lost. It certainly was strange spending Christmas so near to Bethlehem, where had been born the Babe whose advent founded Christendom ; but it was so wet and wretched, that I had considerable sympathy with Nic, who, when I began to rhapsodize, exclaimed : " Here 'Appy, cut the poet stuff out and fill up the mug."

During the first three months of 1918 we encamped at various spots behind the line, and this period of rest to refit the Regiment and recuperate the men forms in my memory one of the happiest periods of the War, although throughout January it rained consistently and very heavily.

Towards the end of the month, my troop was detailed for a week's special duty in a little Jewish colony, known as Wadi Hanein. Here a quaint old cuss,

who called himself the " Mayor," had been very good
to myself and my fellow-sergeant, at this time a very
dear kindly, cultured fellow, with a surprisingly naive
and subtle wit, known alternately as " Cassius " or
" Hungry " on account of his rather abnormal length
and leanness. The " Mayor " had allowed us to sit
in his parlour, with himself and his aged wife, during
the rainy evenings. He loved to try his broken
English on us, and sometimes if he felt he had made any
valuable acquisitions to his vocabulary, and if we
showed no signs of going back to camp without it, he
would produce a very small glassful of wine as a night-
cap. It became a kind of silent trial of endurance
between himself and us, as to which could sit it out the
longer. We would all sit for as long as twenty
minutes without speaking, we wondering how much
longer it would be, he speculating whether he would
get us off and go to bed without producing it. It was
a great trial of patience to me, but " Hungry " was
splendid at a siege, and when I showed signs of falter-
ing cheered me up with many a pregnant glance, like
Joe Gargery and little Pip. Thanks to " Hungry's "
indomitable fortitude we won most evenings.

This " Mayor " had explained the rains to us ; that
their duration was always for twenty-three days,
that he knew exactly when they were going to start
and precisely when they were going to stop. He was a
very clever fellow. As we left Wadi Hanein, we went
to wish him good-bye. He came on to the verandah
of his bungalow and looking up through the showers
of sleet at the leaden sky, pronounced the oracle :

" It will rain for but two days more—this is the
last burst."

Two days later we rejoined our squadron. It was
still pouring as I entered the little bell tent where the
sergeants messed. They had dug a circular trench
inside the tent, so that they could sit on the ground,
put their feet in the trench and use the circular
portion of ground left around the pole as a table.

They all looked wet and thoroughly miserable, so to cheer them up I breezily shouted :

" This is the last burst, boys, I've been staying with the Mayor of Wadi Hanein. He knows all about it. This is positively the last burst." I then brought my imagination to bear upon the wine.

" What ! You come back again, you noisy blighter," was Nic's only reply.

Thinking the trench in the tent a good idea, " Hungry " and I, whenever the rain softened to a drizzle, dug away at a huge square grave, about three foot deep. Our excavations finished, we placed our " bivy " sheets over this hole and thus had more head room for our heights, and could almost stand up with comfort. Moreover, the ledges of earth inside the "bivy" made convenient shelves for small kit. We dug a huge trench around it so that the water could run away, and settled down to listen to the raindrops rattling on the " bivy " sheets, and laugh at the other fellows lying on the surface of the ground in far less comfort than ourselves.

From that very night the fury of the rains increased and a regular gale sprang up, accompanied by sleet and hail and thunderstorms. The horse-lines became rivers, and everywhere was churned up into two or three feet of mud. It was as much as we could do to get the horses to water ; no other parades were attempted.

I was the standing joke all this week. I had only to show myself to another sergeant to be greeted : " Last burst, 'Appy," and still it went on bursting.

The fourth night of this storm the wind and sleet rose to Atlantic fury ; still, " Hungry " and I settled down snugly to sleep in our grave, and listened to the constant pit-pit-pit of the rains and the slushing of the torrents in the trench. We went to sleep. In the middle of the night I awoke suddenly to find myself almost covered in water, and hurriedly finding a match from the waterproof case on the ledge, saw at a glance that the water was pouring in great torrents into the bottom end of our " bivy." Our trench had burst its bulwarks and we were now in direct line of route to the sea. I grabbed at " Hungry "—he was just about coming up for the third time—and, naked but for our shirts, with sodden blankets wrapped around us, we bolted through the storm and mud to the mess tent. We huddled together in this, but within an hour that blew down upon us, so we left it where it was and crawled into the trench underneath the sagging canvas. There they found us at réveillé, amid cheers, as you may well guess, of " Last burst, 'Appy, the Mayor says it's the last burst."

We spent the morning delving in the icy-cold waters of the " grave bivy " to recover what few articles of clothing had not been washed away by the stream.

However, the rains ceased in a day or two and with the advent of warm sunshine we soon began to get horses and saddlery spick and span again.

As soon as the weather was settled enough we moved back to Deir el Belah on the beach, where General Allenby had made his store base for the Gaza show.

The night we arrived at Belah long remains in my memory. We put down horse-lines on a stretch of sand near the sea, about 4 p.m., and having made our long-faced pals comfortable for the night we sat down on the sands for our own meal. In a very few minutes everyone was wriggling, itching and scratching all over. I opened my shirt, simultaneously with the others, to discover dozens of little red sand-fleas. We were for it; inadvertently we had pitched down on some old camel-lines and the sand was just alive. I itch as I think of it. Everyone was very unhappy, but it was impossible to move again that night. I held a hurried consultation with Nic and Mick, and we agreed on a plan of campaign. As we had ridden into the camp we had passed, about two miles back, a grove of date palms in which were the headquarters of the Tank Corps. The tanks had been used for the attack of Gaza and caused considerable dismay to the Turk, as two had climbed right into the main defences on Samson's Hill before being put out of action. We decided to slip away after dark and visit the Tank Sergeants to see if they had any " Wallop."

We shook our shirts as clear of the pests as possible and started off over the loose sands under a beautiful starlight night to seek hospitality from this new arm of the Service. We found the encampment all right, and, after some little difficulty with the guard, entered the compound and eventually located the sergeants' mess. Now it was a custom in the Yeomanry that any sergeants of any other regiment should be made welcome in the mess were they trekking through or camping near by, and so as we blustered in with a cheery " Hullo, folks, I suppose we can buy a drink here ? " We were surprised to be received with a stony silence. We explained, however, that we had come down country, had not seen a drop of liquor since Christmas-time and they allowed us to fraternize. We stood a few " drinks all round " and after singing them a song or two they soon became firm friends and " did us well." In fact, so well, that it was in the early hours of the morning when two of them led us past the wire. Out in the cold air our potations duly took effect and we were rather fuddled as to which direction our horse-lines lay. However, we linked arms and set off across the sands. I fear we stumbled down many times, but finally reached our lines. There, huge bonfires were blazing and the men were all awake, walking about, cursing, itching and scratching. We " kipped " down quietly and I solemnly believe we were the only three who were able to sleep that night, the fleas got " tight" as soon as they bit us.

We shifted camp early at dawn a mile or so higher up the beach towards Gaza, and there remained for nearly a month, training and entertaining.

The " Sharps " and " Roughs " were camped quite near and we spent many happy evenings together.

" Hungry " and I composed a squadron mess song, hitting off the peculiarities of most of the members— the verses are too lusty and ribald to quote ; and a great turn nightly in request was Mick's rendering of

> " At Low-es-toft her keel was laid
> And she was built for the herring trade."

We also wept crocodile tears of emotion at the pathetic singing of one of the farrier sergeants who in a drawling crying voice would give us :

> " It is an old fashioned cott-i-age
> With ivy round the dow-er,
> It's a dear old kitchen
> With sand upon the flow-er,
> There's a dear old lidy
> An' wherever I may ro-am
> I'll fink of my muvver
> And the dear old ho-am."

We had also with us a banjoist, a rather simple soul, who could not always appreciate when his " leg was being pulled." I shall long remember the sight of this fellow when we " kidded " him to try a little snake-charming. We found a small sand-adder and enlarged upon the powers of music to such an extent that he sat on the sand beside it playing and singing to it " With my 'igh 'at on—my high 'at 'on," " Roger of Kildare," " Hello, my dearie, I'm lonesome for you," and other ditties for nigh on an hour whilst we hid like Sir Toby behind the boxtree, and nearly exploded with laughter.

It was at Belah on a warm spring day—spring breaks early in Palestine—that we held a Brigade mounted sports meeting. A fine course of jumps was put up and we had some excellent sport. I again captained the wrestling on horseback team, but this time we were not so fortunate ; being rather badly beaten in the final by the " Roughs." The meeting will long be remembered for its early termination. Three dozen barrels of beer had been ordered for the Brigade and a canteen with a canvas surround erected on the sands. I am afraid there is rather a deal about beer in this yarn, but most Yeomen are fond of their pint, and when he only has a chance of it once a month or so he remembers certain occasions very distinctly. Now, when the canteen opened in the morning at 11 o'clock it was found that the three dozen barrels contained not ordinary bitter beer but, if you please, Younger's XXX Scotch Ale. The result of drinking this in the heat of the day may well be imagined; by three o'clock in the afternoon the sports fizzled out, and a deadly silence reigned over all save for the sonorous snores of dozens of recumbent figures sleeping 'neath the palm trees.

There were about half a dozen Irishmen who had been drafted to us from " de Thurd Hussaars "—I honestly believe because the Regular regiment could do nothing with them. They were always " agin " the Government, always holding secret conclave and singing " The Shaun Van Vocht " with mystic ceremony; there was no private row in which they would not lend a hand. In a Regiment such as ours, which relied more on the spirit of " playing up " than strict military discipline, they were a thundering nuisance. On this particular night they must have felt themselves getting " younger " every hour, for about eleven o'clock the night guard found them in a highly revolutionary frame of mind, fixing up the Hotchkiss gun and training it upon the sergeants' mess. The timely discovery probably saved a stupid fatality; they were put to bed and given thoroughly to understand that any similar act would be made into a serious case.

On February 22nd we shifted camp to Gaza; and more important still came the welcome news of the Fall of Jericho the day before.

General Allenby had found this operation necessary to strengthen his right flank; as the hilly country held by the infantry across the Jerusalem–Jericho road after the capture of Jerusalem caused con-

THE BRIDGE AT GHORANIYEH ACROSS THE JORDAN

A GOOD "BAG" OF PRISONERS TAKEN AT WADI MALEH

siderable difficulties for transport of food, ammunition and supplies. The operation took two days to complete and was carried out mainly by the 53rd and 60th Divisions and the Australian and New Zealand Mounted Division. The 53rd Division carried out what was a holding action across the Jerusalem-Nablus road and the 60th Division attacked strong Turkish positions on commanding heights on either side of the Jerusalem–Jericho road. Meanwhile the Cavalry Division which had concentrated near Jerusalem and Bethlehem made an enveloping movement down to the plain of the Jordan and through the wilderness of Jeshimon.

An attack was launched at dawn on February 19th, and after severe fighting the 60th Division managed to drive back the Turk to his next line of defence. The key to the position in the hills was a height known as Talaat el Dumm, where stood the remains of the traditional Good Samaritan Inn. This height was successfully stormed by London regiments, which pressing forward were able to occupy the heights commanding the sudden descent into the Jordan valley and overlooking the little town of Jericho nestling at the foot of the hills. Having thus cleared the hills, the Australians and New Zealanders were able to advance from the south up the valley by the north-western shores of the Dead Sea, and occupied Jericho at about eight o'clock on the morning of February 21st.

The position in the hills was consolidated and the cavalry pushed out patrols to drive the Turk right back to the Jordan where he held a bridge-head at El Ghoraniyeh.

From our new camp at Gaza we were able to explore the ruins of the city, and we were amazed at the formidable trench systems of the enemy that had been so gallantly carried by the P.B.I. in the last advance. Across the main ridge known as " Samson's Ridge " were the two battered and abandoned tanks ;

whilst in and about the enemy trenches a hand or a
leg protruding from the soil indicated many a hasty
burial. The famous mosque, which had been used by
the Turks as an observation post and an ammunition
centre had been nearly blown to pieces by our shells,
and was now full of exploded ammunition, large and
small. All around the town were many shells which,
owing to a faulty fuse or some other defect, had failed to
explode, and these were very dangerous ; in fact, we
lost several horses through a hoof suddenly striking a
fuse-head half buried in the sands. There were many
large unexploded shells, some as much as three feet
high which had been fired from the monitors at sea,
and we were careful to give all such pregnant danger a
wide berth. One such huge shell was half-balanced
across a jagged edge of rock ; it had been seen by us
for days. On one occasion riding some half-mile away
from the spot we noticed that a little Arab boy had
come out of the town and was sitting cross-straddled
playing on this dangerous mount. We shouted to him,
but even as we did so the shell seemed to slide sideways, topple and explode with a blinding burst of
flame and a cloud of smoke, rock and dust. Hardly a
vestige of the little fellow could be found.

We began training again in earnest at Gaza and
several sergeants from the Army Gymnastic Corps
were attached to the Regiment. Thus we had about
three hours' P.T. a day, and although it gave us "gyp"
it was thoroughly enjoyed by all of us. Then a
sergeant who admitted he had never been in the firing
line taught us the new ferocious "put-the-wind-up-
him" bayonet drill. You snarled and shouted
"Errk" as you stabbed the sack—we presumed in
action you wiped the blood off on the seat of your
pants and shouted "Next please."

A Brigade Rugger contest was started and we had
some splendid games, although the ground was so
hard and sandy that a good tackle meant a good
"septic" for a week or more. We did very well in

this as we managed to muster quite a good team. If I remember rightly we beat the " Warwicks " by a try to nothing in the semi-final and lost to the " Sharps " in the final.

One game of Rugger I shall long remember, a Brigade team played a team from the 4th Light Horse, and it was a battle royal. We took our knock and gave our knock that day, and though defeated we all enjoyed the game immensely—and weren't the Aussies just pleased with themselves !

Boxing contests were organized and the finals took place in a ring set in a natural coliseum in the Gaza hills. It was a beautiful spring day and everyone rode down to the circular stadium, nicknamed Dingley Dell ; horses were tied to posts and rails and then we sat on the hill-slopes, tier upon tier of men with eyes riveted on the ring below. There were many splendid bouts, but the top line was a contest at about 8st.6lbs.,between a fellow named Jordan of the " Staffs" and a lad in the Roughriders named, I believe, Touse. They had met each other twice before and had been accredited with a victory apiece. Jordan was tallish, slim, with long arms, a very clean-limbed lad ; Touse was short, stocky, with a fine chest and back and a very heavy punch. Their styles were consequently in as great a contrast as their physiques. If one may draw a distinction kindly, Jordan boxed with the long straight left, piston-swinging public-school style, and Touse with the sharp snappy heavy punching in-fighting style of Hoxton Baths and Wonderland. Betting had been fast and furious as to the result and these boys gave us a wonderful display. In a long experience of watching boxing of all kinds, I never remember a bout that thrilled me so. Jordan with such grace and ease, boxing off, side-stepping ; Touse with jaw set and head forward following in landing terrific punches whenever an opening occurs. Jordan is the cleverer, speedier boxer, but Touse is the harder hitter. Touse follows Jordan round, almost cornering him on the ropes ; a side-step, a dodge and he is away. Touse is after him again, caring nothing for the straight swinging left and rights to the head. Now he has him on the ropes again and all seems up with Jordan, but somehow his pluck has pulled him through a bad minute and he is out boxing off hard again. Four rounds superb fighting by each lad. In the fifth, Touse is tiring and visibly becoming slower ; Jordan who has taken no end of body punishment seems to assert superiority. His lefts and rights flash out, he makes all the fighting now ; a perfectly timed punch, a left to the jaw, Touse falters, another left and Touse totters and falls by the ropes. Well fought both, a contest fit for the gods of Olympus !

One other day's sport must be mentioned. The 22nd Mounted Brigade, the Staffs, Lincolns and East Riding Yeomanry, organized a race meeting and invited the rest of the Division. The Division entered into the spirit of the thing, and we had a most wonderful day out. A race-course had been laid out for both flat and steeplechasing behind the city of Gaza, and on the appointed day, every Yeoman began his pilgrimage to this course as if to the Derby. The road down to Gaza was a sight; transport waggons decked in colours, some men riding, some men walking, all " chi-ik-ing " one another as they passed, all emulating times they had ridden along the road to Epsom Downs. Such banter and fun on every side, such sporting of colours, such yelling of tips, bragging and boasting of regimental favourites, such singing, such wagering—such fun and laughter everywhere.

I have the programme before me as I write ; there were seven races, and among other well-known names in the racing world I notice those of Mr. O. Anthony, Mr. Gilpin, Mr. Wootton, Mr. Sheddon and, of course, our own Colonel's, Sir Mathew Wilson. The two great races were, to quote from this programme :

Palestine Grand National. Value a Cup and P.T. 500 to the winner. P.T. 1000 to the 2nd. P.T. 200

to the 3rd. A steeplechase for all horses in the Desert Mounted Corps. Catch weights over 11 st. 7 lbs. To be ridden by officers. Distance about two miles. Entrance fee P.T. 150.

Gaza Hunt Cup. Value a Cup and P.T. 500 to the winner. P.T. 1000 for the 2nd. P.T. 200 for the 3rd.

An open Flat Race for all horses of the Desert Mounted Corps. Catch weights over 12 st. To be ridden by officers. Distance about one mile. Entrance fee P.T. 150.

There were, of course, several races for troop horses confined to men of the 22nd Brigade, but the National and the Hunt Cup were the great open races. As is usual at race meetings we all lost money except the bookies, but the day is long talked of as a grand day's sport whenever men of the Yeomanry Mounted Division meet together.

In the evenings we were much entertained by a splendid Concert Party of the " Sharps " known as " The Tanks." " The Tanks," of whom Edwards and Riley will long be remembered for their drolleries, was different from many Concert Parties in that every member of the " troupe " was also a member of the Troop. That is to say, not one of them was ever excused a parade of any kind, all their rehearsals were accomplished in odds and ends of times between stables and night guards. They were a wonderful combination and they brought to us all those songs which were so popular in London at that time from the *Bing Boys* and other plays. They had a perfect leading lady and all who heard them will long remember " Everybody calls me Teddie," " Hello, my dearie, I'm lonesome for you," " Carolina Jane " and their concerted number, " Let's put the best foot forward for the fun of the fair."

Whenever doing a turn myself at one of the concerts, I relied on old favourites or a song with a splendid chorus I had managed to pick up some two years previously. It was a song that ripped along with a swing and was a great favourite with the London lads on account of its theme :

> " If you're going back to London,
> If you're going back to town,
> Say, in Trafalgar Square,
> Greet the Lions there,
> Shout—Hello ! Hello ! Hello London !
> Tip the man in blue a fiver,
> Kiss the girls, don't be afraid,
> Tell every London pet
> She's not forgotten yet
> By the Boys of the old Brigade."

You can well imagine a crowd of lads on a strip of desert to whom the magic word London meant light and laughter, sweethearts and wives, dinners and shows and lots of fun, singing this song with a real swing—hear the crescendoes on the " Hello ! London ! "

A little parody I wrote on " Take me back to Blighty " also proved a successful number. The verse imagined a fellow after the War, who could not get work because a woman had his job, standing selling matches in the Strand, tired of London and longing for the old Army life again : the chorus ran :

> " Take me back to Deir el Belah,
> Put me on the train for Abasan,
> Drop me over there, leave me anywhere,
> Ras Deiran or Sidi Bishr.
> Well, I don't care,
> A ' bint ' will do for me as best girl,
> Though much of her face it's difficult to see,
> Oh ; Hi-ti-illiddley-ity, I'm fed up with Blighty,
> Egypt is the place for me."

One night whilst sitting up late in the sergeants' mess at Gaza with Nic and Mick—we were quarrelling about Mick's art-collecting tendencies, I believe— we heard a devil of a shuffling and scuffling, shouting, swearing and coaxing on the outskirts of the camp. We flung open the hut door, and peered across the desert. There was but little moon that night, and

it was difficult to discern the cause of the distant
commotion, but it looked like a crowd of Arabs in
white robes massing to attack the camp. We stood
spellbound for a moment or two, and as the mass drew
near heard many well-known expletives and ex-
hortations that could only have been uttered by an
English Tommy. Nearer and nearer the drove came,
and suddenly we began to laugh, as a rich deep voice
we thought we recognized shouted : " Is this the
b——y Middlesex, 'cause I'm not going a step further
to-night, I'm kipping right here."

" Harry Biggs, for a wager," I shouted through the
dark.

" You're right, my son, and I've got three hundred
b——y donkeys here, and I'm d—— if I'm going a
step further to-night with the cow sons." Harry
loomed up, big, fat and greasy, mopping his forehead,
sitting astride a milk-white donkey, balanced well on
the moke's posterior. I hastily smothered a reference
to Balaam, remembering that Harry was now an
officer. Harry, an old regular, of the Carbineers, had
been one of the most popular sergeants of the
" Sharps " and had been drafted to the Camel Corps,
and after being their Quarter bloke had taken a
commission. We took him into the mess, while he
disgustedly explained :

" Yes, early this morning they sent me down to
railhead with a party to draw mounts. When I gets
there, they dishes me out with three hundred of these
b——y donkeys to take to Divisional Headquarters.
They've got to be posted so many to each regiment.
I don't know what we're coming to, straight, I don't.
I've had a proper game with them, I can tell you,
about one man to a dozen donkeys." He soon had
them picketed down, and in the morning we all assembled to give him a cheer as he rode off at the head
of this curious convoy.

Shortly afterwards they issued these donkeys and we
quite made pets of them. They were posted one to a

Troop, and we used them in camp for riding short distances over the loose sand, instead of saddling up a horse ; and whilst on the march as an extra pack animal. We nicknamed the four in our squadron, " Shadrach," " Meshach," " Abednigo " and " Habbukuk." I shall long remember dear " Bully's " smile as he saw our donkey in the lines for the first time, and asking his name, I replied, " Habbukuk, sir, but I'm afraid I shall have to rechristen him, as I regret to say observation tells me that his thoughts are not always pure."

The padre about this time gained a signal victory over military procedure. It is well known how irksome the Sunday morning compulsory church parade has always proved to be to all troops. The men used to ballot as to who should have to attend, and the padre realizing this, went to the Colonel with a scheme. He suggested that the compulsory parade be abolished and that he would hold a light voluntary service in the early evening, and he guaranteed that the attendance at church would be doubled. The Colonel gave permission for the experiment, and without exaggeration the Regiment supported the padre to such an extent that practically the whole of the men turned up—we roped in every one—" the black squad " included. And jolly services they were too. Removed from the restrain of spit and polish the men sang the old hymns with gusto, and the padre beamed through his glasses till the tears were in his eyes. He also, good soul, was for ever arranging concerts and sought to entertain us on one occasion by inviting the Pipe-Major and Pipe Band from the Black Watch over to play to us. They arrived in high glee in a lorry. They entertained us and then we entertained them, and they departed all lying in the bottom of the lorry with their pipes folded gracefully above them ; save one—the Pipe-Major, who could not be found. The last dying squeal of a pipe somewhere out on the desert sent us on a search that proved, alas, to be in vain.

Just before réveillé a shrill and crooning tuning-up could be heard and in the half-light of dawn the Pipe-Major could be seen swirling his way homeward across the desert, with his chest well out, blowing his pipes as if he led a phantom army not only of " Docks " but " Dorises."

Mention of pipers, recalls a traditional Army story, claimed by many regiments to be their own ; at any rate it was much in vogue at this time. It concerns a regimental concert at which the Colonel rose to make the following announcement : " Officers, Non-Commissioned Officers and Men, I very much regret that my old friend Colonel B——, who usually sings so delightfully at these concerts for us, has sent a message saying that owing to a severe cold he is unable to be present here with us this evening. I am sure we all are very sorry of his indisposition, and that you wish me to convey to him our best wishes for a speedy recovery. ('ear, 'ear.) However, hoping to add to the hilarity of the evening, he has sent his regimental piper to play to us. ('ear, 'ear.) I have now much pleasure in calling on Pipe-Major MacTavish to play to us " (roars of applause).

With a flourish of his pipes and a swishing of his kilt, the Pipe-Major strode on to the platform and began to make the most hideous row imaginable. The men, out of respect for the artist as their guest, stood it as long as possible, but the piper, now well into his stride and thoroughly enjoying himself, failed to notice the growing impatience of the audience and played on from one tune to another. The men became restless, then fidgety, and finally began to mutter and talk. At a pause, when the piper looked like regaining his breath to start again, a loud voice from the back of the audience was heard to exclaim : " What a blighter ! " (Soldiers always say " blighter.")

" Stop, stop," the Colonel jumped to his feet, " who called the piper a blighter ? "

No response.

P

" I will not allow this concert to proceed until I know who called the piper a blighter."

Still no response.

The Colonel now waxed furious : " Gentlemen, this is an insult to my old friend Colonel B——, that he should send his piper here to entertain us and that he should be treated in this fashion. I demand to know who called the piper a blighter."

No answer, was still the stern reply.

The Colonel was now nearly apoplectic. Red in the face, and gesticulating violently, he continued to shout : " Who called the piper a blighter ? The Regiment shall be confined to camp until I know. Who called the piper a blighter ? In fact, not a man shall leave this hut until I know. Who called the piper a blighter ? "

Voice from the back, unable to contain himself longer : " Who called the blighter a piper ? "

Another traditional story too good to be true may be new to some folk, I refuse to vouch for its veracity.

A Colonel of the hearty robust type, with a keen sense of humour, entered his orderly-room one morning, rubbing his hands and chuckling, feeling just fit for anything that should come his way.

" Morning, Adjutant, anything special to report ? "

" Well, no, sir," replied the Adjutant ; " nothing of military importance, but there was a devil of a row down the horse-lines last night."

" Oh oh ! what was that ? "

" Just those two Irishmen fighting again, sir, Troopers Carroll and O'Daly ; they're always at it."

" Ha ha ! and what was the trouble this time ? "

" Well, sir, it appears from what the sergeant-major says, that after a pint or two in the canteen, they started an argument as to which smelt the worst, a goat or a Turkish prisoner."

" Well, I'm damned, what a thing to fight about ! Ha ha ! silly fools, which said which ? "

" I think Carroll was backing the goat, whereas O'Daly rather fancied the Turkish prisoner, sir."

The Colonel roared—" Ha ha! Well, which does smell the worst ? "

" I'm afraid I don't know, sir," then added the Adjutant tentatively, " I should think the goat, sir."

" Damn it, I bet you're wrong," answered the Colonel emphatically. A bright idea suddenly struck him—" I'll tell you what—we'll prove it and then the sergeant-major can tell the men which really is the worst," and as if to justify his whim, " can't have them fighting about anything so damn silly."

Accordingly a goat and a Turkish prisoner were brought and placed at a convenient distance from the orderly-room, where the Colonel had arranged himself comfortably in the position of chief adjudicator.

" Bring in the goat," roared the Colonel, in high glee at his jest. The goat was led in and the Colonel, leaning over, took two or three deep sniffs, rapidly changed colour, spluttered a bit and finally fainted.

When he came to, he coughed and said : " Well, well, that was bad, damn bad—Carroll said goat, didn't he ? I suppose I'd better stick it out and try the other."

Then in stentorian tones : " Bring in the Turkish prisoner."

The goat fainted.

Just one more, also untrue.

An infantry battalion had achieved a successful forced march of some fifteen miles across the loose sand of the open desert to take up a required position. On reaching their objective the Colonel gave orders for the officers to fall out for lunch whilst the men sat down to their biscuits and " bully." The Adjutant, studying the map, suddenly pointed out to the Colonel that they had come to the wrong place and that their real objective was a further fifteen miles to the right.

The battalion was hastily paraded and the Colonel addressed them :

" My men, there has been some—er—slight mistake. The battalion will be required to march another fifteen miles. Now if there is any man who feels he can't manage another fifteen miles, let him take three paces forward."

To his amazement, the whole battalion moved, except one man wearily swinging on his rifle in the back rank.

Disgustedly the Colonel shouted :

" Hm ! I'm astonished at this sign of weakness in the battalion, but there—anyhow—I'm pleased to see that there's one man who can march another fifteen miles."

" Me, sir, I can't take the three paces forward."

I have dwelt at length on these three happy months behind the lines, as generally when old soldiers foregather it is of such times they yarn. The good times and jokes are more readily remembered than the disasters and discomforts of campaigning, and a carouse recalled more often than a battle.

CHAPTER X

THE VALLEY OF THE JORDAN

" One more river, and that's the river to Jordan,
One more river—there's one more River to cross."

WHILST we were thus recuperating and refitting on the plains, General Allenby successfully carried out his first raid across the Jordan into Gilead, the objectives being the towns of Es Salt and Amman. Amman was an important junction on the Damascus–Hedjaz railway, and it was contemplated that a smashing of the railway would seriously hamper the lines of communications to those Turkish forces engaged against the Sherifian troops under the direction of Colonel Lawrence in the Hedjaz country. The force detailed to undertake this raid across Jordan was known, from its commander, General Shea of the 60th Division, as " Shea's " group, and mainly consisted of the Australian and New Zealand Mounted Division, the 60th (London) Division, and the Imperial Camel Corps, with attendant artillery and bridging trains.

The River Jordan was well in flood after the winter rains, and was found to be absolutely unfordable; moreover, the steep drop in the river-bed as the stream approaches the Dead Sea creates a strong and treacherous current. The banks of the Jordan were marshy and sodden, rendering the surface muddy and slippery, and across the other side was a strip of jungle, almost tropical in its density and apparent impenetrability.

It was decided that the most practical places for

throwing over bridges and establishing bridge-heads were at Ghoraniyeh and Hajlah. Ghoraniyeh is the traditional site of Christ's baptism, and is known to pilgrims from Jerusalem as the " Place of Baptism," and Hajlah is some five miles further south, almost equidistant from Ghoraniyeh and the Dead Sea. Around Hajlah the undergrowth is very thick, but the river is much narrower ; there is a disused monastery near this point which many say marks the site of the destroyed city of Gomorrah.

To the 180th Brigade—2/17th (Poplar and Stepney), 2/18th (London Irish), 2/19th (St. Pancras)—was given the task of effecting these two crossings. The Ghoraniyeh bridge was to be a heavy barrel-pier bridge for the infantry, the Hajlah bridge a short steel pontoon bridge for cavalry and artillery. To deceive the enemy, feint attempts to cross over were made at the fords of Mandesi, Enkhola, Yehnd and Henu, which kept a number of enemy troops actively engaged at points opposite to these small detachments.

Attempts were first made to cross the Jordan at midnight on the night of March 21st–22nd. The river is fairly wide at Ghoraniyeh and all attempts either by swimming, by punts or by rafts were frustrated by the heavy current. Moreover, the splashings and noises from their unsuccessful efforts soon attracted the attention of the Turks, and brought reinforcements and a heavy fire to bear upon those engaged in the already difficult operations.

At Hajlah, however, after several efforts, swimmers got across the Jordan unobserved. Imagine a little group of some dozen men stealing down through the undergrowth by the slippery banks ; undressing, and slipping silently into the swiftly running, muddy stream. Hardly seeing the other side and not know-ing the strength of the current they struck out, carry-ing a small rope with them. Several were washed back again and clung helplessly on to twigs and

branches from the overhanging bushes ; but two or
three swimming strongly, made an oblique crossing
and eventually hauled themselves up naked on to the
other side. Actually the first men to swim the Jordan
were Second-Lieutenant G. E. Jones and Corporal E.
Margrave, both of the 2/19th London, but a number
of others followed. A heavy rope was drawn across,
and the first raft of troops containing twenty-seven
men was hauled across Jordan at about 1.30 in the
morning. Men were ferried across by raft as quickly
as possible, but it was naturally a slow operation,
especially as immediately dawn broke the crossing
was discovered by the enemy, who brought such concentrated fire to bear on the rafts that only eight men
lying crouched in the bottom of the raft could be
ferried over at a time.

The Ghoraniyeh crossings having been abandoned
for the time being, reinforcements were brought down
as a covering force to engage the enemy, which proved
so effective that by eight o'clock in the morning the
first pontoon bridge was completed across the Jordan.
This rendered it possible to rush troops across the
river in greater numbers, and the enemy was driven
eastward and northward as a bridge-head was established.

The Hajlah bridge-head was held successfully all
through the day and night of March 22nd, against
counter-attacks of the enemy, whilst under cover of
darkness several further attempts were made to cross
at Ghoraniyeh. Enemy fire and the current combined
to render these attempts abortive ; so a concentration
of machine-guns was made on the west bank of Jordan
which at dawn opened up such disastrous and continuous fire on the Turks that in a few hours the immediate further bank was completely cleared of the
enemy. Thus in daylight, able to see their destina-
tion and judge the currents, strong swimmers were
able to cross the river by swimming obliquely to the
stream. It was, of course, impossible to land opposite

their starting-off point, but by continual battling with
the current they reached the opposite bank some
eighty yards downstream. Rafting was now commenced here, the engineers working with a will.

Meanwhile a small Naval detachment lent a helping
hand. This detachment had, some time previously,
by great skill and almost superhuman efforts, brought
in sections three motor-boats down that mountainous
Jerusalem–Jericho road and fitted them up on the
Dead Sea. Making several journeys early on the
morning of March the 23rd, they established a landing
party on the further shore of the Dead Sea, and these
moving up country soon established touch with the
Hajlah bridge-head. The land to the south now being
clear of enemy the Auckland Mounted Rifles, who
had crossed the Hajlah at dawn and been held in
readiness, now moved northward, and galloping
several Turkish positions cleared all the ground in
front of Ghoraniyeh, capturing sixty-eight prisoners
and several machine-guns. The engineers could now
work unhampered by enemy fire and by midnight of
March the 23rd there were four bridges across Jordan,
two at Ghoraniyeh and two at Hajlah.

The Jordan safely crossed, the raiding parties now
began to fight their way north-eastward and eastward
towards Es Salt and Amman. The main track up the
precipitous hills of Gilead was more difficult to
negotiate than the Jerusalem–Jericho road, and as the
flanks had to be cleared on either side and a strong
holding force stretched across the Jordan plain, the
Turks were able to bring considerable resistance to
bear and they had to be dislodged by continual heavy
fighting. However, Es Salt was captured by the
181st and 179th Brigades, and this strategic position
once held, the cavalry could press forward towards
Amman. The 2nd Australian Light Horse Brigade
had attempted another pass through the hills, and
soon found that further wheeled transport was impossible, so that all ammunition had to be loaded on

to camel and pack-horses. As they advanced in single file the track became as bad as that in the Judæan hills around Fokka ; and the horses and camels had to be dragged, shoved and sometimes almost lifted up the slippery slopes and over the shifting boulders. Their discomforts were added to by a continuous rain, but finally, with that indomitable Australian endurance, they arrived south of Amman, and raiding the railway line in several places, blew up sections, and achieved considerable damage.

They found Amman very strongly held by the enemy, and had to wait for the arrival of further cavalry and infantry, via Es Salt, before a concentrated attack could be made. It appeared that the enemy was determined to hold Amman and thus secure his line of communication to his Southern Arabian troops at any costs ; for he rushed up reinforcements from Damascus and other centres as quickly as he could.

After two days' continuous fighting, in which casualties were very severe on both sides, Amman was occupied on March 30th, but the arrival of very heavy reinforcements before both Amman and Es Salt, rendered the occupation by so small a force impossible, and the withdrawal was ordered the same night.

It would appear that the Turk believed this raid the beginning of another advance, for he now concentrated large bodies of troops before Es Salt and began to attack in force. The gallant little garrison at Es Salt were now in a very awkward position ; if they gave way the whole of their comrades at Amman would be surrounded and captured, and by desperate fighting they kept the enemy at bay whilst the forces withdrew from Amman. The London Scottish and the 2/13th (Kensingtons), 2/15th (Civil Service), 2/16th (Queen's Westminsters) Regiments held on like grim death to Es Salt until the last of the Amman force had passed through with their wounded painfully

swinging in camel cacholets. Although knowing
the town of Es Salt to be almost surrounded, and the
Turks about to enter, the 179th Brigade marched out
unconcernedly on April 1st. Although they had had
ten days' continual fighting and storming of precipitous heights, the Scottish pipers were sent for, a
couple of Turkish drums were found from somewhere,
and with chests well out and an undeniable swagger
those London boys marched out of Es Salt as serenely
as they would pass the Mansion House on a Saturday
afternoon route march, just as Johnny Turk entered
the town the other side.

A squadron of thirteen enemy planes had made
several bombing raids on the dressing-stations on the
plain ; but the whole force retired back across the
Jordan, bringing with them a thousand prisoners and
leaving a well-established bridge-head on the further
side of Ghoraniyeh by the night of April 3rd.

Some time later, about the middle of April, the
enemy made a strong attack on the Ghoraniyeh bridge-
head, but the assault was beaten off with considerable
loss to the enemy.

Towards the middle of April a real tragedy befell
us ; we lost our best pals, the " Roughs " and
" Sharps." Owing to the German break-through in
March on the French front, General Allenby had to
spare every man he could from the Egyptian Expeditionary Force, and thus two regiments from each
Brigade of the Yeomanry Mounted Division were to
be sent to France dismounted. We were fortunate, as
being senior regiment in our brigade we were to remain
mounted. We felt very sorry for our old friends, with
whom we had fought for nearly four years, as they
camped near to us for the purpose of handing in their
horses to remount depot. We felt pity for them at
being parted from their mounts after so much cavalry
campaigning, and we felt sorry for ourselves at losing
them, for we had become so intimate with both
regiments that the London Mounted Brigade was

indeed a " happy family." We had always been able
to rely on these our sister regiments in time of stress,
and we had been just the best of friends at sport and
play.

The last thought of these two regiments was,
indeed, typical of the splendid feeling that existed
among us all. The day before their horses had to be
handed over, our Troop sergeants went through their
horse-lines, at their invitation, and we took the very
best of their " cattle," exchanging for them the worst
of our " crocks." We had to do a deal of alteration of
numbers on the hoofs, etc., but it fitted us up with
some splendid horses and gave us an opportunity to
get rid of some of our duds. Moreover, the parting
from their horses was less intense where they could
hand the horse over to a pal and know it would be
well cared for, rather than see one's " four-legged
friend " just sent back to depot.

The night before they left for France, we entertained them well and a great combined concert was
held. We really were very sorry to say good-bye to
these brothers of ours, and in the morning, as we
turned out to cheer them as they marched away dismounted, our throats were more than a little choky,
and hardened sinners as we were, our " e'en a wee bit
moist."

Quoting from Kipling, it was truly a case of :

" We've rode and fought and ate and drunk as rations come to
   hand,
   Together for a year or more around this stinkin' land ;
   Now you are going home again, but we must see it through.
   We needn't tell we liked you well. Good-bye—good luck to
   you ! "

" There isn't much we hav'n't shared since Johnny cut and run.
   The same old work, the same old skoff, the same old dust and
   sun ;
   The same old chance that laid us out, or winked and let us
   through ;
   The same old life, the same old Death. Good-bye—good luck
   to you ! "

About a fortnight after this farewell we amalga-
mated with two other senior regiments that had been
left behind, the Dorsets and the Staffordshire Yeomanry, to form one brigade under Colonel Hodgson,
and then commenced to trek up country again to take
part in the second raid into Gilead.

It was good to be on the move again, and we
enjoyed the trek up through Askelon and other places
where we had been actively engaged on the first
advance. Instead of continuing on through Ramleh,
we cut inland and halted one night near to Junction
Station. I shall always remember the night spent
here, as taking a stroll a little way out from the horse-
lines with Nic, we suddenly heard the strains of a
guitar, and several beautiful passionate tenor voices
singing " O Sole Mio " and such like songs. We
walked on in the direction of the singing, and stumbling up a small hill, found on the other slope a small
encampment of Italian Bersaglieri. They greeted us
with great " bonhomie," pressing us with cigarettes,
and playing and singing to us in their very best
manner. Their camp, however, was perhaps a little
deficient in sanitary services, for the smell was so
objectionable that we decided to make the visit a
short one. As we rode off next morning we saw this
little body out marching with their quick short step
and their black feathers flowing out in the early
morning air.

On through Latron, with its tall and solemn poplar
trees and its white stone monastery, up into the hills
to camp the night in the little valley of Enab just
below Jerusalem. The column moved on later the
next day up the curling, curving, switchback road to
the Holy City. It was after dark when we marched
through : there was not a soul in the streets
and the horses' hoofs and the rumble of the gun-
wheels rang out clear and crisp through the cool night
air. It is very cold in Jerusalem at nights on account
of its height above sea-level and we felt it immensely,

but we rode on and out of the city down past the
Mount of Olives to halt in the olive groves on the
slopes above Bethany.

I shall long remember this ride as it was the first
time I myself had entered the Holy City, and I could
not help feeling some of the awe and majesty of this
silent city, the Mecca of Christendom. The stars
hung low in the sky and the moon shed a pale radiance
over the landscape as we rode down by the Garden
of Gethsemane and skirted the Mount of Olives, with
the minarets of the Russian Church cast up in sharp
relief against the sky. And, as finally I kipped down,
rolled in my blanket, just by Bethany, I wondered
which of those little white stone huts had sheltered
those two sisters and friends of Christ, Mary and
Martha.

On again next morning, up and down the zigzag
track, with its steep hairpin bends, that leads to
Jericho. As one reached the bottom of the valley
it was strange to look up at the way one had
come and see the zigzag of the column, some parts
of which would seem to be riding in the opposite
direction.

Then the steep climb up, with a sheer drop of two
hundred feet or so over the one side of the road to
Talaat el Dumm, where the ruins of the Good Samaritan Inn remain to remind all and sundry of their duty
to their neighbour.

For over a mile I had a most uncomfortable experience. My horse Emperor had a dread of camels, and
on the approach of that scented animal would rear
and cavort all over the place. As we approached
Talaat el Dumm we met a convoy of camels coming
from Jericho on the near side, and Emperor did his
best to prance about like a circus horse on the very
edge of the precipice. Most uncomfortable, I can
assure you. I was reminded of Hazelton's remark to
him, on a similar occasion. Hazelton had been taking
him to water and, having run into camels, he had been

led a fine old dance. So weary had the lad become with his rearings and dancings that in desperation he shouted, " Aye, if tha' doan't like em, doan't b——y well look at 'em."

We watered near the Good Samaritan Inn, on a dust-blown barren patch, and then on over the old and boulder-strewn road to Jericho. It was dark before we were out of the hills, the column rode almost silently in a cloud of dust so impenetrable that it was impossible to see the horse in front of you.

Throughout this trek Nic had ridden at the rear of his troop and I had ridden at the front of mine, so that we could be together. I have always had a passion for onions, and nearly always carried a few small ones loose in one pocket of my tunic. Whenever near a cookhouse I replenished this store. I loved to munch one occasionally whenever on trek, as they seemed to stop the throat from becoming too dry, and I found them a good antidote for thirst. Chewing these onions, I think I must have got on Nic's nerves a little. For about two hours I thoroughly bored him with one of my pet topics, " The Meistersingers." I explained to him the plot, the philosophy underlying the plot; I hummed him airs, I rhapsodized on the blending of the motifs, trying to hum two at the same time to illuminate the counterpoint ; when he made what for him was quite a speech.

" 'Appy, sometimes I hate the sound of your voice ; it just makes me sick. I know you enjoy it yourself, but I can't share the pleasure. I don't mind listening to your crackpot ideas on music, not that it's any good, and mind you, I much prefer hearing Edie Veno at the ' Bedford ' singing, ' My old man gets a bull's-eye—gets a bull's-eye every time ' ; but I do object to your smelling like a garlic-chewing dago. Blimey, that mob we met the other night would suit you down to the ground. You never could b——y well ride so they're just your mark ; you ask the Colonel to get you a transfer to the b——y Bersaglieri—they'd take one sniff of your breath and make you a Brigadier."

The rest of his remarks were cut short as we suddenly felt our horses almost dropping away from under us as they began the steep descent into the Jordan valley.   What with the darkness of the night and the impenetrable cloud of dust raised by the column it was impossible to see the half-section in front of you.   The road sloped so precipitously that it was somewhat of a nightmare of a ride, the column continually bunching, then opening out concertina fashion.   Your horse would suddenly draw up on its haunches on top of those in front, then they would disappear and he would dart off down the slope after them.   Eventually we found ourselves on the level, and as the moon now arose we beheld the few stone buildings, mud huts and ruins set about with cypress trees which form the tiny township of Jericho.

We camped down on the open scrub land on the plain some three miles from the Jordan, and through the next two days, ourselves a constant target for enemy aeroplanes, we watched the battle of the second raid on Es Salt taking place on the other side of the river.   We could see the white puffs of smoke where the shells burst on the red mountain tracks, and with field-glasses could occasionally distinguish the movement of troops.

Since the first raid into Gilead the Turk had reinforced his troops east of Jordan, and the whole of his Fourth Army was now located on that bank of the river.   The Turk held strong entrenched positions watching the Ghoraniyeh bridge-head at Shunet Nimrin where the waters of the Nimrin gurgled over its shallow stony bed on its passage to the Jordan. These outworks were attacked and taken by the 180th Brigade of the 60th Division, and once the Turk had been driven out from here, two brigades of Australian Light Horse, each by different routes, had made a forced march to reach Es Salt, capturing the city just as the General Headquarters of the Turkish Fourth Army moved out.

Johnny Turk attacked in great force on May 1st, and our own Brigade were rushed across the Jordan to hold up the action and cover the retirement of the Light Horsemen from Es Salt. We marched down a sidetrack till we entered the curious formed Salt Hills around the stream of the Jordan, and then across the swaying pontoon bridge at Ghoraniyeh, through a cut made in the dense undergrowth and then up the side of the brook Nimrin. We then rode in line of troop column up through the scrub to take up a position at Shert at right angles to the Jordan, across the plain, covering the left flank of the road down from Es Salt.

The enemy now attacked in large numbers and our cavalry in Es Salt were almost surrounded, their only line of retreat being a rugged mountain track down to the plain. The Turk came down the plain in thousands, so that our little holding force was outnumbered some twenty to one; but everyone engaged hung on desperately to give our Aussie cobbers time to get clear. The Light Horsemen suffered badly from casualties and from forced marching in the heat, but in spite of all they came out of those Mountains of Gilead a cheerful crew. I shall long remember the sight of one stalwart, white as a lump of chalk, riding his jostling whaler down that stone-strewn track, with a cigarette gripped in his tightly-closed lips. It was not until one saw his off side that one noticed his leg was smashed and shattered at the hip, the bones so broken that the lower limb was almost falling off, yet he was making his supreme effort to keep going and get back.

The Turkish forces sweeping down the plain were now but some two hundred yards from the nozzles of the batteries of " A " Battery H.A.C., and the Notts Artillery. The gunners stuck to their guns firing point-blank into the massed crowds of infantry and cavalry before them. A gallant effort to get the guns away over the plain, cut as it was by gullies and gorges, failed, and the guns had to be abandoned to the enemy, who incidentally captured a large field ambulance station which had been advanced to deal with the wounded from Es Salt.

A stronger line was now taken up by the Red Hills, and the action continued in desultory bursts through the days of May 2nd and 3rd. Meanwhile even greater reinforcements were being brought up by " Johnny T.," and it was evident he was going to attack in tremendous force.

Throughout the day of May 4th my little troop, after three consecutive nights on " outpost duty," held a slightly covered position on a little hillock, and whenever a Turkish head showed up for a second we did what damage we could with the Hotchkiss. Just at dusk two scouts went out to our front and reported thousands of the enemy about one hundred yards to our front massing under cover of a ridge. We were disinclined to believe this as throughout the day we had only spotted a few just here and there. I openly told my men that it was " old woman's talk," " windbags, etc." There was almost a deadly calm when night fell, and I put forward picquets to the outpost line. About eight o'clock, however, in the pitch darkness, just on our right by the foot of Red Hill, a furious gun and rifle fire broke out. It sounded like hell's furies let loose. To be frank, I now got the wind up, and began to believe we were in for extermination. A further scout reported that it was infantry to our front and that they were advancing slowly. I rushed back to the horses and with the aid of a horse holder we gathered all the horse bandoliers and stumbled back in the dark to give every man a double supply of ammunition, and then we lay straining our eyes to the front.

We did not know at this time that a general retirement had begun, that all were safely out of the hills

Q

and that we had been left out as the last covering
force. Huge black masses could now be seen to our
front, and we were awaiting orders when a whisper
came all along the line, " Retire."

We bolted for the horses, mounted, and began what
was afterwards known as the " Ghoraniyeh scurry."
We kept some sort of troop formation, but in the
broken country and at the pace we were going we
soon lost touch with the Regiment. In the pitch dark
our horses stumbled and blundered, but everyone
imagined " the breath of the Turkish cavalry to be
on the back of his neck " and we rode like mad. On
account of the broken nature of the land and the
patches of impenetrable scrub, the various sections of
my own troop soon became separated, though I did
all I could to hold them together. I was pleased soon
to hear the hoofs of my horse splashing through water,
though the density of the night and the thickness of
the dust cloud made it impossible to see the ground.
I knew then we were recrossing the Nimrin, and
were not far from the bridge-head.

We soon found ourselves among other troops, all
racing for the bridge, and there was then a proper
bustling, jostling and barging of all branches of the
Service. By this time everyone had completely lost
touch with their regiment, squadron, and many with
their troop, it was one desperate hustle to get across
Jordan. It was not a " disorderly rout " ; it was like
a man who whilst pretending not to hurry was walking
just as fast as ever he could without breaking into a
run. As the pathways converged to the bridge the
" traffic jam " became more intense. Through the
clouds of white fine chalky dust thrown up by the
tramp of the men and the hoofs of the horses a hetero-
geneous force could be seen. One moment we were
riding beside stragglers from the Camel Corps, then
a group of British and Indian infantry all mixed up
together : ambulance waggons, guns and limbers,
camel cacholets, tall Indian Sikhs, short Indian

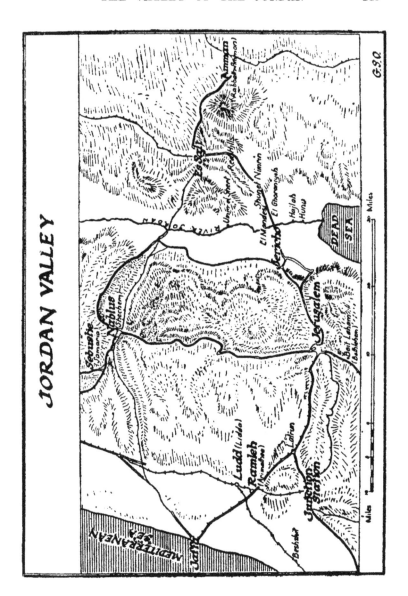

Gurkhas, London lads, Australian bushmen, all "going the same way home."

Once across the Jordan, we deployed out on the plains and camped down anywhere, leaving it till the morning for the Regiments to sort themselves out. The whole raiding force had safely crossed the bridge during the night and had left an established bridge-head on the eastern shore of Jordan. The truth about this raid is that we narrowly escaped a damned good hiding, but when the papers reached us from England a month or so later we were delighted to read that "it was a famous victory."

We remained for about a week on the plain west of Jordan between Jericho and the river. We shifted camp three times during the week and were bombed every morning by enemy aeroplanes. Sometimes at dusk also they would swoop "phut-phut" a machine-gun along our horse-lines, but we usually drove them off with rifle fire.

Somewhere about the middle of May we rode back across the Jordan and took a camp inside the bridge-head, and commenced a series of day and night patrols to various points in front of the wire.

We little knew that we were doomed to spend a whole summer in the Jordan valley and that the next three months were to be from all points of endurance the most trying and wretched of the whole War. Emphatically the Jordan valley is not a place for a summer holiday. Notices dropped from German aeroplanes attempting to cause disaffection, informed us that no white man could live through a summer in the valley and that even natives retired to the hills. Once again we were to prove there is nothing impossible to the British soldier.

We camped below the Ghoraniyeh Bridge about fifty yards from the river. As is well known, the Jordan lies some 1200 feet below sea-level, hence the air pressure is much greater than normal and it was the extreme density of the atmosphere that made the other discomforts so difficult to bear. The daily temperature averaged 125 degrees in the shade, and the heat was damp and humid. On an open desert where the heat is dry and the air crisp 125 degrees can be borne with fortitude ; but here in the valley the damp muggy heaviness seemed to sap away all energy. In addition there were flies in greater numbers than anywhere else we had yet encountered them, terrible hot dust storms and at night such thousands of mosquitoes that although encased in a mosquito net one could hardly sleep for the noise of their "ping-pinging" against the outsides. Our "bivies" had mosquito nets which just fitted along the inside, and if we had to ride out of night patrol anywhere near the water, we wore muslin veils around our pith helmets and muslin gauntlets for the protection of the hands.

The scrub and ground generally was alive with small adders, tarantula spiders and, worst of all, huge black scorpions. It was as well to thoroughly shake one's blanket at night, for as the sun went down and the earth became cooler the adders and scorpions found them comfortable havens till morning. I have never been stung by a "scorp"—they sting by whipping the tail over the head—but I know fellows who have, and they say the pain as the poison courses through the blood is something terrible to bear. I saw a fellow's arm swell twice its size in less than ten minutes after a sting from one of these "flat irons" as we sometimes called them. The nearest I ever approached to such distinction was to wake from an early morning "kipp" to find one resting on the back of my hand ; I had to lay rigid without a movement for nearly a quarter of an hour before he eventually crawled off.

A gladiatorial contest occasionally staged by the troops was a fight between a tarantula and a "scorp." The tarantulas have a kind of four-sided jaw, are most horrible to look at, can eat flies and hornets by the dozen, and I have been told that they have been seen to eat a small mouse. Anyhow, whether the cock-fighting laws forbade it or no, if one could coax a tarantula and a scorpion into a small rock-enclosed arena a battle royal would take place. The tarantula nearly always proved victorious, for when the "scorp" found himself badly injured and unable to carry on the combat, he stung himself behind the head and thus committed suicide.

During the first part of my sojourn in the valley we kept a small chameleon in the rush hut we called a "mess," and he became quite a pet with us. It used to amuse us to watch his tongue roll out like a Christmas squeaker and gather in the flies. Bert, who had always been a little sceptic about "this changing colour business" was now convinced, as "Horace," as we called him, moved from brown bough to green leaf. Not satisfied with nature's demonstrations Bert put him in the centre of a small Union Jack one day, exclaiming with a chuckle : "That's b—— you, my son."

The flies were a perfect plague both from point of view of number and pertinacity. We had encountered flies on Gallipoli and along the Suez Canal, but here all insect records were easily beaten. It made any attempt at meal-taking a quarter of an hour's sheer exasperation. One had to keep waving your left hand over bread and jam the whole time, and then they would settle in dozens on the other end as you placed one end in your mouth.

After a week or two of this constant hand-fanning I began to realize why the Jews wave their hands about so much in talking, it is obviously an hereditary trait acquired throughout the ages by countless ancestors "swiping" flies off their bread and jam.

There were dense patches of vegetation in the Jordan valley, around the streams, and animal life abounded in the jungles. When on night outpost duty at any of the fords to our front, a careful watcher would see dozens of wild deer, wild boar, a kind of jackal, and other creatures stealing down to the water to drink.

Mick once reported seeing a panther, but as he'd gone out with a bottle of Sergeant-Major Antiquary we all had our doubts as to the dependability of his vision.

Indian cavalry which had been sent out from France joined us in the valley and the cavalry brigades were reconstructed with one Yeomanry regiment to two regiments of natives. We were brigaded with two crack corps—the Jacob's Horse and the 29th (Patiala) Lancers. Fine fellows these Indian cavalrymen ; of good caste, most of them were sons of landed proprietors in their home provinces ; the Jacob's Horsemen were of shorter hussar build, but the lancers were tall, handsome, heavily bearded men. We missed our old friends the " Sharps and Roughs," but once we had mastered the many things we had to refrain from doing near the native camps, we became firm friends with our new comrades. The most difficult observance was that if the shadow of a white man fell across their sheep or food we rendered it unclean, and we had to be very careful not to give any offence when visiting their lines. They considered it a great honour to talk with the British cavalry, but for many reasons Headquarters viewed with disfavour too close a fraternization between English and native troops.

Our work in the bridge-head consisted mainly of either day or night outpost duty and we were in constant touch with the enemy scouts, many little brushes occurring almost daily, but operations or " scraps " of any size were few. The oppressive prostrating heat of the day rendered military operations almost impossible for either side. The bridge-head, however, was occasionally shelled and we were often bombed by enemy aeroplanes. Mick had a marvellous escape on one occasion ; he was lying half-naked in a sheltered "bivy" placed against the chalk face of a cliff, when a shell went clean through the " bivy " sheet and embedded itself in the earth at his feet without exploding. The look of blank amazement on his face was wondrous to behold.

Our patrols would ride out of the wire just before dawn, always a most magnificent sight in the valley. Whilst we, under the shadow of the Mountains of Gilead, were in cold grey gloom, the sun's rays would light the red and purple rocks and hills across the valley, throwing into sharp relief the crags and crevices of the hills of Judæa. As the " Hunter of the East " arose one could watch the shadow-line coming nearer and nearer to us across the plain, until we ourselves were bathed in the warmth of early dawn.

The patrols took up picquet posts at important cross-roads and fords across the various streams; the patrol work was fairly popular as, although the heat was everywhere heavy, damp and overpowering, there were less flies on the plain than in the camp by Jordan. A good deal of the enemy could be seen during these patrols and often one would round a belt of vegetation and come upon an enemy scout quite suddenly; almost every occasion it was the policy of the Turk to run rather than give fight, and thus our casualties from gun- and rifle-fire were very light at this time.

One night, however, Mick and Nic advancing on a night reconnaissance up a wadi bed, suddenly found themselves in the pitch darkness in a Turkish ambush. The presence of mind of Nic, who acted directly against the orders of a new officer just out from England, saved the situation, and the Turks, thinking themselves against a much greater force than two troops after a few rounds rapid, retired.

The whole bridge-head was attacked in some considerable force towards the end of May, but the enemy was driven off and suffered very heavy losses; the timely arrival of " Jacob's Horse " saved our regiment from another long outpost fight against superior forces. If casualties from fighting were few, those from sickness were very great indeed. In spite of the morning quinine parade, when every man lined up with his mug and drank his ten grains of quinine, by numbers, in the presence of the doctor, dozens of men fell sick with sandfly fever and malaria. The heaviness of the atmosphere and the dampness of the heat made the climate that of a typical hot-swamp region, and men who had been on constant service for four years had not sufficient reserve of strength to withstand the conditions, so that the sick parade every morning was a sorry sight. Moreover, the waters of the Jordan although chlorinated acted on the blood in some peculiar way to produce a large and painful variety of " boil." We called these " Jordan boils," and those of us who had sufficient recuperative powers to battle out our bouts of malaria without leaving the regiment, suffered a good deal from these boils and septic sores.

As is always the case, those who are the stronger eventually have the more work to do, and we were losing men from sickness at such a rate that very shortly each man was looking after three horses apiece instead of one. It is difficult to describe the relief one felt, after a terrible day's heat, at the approach of sundown. All stable work, if not in patrol, was done by 7.30 a.m., and except for the midday water and feed, the men remained naked under their mosquito nets prostrate for most of the day. In fact, it was almost unbearable from 9 a.m. till 4 p.m. Usually about half-past four, after evening stables, we would stroll down to the Jordan where a swimming run had been constructed for good swimmers. The bushes had been cleared a bit from either side, and two posts with ropes attached driven into the bed of the river on the opposite side, one fifty yards down, and the other fifty yards upstream. You dived into the hot muddy waters and attempted to swim across, but by the strength of the current you were carried across to the lower post. You then got out and ran a hundred

yards upstream to the other post, dived in again and
the current brought you back to the starting-point.

The Jordan was very dangerous to non-swimmers
and several lads were drowned here. It must have
been well stocked with fish, as in swimming one could
often feel them hitting against one's thighs, and I
believe several fairly large cat-fish were caught from
time to time.

After a month in the line we retired across Jordan,
each man leading two horses to a dust-heap on the
plain by Jericho and remained in camp here a fortnight.
It was better in the bridge-head, as here we had constant fatigues to do, and what with the heat, the dust
and the flies, life seemed most wretched.

One little incident is worthy of mention. Overlooking the town of Jericho is an almost sheer precipice
of rock known as the Mount of Temptation, and half-
way up the face of this cliff, cut and built clean into
the rock itself, is a small monastery of white stone.
It is a most wonderful sight and must have taken
years of great patience to build. Nic and I decided to
visit this hermitage, and so saddling up just at dawn
one morning we arrived at the base of the mountain
about 5 o'clock. We tied up our horses and began
the ascent up the steep and stony pathway. It was a
difficult climb, but in places the monks had cut steps,
and having scrambled up some two hundred feet we
found ourselves at the little wooden entrance. It was
opened by a courteous Russian monk who spoke a little
English and French. Would we come in ? He would
be too enchanted to show us round. It seemed
strange indeed to find this little religious colony of not
more than twenty souls living a life of such solitude
in the wilderness of Jordan. He explained that the
monastery was on the Mount of Temptation and that
the monks were building another temple on the top
of the Mount to mark the place where our Lord was
tempted by Satan. He took us another steep and
perilous climb to the top to show us where the founda-

tions and outer walls of this new Temple stood. In the monastery itself the little cells were just cut clean into the cliff with a stone slab on which to sleep. There was a small refectory where we were offered boiling-hot black coffee, and a most wonderful little chapel. Perhaps not much larger than an English drawing-room in size, it was yet one of the most beautiful places of worship I have ever entered. The craftsmanship of the monks of the ages had combined to beautify this little retreat from the world, the flesh and the devil. The carving on the wooden panels and pews, the paintings around the walls all were most beautifully executed ; and it was with conscious awe that dust-stained and dirty we tiptoed up to the carved and ornamented altar. Our guide explained that it was the first care of the monks to keep this little haven of peace beautiful for meditation. He told us that the monastery was used as a place of exile for monks who in larger monasteries in Russia had been guilty of some misdemeanour or other. It was wonderful to think of this hermitage so peaceful and so quiet standing high above the plain where but recently thousands of men had been engaged in bloody battle.

From Jericho we moved again south-east toward the Jordan and camped in the groves around a ruined monastery near to the Dead Sea and opposite the Henu Ford of the Jordan. In the groves around this monastery were pomegranates, grapes and figs galore, and though the sickness amongst the men was still heavy, here good shade could be had, and there was moreover a large stone cistern in which one could bathe. We took turn about with the 29th Lancers to patrol across the Jordan to a place known as Henu Post and down to the Dead Sea on our right. Naturally we took advantage of this chance of proving our school teachers wrong, by bathing in the Dead Sea. Our masters had been right as to the impossibility of sinking in the Sea, but what they hadn't told us

was the chronic soreness of the skin from the salt that
we felt on coming out from the water. The northern
shores of the Dead Sea are just the very apotheosis
of desolation. The first time I stood upon its banks,
a mental picture I have gained from " Childe Roland
to the Dark Tower came " somehow flashed up in my
mind :

" I think I never saw such starved ignoble nature."

The 29th Lancers were much incensed with the
enemy. Two of their number had been shot during
patrol, and when a squadron had gone out in force to
get their bodies, it was found that the Turks had
mutilated them, as was the custom with certain of
the Bedouani. The dead men were found with their
private parts cut off and stuffed in their mouths.
The 29th Lancers swore a terrible vengeance and it
came shortly afterwards.

We were carrying out a reconnaissance in force to
the north-eastern shores of the Dead Sea, when we
came under very heavy fire from the flank ; certain
armoured cars came to our aid and drove off the last
detachments of the enemy. Some of these retiring
were spotted by the 29th Lancers, who promptly
charged them with the lance, giving no quarter to any
who came into range of that deadly weapon.

In the second week of July, after more than two
months in that infernal " damp chemical oven," the
valley, we came out through Jerusalem down on to
the plains and spent a month's easy at Latron,
Zenouka and Richon Le Zion.

From Latron, at the foot of the road up through the
hills to Jerusalem, small parties obtained leave to visit
the Holy City and its sepulchres.

Frankly, we were disappointed, as the sacred places
were so over-adorned with cheap tawdry tinsel
decorations. Whoever had the churches in their
keeping had no artistic sense whatsoever ; the
serenity and simple quietude of that little chapel at

the monastery on the Mount of Temptation was finer than all the churches in the heart of Christendom.

The Allied forces treated the various sacred shrines of all the religions in Jerusalem with the same genuine respect, but there is a story told of a mild vandalism.

An Australian was being shown round a church by a very garrulous guide to whom he had listened as patiently as possible. Presently they came to a little oil lamp burning in an alcove at which the guide apostrophized :

" It is so arranged that this lamp can be filled without ever being put out. This lamp has never been put out. For over a thousand years this lamp has been burning now, and has never been put out."

" Say, cobber, then I guess it's time it was," was the answer as he leant over and giving a puff, out went the light.

Rumour had it that by order of the Commander-in-Chief the Aussie in question was also temporarily "put out" by a very heavy sentence.

They were pleasant days at Latron, " Hungry," with whom I " bivvied " at this time and myself having three notable successes.

Firstly, we managed to procure copies of the *Palestine News*, a paper issued by the Military Authorities, and spent much time working the acrostics. Under the pseudonym of " Hathol " we won a real prize, a copy of the *Palestine News* free each week for a month.

Red wine made its appearance again, and managing to obtain from a secret source in the village a couple of bottles of vermouth, we made ourselves extremely popular by dispensing in large quantities the " Hathol " cocktail—drunk in pint mugs.

Our third success was a splendid row, neither of us knew what started it or what it was about ; but we both went livid and cursed each other's ancestry back to feudal times. We had always been the best of pals and always have been since, but on this particular day each of us could cheerfully have rended the other limb from limb with naked fingers. We just wanted to tear each other's entrails out and we avoided one another as much as possible to prevent open friction. I think in the evening we just took one look at each other and burst out laughing.

An outstanding event in my mind at this time was that Charlie, the finest cook in the world, now well over sixty, went on leave. He had stuck it right through and his leave-taking from the regiment was a notable one. The eve of his departure he spent in, " everybody's to 'ave a drink with me. And when I get back to London, I won't half tell 'em neither."

He went clean out and was still clean out the next morning. Finally, we put him in the bottom of a limber, covered him with straw, and quite unconscious of the cheers they drove him through the lines and off to railhead.

We continued our holiday at Zenouka and Richon Le Zion, where we received a substantial draft of Yeomen who had been down the line sick. Richon Le Zion, where the best Palestine wine comes from to-day, was a really beautiful Jewish colony set about with olive groves and orange orchards.

The wine was exceptionally good when we stayed there, and could be purchased at five piastres (one shilling) a pint. It was rather like port, but perhaps a little sweeter. Two pints, and one brought out the family album and talked affectionately of all one's poor relations. Sergeant Stevens of the " Warwicks," one of those fair-haired boys too handsome to be true, was posted to us at this time, and deserved extermination for introducing as a test of sobriety the phrase :

" Whisky when I'm well makes me sick, whisky makes me well when I am sick."

I shouldn't be surprised if I haven't written it down wrongly now—I never could say it myself.

Under the auspices of the padre we had several good concerts there, and certainly regained much of the good spirits which had reached rather a low ebb in the Jordan valley. The Colonel, Sir Mathew, was recalled home to the House of Commons—lucky old dog—so now the War would be soon over !

Whilst we were thus taking a breather " we missed a lively little scrap " in the valley. It appears that a composite battalion of Austrians and Germans, together with three or four battalions of Turks, was deputed to make a determined attack on the Ghoraniyeh bridge-head about the middle of July. The attack began at dawn with the German battalion leading. Finding a stubborn resistance the Turkish battalions in support immediately retired, leaving the poor Fritz well in " the soup." A regiment of Light Horsemen rode out to counter-attack and finished off the engagement with the butt-end of the rifle.

An Aussie who had thoroughly enjoyed the show described it to me somewhat as follows :

" Well, cobber, somewhat about dawn about three Turkish regiments and a crowd of Germans kicks up a fuss in front of our wire. They puts the Austrians and Germans in the front, and when we can see what we're a-doing of, and letting 'em have one or two, the Turks remembered they 'ain't 'ad no breakfast, so they does a guy and leaves the other poor b—— up in the air. It was a shame to take the money, we just rides out bareback in our shirt-sleeves and hits a few over the head with the butt-end and one or two under the jaw. They sees its hopeless, so we brings them in and gives 'em a good feed right away."

About three hundred prisoners, chiefly Austrians and Germans, were marched through Jerusalem at a subsequent date, and their appearance did much to smother any latent disaffection among certain of the inhabitants.

In the middle of August we started off on trek again

for our second tour of duty in the Jordan valley, and
eventually found ourselves back in the bridge-head
at Nimrin doing the same old patrols.

Just by the bubbling brook of Nimrin we saw a
large grave, where had been laid to rest many a gallant
laddie of the London Scottish who had been killed in
a valiant defence during the second raid into Gilead.

Our second sojourn was worse than the first; it was
hotter if anything, and we suffered the same wearying
discomfort from flies and dust, the same depletion of
strength from fever, boils and malaria, until the
regiment almost ceased to exist except as a skeleton.
This last month in the valley remains a nightmare to
all who endured it.

Suddenly one night in September we had orders to
move and, this time officers and men riding one and
leading four other horses apiece, we recrossed Jordan
for the last time, and by stealthy night marches and
laying up by day, found ourselves once more on the
coast, well behind the Turkish lines at Medjel.

As we left the valley, the plain around Jericho was
one huge camp with rows upon rows of tents and
squares upon squares of lines. Hush! they were all
empty.

General Allenby had deceived the Turk by the two
raids on Es Salt that the main attack, if any, was to
come on the right flank by way of the Jordan valley.
He now deceived them further, as by erecting this
"phantom camp" the enemy was given to understand that a large concentration of troops was taking
place on the west bank of Jordan with Jericho as the
base.

CHAPTER XI

ON TO DAMASCUS

" Mount—March, Ikonas ! Stand to your 'orses again,
  Mop up the frost on the saddles, mop up the miles on the plain.
  Out go the stars in the dawnin' ! up goes our dust to the sky.
  Walk—trot, Ikonas ! Trek you—the old M.I."—*Kipling.*

WE had camped but three days, and were about to toss up which of the remnants had prior turn to go sick, when we received a large draft of men from all regiments under the sun, to take over some of our spare horses. There were even men from the Dublin Fusiliers—I think they had been wandering about since the Boer War looking for another job.

We had a week's comparative easy to recuperate from the effects of the Jordan valley, and then, suddenly dumping every shred of kit, except a blanket, a " bivy " sheet and the clothes we stood up in, we began night marches up to the line through Yebna and Ramleh and eventually hid ourselves in the fruit groves at Sarona, just behind the Turkish lines.

There was a great concentration of cavalry here, and it says much for the excellent Staff work, and also the " nous " of individual units, that the Turks were still thoroughly under the impression that all the cavalry were encamped in the Jordan valley. There were no less than three whole divisions of cavalry, as well as five divisions of the infantry, together with some three hundred guns, hidden away among the orange groves and the clusters of olive trees between Ramleh and the front line of the coastal sector. Yet Johnny Turk was ignorant of all this, and kept his left eye the wider open watching that skeleton army down in the Jordan valley.

Lying lazily on our backs beneath the fruit trees, gazing up at the little patches of blue sky between the dark green leaves, musing and sleeping away the hours, we little guessed that the morrow morn would embark us on the greatest cavalry drive of all time. Those of us who had survived that dreadful summer in the Jordan valley were very thin, and could still show boils and septic sores to witness the impoverishment of our blood and the low state of our health generally ; but the new drafts, if unseasoned soldiers, were lusty and willing young fellows, whose strength and enthusiasm did much to invigorate a regiment whose powers of endurance had now been worn nearly threadbare by four long years of war.

As we woke our men silently at 0200 (2 a.m.) on the morning of September 19th, rumours of an attack were in the air, but we scarcely dreamt that for Mr. J. T. it was the beginning of the end, or that we were to participate in an offensive which was to finish off the war in Palestine, and strike one of our " opposed numbers " clean off the list.

We rode out at 4 a.m. and took up a position in rear of the 7th Division, a Division composed mainly of Indian troops, Punjabis and Gurkhas, with a good seasoning of white troops in the shape of those famous regiments, the Black Watch, the Seaforths and the Leicesters. An intense bombardment from every gun on the front commenced, but it was of short duration, lasting little more than a quarter of an hour, and then the infantry attacked with a will. Their assault was more than successful, for in less than a couple of hours they had broken right through the Turkish defences and rolled back the whole of their left flank a distance of ten miles, so that there was a great gap by the coast for the cavalry to go through.

Shortly before nine o'clock, with the other regiments of our brigade, the 29th Lancers and

Jacob's Horse, in line of troop column, we rode off
through gaps in the wire and quickly passed over the
Turkish trenches. The signs of battle were fewer
than would be supposed. Here and there the loose
huddled body of a dead Turk, or one badly wounded
calling for " moyah," a few forsaken machine-guns,
an occasional field-piece, several dead donkeys and
pack-ponies ; but nowhere were the heaps of slain
that had formed such a grim testimony to the attacking troops at the smash-up of the Beersheba–Gaza
line. Just a few " pip-squeaks " burst here and there,
and occasionally a " puff and phut " of shrapnel,
but otherwise we might have been on an ordinary
trek.

It had been impressed upon us in our reconnaissances before Beersheba, and also whilst in the Jordan
valley, that, wherever possible, we were to indulge in
" shock tactics " ; that dismounted action was only
to be employed as a last resort, and that in all cases
the enemy was to be charged at sight. The necessity
for mounted action was again repeated to us, and
throughout the next fortnight we obeyed this order
up to the hilt, and gave fair value for money. Towards the afternoon the advance guard came under
fire from the right flank, but the leading regiment,
Jacob's Horse, galloped the position in style and
captured two hundred and fifty prisoners. Our
regiment encountered no opposition and we rode
rapidly on to reach Kakon, a position well behind the
Turkish lines, by nightfall. We enjoyed a snatched
three hours' halt and a short " kipp ", and at 1.30 a.m.
we saddled up again and were off to make the Musmus
Pass, which should lead us through the hills down to
Megiddo in the famous battle-plain of Esdraelon.

After wandering like Moses in the Wilderness for a
while, we eventually struck the Pass, which proved
to be a rocky goat track, so that we slipped and
slithered through in single file to deploy out upon the
plain at about 6 a.m. We advanced on Megiddo,

and the leading regiment of the Division coming into touch with a large body of Turks and Germans immediately charged and captured about five hundred prisoners. We passed these poor Johnnies squatting disconsolately on the ground, and they were actually the first group of the enemy we had seen during this stunt.

The whole column now swung eastward towards the Jordan to complete the encircling movement, so as to surround absolutely the Turkish VIIth and VIIIth Armies, and to render all retreat impossible west of the Jordan. Way on our right we could just see the white stone houses of Nazareth, set among the olive trees upon the slope of a hill-side, and throughout the day, wherever one looked to left or right, miles upon miles of moving cavalry met the eye.

On we rode rapidly and continued the march to reach Beisan upon the Jordan by midnight—eighty miles since the previous morning.

Although completely unaware of the fact, the two Turkish armies west of the Jordan were now surrounded, and as the infantry were still pounding away at them on the original line and driving them into the hills ; and the troops down in the Jordan valley, the Chaytor Force, were also engaging the IVth Army, we realized that before long they would be driven back on to us. The infantry were advancing rapidly and the engineers were well supporting them, for the second day they laid some six miles of water-piping in eight hours, so that the men could be well supplied in the arid hilly terrain in which they were fighting.

As we reached Beisan the 5th Cavalry Division captured Nazareth, and with it the Army Headquarters. Marshal Limon von Sanders Pasha himself had a narrow escape, as he was in the city as the cavalry entered. At the first alarm he rushed out of his quarters in his pyjamas only, and made off in a motor-car ; but finding the Turks were putting up a good resistance, he returned, dressed, and removed some of his papers just as the cavalry won through, and the town capitulated.

We remained two days at Beisan and were afforded many opportunities of estimating the rapidity of our advance, as the main army was still unaware of their perilous plight. A German aeroplane from the north landed in the aerodrome at El Afule, and the pilot was surprised when he was captured, as he was unaware the town was in the hands of the British. On occasions German lorries drove up to us to draw rations and were promptly seized. Rumour had it that the Quartermaster-Sergeant of " B " Squadron was accosted by a German paymaster with money for the troops, who promptly dumped the " verluche " and bolted, on finding the place occupied by English. Stragglers were surrendering in hundreds, and groups of men readily threw down their arms to any stray Tommy who would show them the way to the prison camp.

Beisan itself was an unhealthy spot, being on a hot swamp. The ground was low and marshy, and the whole place a hotbed of malaria, and the Regiment was afterwards to suffer severely for its activities in this infected region.

Leaving a camp established at Beisan on September 21st, we marched southward along the west bank of the Jordan to establish contact with the retreating enemy. We soon came under shell fire, and about noon ran into a considerable force of the Turks. We moved round the flank, whilst the 29th Lancers charged the centre of the position, capturing eight hundred prisoners and fifteen machine-guns. Jacob's Horse operating on the other bank of the Jordan had two charges held up by overwhelming numbers of the enemy, and the gallant Hants battery, our companion in many a scrap during this stunt, galloped up their guns into the open to assist the action of the Indian horsemen. They in turn came under heavy fire from the concealed battery of the enemy, and the whole engagement looked like coming to a standstill.

Our " B " Squadron, cleverly finding a place to ford the Jordan, crossed the river, deployed upon the plain and charged the Turkish batteries with the sword, capturing four guns and putting others out of action. The enemy withdrew and, being harassed by machine-gun fire, abandoned large quantities of stores and ammunition. These captured stores were useful, as we were now far in advance of our rations, and even Turkish bread and date cakes formed a welcome feast to hungry men.

A night of outpost duty and then to march further south again the next morning. Near to the Wadi Maleh we encountered a strong force of the enemy, some one thousand two hundred men with machine-guns. As we charged into action the Hants batteries galloped upon our flank and pasted the enemy as they ran in hopeless rout towards the Jordan. This force had been covering the retreat of the main Army, who were now fully exposed to any attacks, without having time to deploy. Consequently our Squadron crossed the river and then attacked the column, capturing large numbers of men and large quantities of material. " B " Squadron had rather a rough time. With drawn swords they charged clean into the massed ranks of the enemy who attempted to make some sort of a stand. Captain Bullivant, our dear " Bully," was killed immediately, and a small detachment of the squadron getting separated from the main body had two killed, all the remainder wounded. However, this squadron alone, perhaps some hundred strong, brought in over one thousand prisoners. The Regiment reassembled and continued to march due southward down the bank of the Jordan, capturing straggling groups of the enemy and hurrying others across the Jordan. We must have marched some twelve or fifteen miles when eventually we picketed down some few miles north of Damieh.

The events of the day and the large captures were talked of with glee. It was certainly good fun being an arm of a victorious army, and if the horses and men looked a bit scraggy and worn, our spirits were up to " champagne " standard. There was on this particular night, however, for all the older campaigners who had left England with the regiment, a quiet and thoughtful sadness. That dear fellow, " Bully," had gone west. He held a rule that he would never ask a man to go where he wouldn't go himself, and on climbing over a ridge to " scout out," he had been spotted and killed at once.

Every man with a sense of feeling, who had ever come into close contact with " Bully," just loved him. That's all that one can say of it. Brave and fearless, foolhardy really, in battle, he was yet of a sensitive, highly-strung temperament. A leader for any man in action, yet as tender and kind as a woman. Throughout the whole of the four years' service his care and thought had always been for his men and horses, and he was ever the last in the squadron to seek food or comfort for himself. He looked upon us as his own sons, and if ever he had to reprove it was with the kindliness of a loving father. We felt his death keenly, and yet there was something just right, complete, about it all. As I had watched him on many occasions rush up over the skyline and stand focussing his glasses on the enemy to get the range, utterly regardless of the hail of bullets around him, I somehow felt he meant to be killed in action. It was the death he wished for—foolishly desired,—for there is great work in the world of to-day for men of " Bully's " goodness and understanding.

Dear " Bully," when war memories crowd upon me, at Armistice and times of Remembrance, I seem to see you so clearly—that wistful smile playing about the corners of your mouth and your eyes so " soft and fawn-like." The memory of you is very green with us all, we admired your courage, we laughed at your whimsical forgetfulness, we even mimicked you ; but we loved your unselfish kindliness, that care and thought for others which made you do so much in times of peace for the poor boys of our London slums. " Bully "—I salute you.

It may be as well at this point to review briefly the events on other parts of the front, for by this evening, September 25th, the last Turkish soldier has been forced across Jordan, the whole of the VIIth and VIIIth Armies were in rout, and Palestine west of the river cleared from the Infidel.

Whilst we had been driving right up the coast and then turning eastward and southward to complete the encircling movement, the infantry in touch with the enemy on their original line of defence had continued a left wheeling movement into the hills to roll up the Turkish flank. They easily beat down all organized opposition, and by the night of September 20th, after a forced march of some twenty-four miles over the roughest broken country, the 10th Division had occupied Nablus, the ancient Shechem, and the chief city of Samaria.

The main attack on September 18th had been so successful that practically all infantry action of any kind finished on September 20th, and, as has been seen, the Cavalry had encircled the Turks so completely that their retreat or capture was inevitable.

As our division of the Desert Mounted Corps had completed the arc to circumscribe the Turkish Army, the 5th Cavalry Division had gone off on a tangent to the coast and occupied in turn Nazareth, Haifa, and Acre, throwing out a small column to capture Tiberias on the Sea of Galilee.

Chaytor's force in the Jordan valley, intended originally as a holding force only, after the first day or two found the opposition to their front considerably weakened, and thus attacked. The enemy began to retire and by constantly harrying the enemy rearguards this little force pressed on until by the evening of September 25th it had captured both Es Salt and Amman, this time to be held for good.

Harassed by Chaytor's force the Turkish IVth Army, which had been operating on the east bank of Jordan, began also to retire upon Deraa and Damascus, and it is possible this army, which had not been so heavily engaged as the VIIth and VIIIth Armies, would have reached Damascus sufficiently intact to have been organized into a defence of that city. Such a force could have held the city for a long time against the relatively small bodies of cavalry, the 5th and Australian Divisions, which were advancing towards it north of the Sea of Galilee, but a new factor had entered into their consideration.

Advancing steadily northward during the whole of August and September, across the arid deserts of Arabia had come the Arab army of Sherifian troops, so marvellously organized by Lt.-Colonel T. E. Lawrence and the Sherif Feisal. The recruitment, organization and adventures of this Arab army have been most graphically described in his own books by that modern Hannibal, Colonel Lawrence himself.

We had heard rumours of their activities and of the coming of this army for some months, but had always discredited the stories as pertaining to a few Arab tribesmen. An interesting superstition held by some of the natives and told to us afterwards was that Kitchener was not dead, but that Colonel Lawrence was none other than the " Conqueror of the Sudan," come to lead the Arabs victoriously against the Turks.

This Sherifian force had now reached such a point on the extreme flank of the Turkish IVth Army as to be within striking distance of Deraa from the east. The head of this column of Arab regulars and irregulars was well to the north of the retreating Turkish troops and, had it been strong enough, could have commenced another complete encircling movement. It contented itself, however, by constantly

attacking the flank of the retreating Turks and helping in the complete demoralization of the army by
swift raids and withdrawals upon selected units.

During September 27th the last Turkish forces left
Deraa for Damascus, unaware that by this time
regiments of the Arab Army had fought their way
round north of the city and thus barred the retreat to
Damascus. This body of the Turks had been so incensed by the repeated raids of the Arabs and so im-
bued with the spirit of frightfulness that it decided
" to make an example " of two villages which seemed
to be on the point of open rebellion.

Accordingly, after leaving Deraa they descended
upon the villages of Tafas and Turaa, and massacred
about eighty women and children with the usual
revolting atrocities. They hoped by this means to
overcome and terrorize the districts through which
they were passing, but this act only incensed the Arab
armies to such an extent that the Arabs, led by Sheik
Tallah, who charged single-handed into the foe, fell
upon the perpetrators of these dastardly butcheries
and not a living soul of that column ever reached
Damascus.

Meanwhile to the north, the Australian Mounted
Division, after a flying march of some eighteen miles
from Medjel on the Sea of Galilee to Jior Benat Yakub,
where there was a bridge across the Jordan, found
themselves temporarily held up by a determined
resistance of the enemy. The Turks in an attempt
to frustrate this threat to Damascus had formed a
circular stronghold of lorries, artillery and machines
after the manner of a Boer laager at the crossing of
the Jordan. The Light Horsemen knew a better way
of " killing their cat " than engaging this force openly
by a frontal attack. One brigade galloped away to
the north and began to force its way across the
marshes of Hule, whilst another brigade moved away
to the south, swam their horses across the Jordan
about a mile below the bridge, and, working round to

the rear with the assistance of the brigade from the north, captured the whole of the laager by night-fall. They were joined that evening by the 5th Cavalry Division, which had ridden across from the coast by Acre.

And now of our own doings during these two days. From Damieh, having seen the Turks safely across the Jordan, we moved back to Beisan to concentrate for an attack on Deraa. The following morning, the 27th of September, we moved off eastward across Jordan to attack the flank of the retreating IVth Army, utterly unaware of the proximity of the Sherifian troops or of the fighting in and about Deraa. The march lay through dry stony hills and, as we had to make a tiresome nine miles through that difficult terrain without water, the horses drooped and stumbled, so that many of us preferred to lead them. The Dorset Yeomanry had been in advance of us, and by means of a highly successful charge had captured Ibid that morning, inflicting heavy casualties on the enemy and capturing large numbers with stores. We soon encountered a camel convoy of wounded Dorsets from this action, coming down a narrow hill-track, and alas, when, exhausted for lack of water, we finally reached Ibid, we found that the wells had nearly given out by the demands upon them of the advance brigade.

The Dorsets that night pushed out patrols towards Deraa, only to find, to their immense surprise, that it had been occupied an hour previously by the Sherifian troops. This was the first contact between our forces and those under Colonel Lawrence, and even then we did not realize the magnitude of his army.

Several troopers of the Central Indian Horse at a first meeting with the Arab troops arrested a British officer under the impression that he was a German serving with the Turks. His prompt ejaculation of "Well, I'm——," however, immediately convinced them of his nationality.

It was now a race for Damascus, between the Australians to north-west, Colonel Lawrence's troops to our right, and ourselves in the centre. Both the other columns had a fine start of us, so we were apparently to be moved up in reserve.

We were amply provisioned before moving off on September 28th, as a forage supply had arrived, but there was no water for the horses until we reached Er Remte at midday. We passed on rapidly through Mezerib, near to the scene of the Turkish massacre, and eventually camped not far north of the ruins of an old mediæval castle and a moated fortress. A party of Hedjaz troops—" Hedgehogs " we quickly named them—visited our lines and gave us many evidences of their delight in making our acquaintance, including a display of riding standing in the saddle and firing in the air with whoop and war-cry. I hadn't seen anything so good since the days of Buffalo Bill.

The forced march over dry, dusty and waterless country continued the next day, the rough and stony roads were strewn with dead Turks who, for the most part, had been stripped naked by the tribesmen, and mules and ponies that had been ridden to death threw up a filthy stench. A short halt at Sheik Miskin and on to a spot near Dilli where we camped the night.

Off again shortly after dawn, one day's rations in hand, but no water; on and on, mile after mile, through El Sanancim, but recently evacuated by the Turks, until about 5 o'clock that evening we overtook the rearguard and remnants of the IVth Army at Khiyara. Our artillery galloped as well as possible into action and began a heavy bombardment, but the condition of our horses, and incidentally ourselves, rendered further pursuit impossible that night. From a rise in the ground we could now distinctly see the column of the Australian Light Horsemen away out to the left, whereas regiments of the " Hedgehogs " were riding alongside on our right.

Utterly worn out and almost falling off our horses for want of sleep and long hours in the saddle with little food or water, we stumbled on to Zerakiye, some twelve miles south of Damascus, the horses having travelled thirty-five miles that day without water, and over one hundred and thirty miles in all since noon of September 26th. One hundred and thirty miles in four days ; no wonder we felt tired. We experienced one little thrill of exaltation as we beheld the fires of the Turkish dumps before dropping wearily to the ground to sink into the dead sleep of physical exhaustion.

Meanwhile the 5th Cavalry Division, together with the Australian Mounted Division, by tremendous hard riding, after their desperate scrapping at Jordan Bridge, had taken Kaukab with over one thousand prisoners, and despatched a brigade to Kiswe on the other Damascus road, which cut the column retreating from us clean in two. The 5th Light Horse Brigade, summoning a last burst of energy, rode due north across the open country a further ten miles, and took up positions well astride the Damascus–Beirut road, north-west of the city. Thus as the Turks rode out of Damascus, weary and battered as they were, they found yet another line of retreat closed to them, and a whole column was trapped as the defile was swept with rifle and machine-gun fire. A great number were killed and over four thousand prisoners were captured.

During the night, the whole of the Australian Mounted Division having come up in support on this road, the 3rd Light Horse Brigade marched east around the northern suburbs of the town to complete the enveloping movement, and by dawn had effectively blocked the Damascus–Aleppo road.

The Turk had to abandon Damascus without making the slightest stand for such an important city ; his IVth, VIIth and VIIIth Armies were broken, and only remnants remained, utterly routed without organization or morale.

The " Hedgehogs " and the Aussies both entered the city early in the morning of October 1st, but both detachments were ignorant of the arrival of the other, and each naturally ascribed the honour to itself. In point of fact a detachment of Light Horsemen under Major Olden entered the city about 6.30 a.m., while Colonel Lawrence at the head of the Hedjaz Camel Corps was a trifle later. At about 8.30 a.m. the town was officially occupied by General Chauvel commanding the Desert Mounted Corps, amidst scenes of wild enthusiasm from the inhabitants at the collapse of four centuries of oppression under the Turkish regime.

Our own réveillé had been about 2.30 in the morning of October 1st, and we were saddled up shortly after 3 a.m. Dust-stained and dirty, with crisp curly beards, we yet made some attempt to " posh " ourselves up for the capture of the city, but we only marched through Kiswe on to Daraya and camped some five miles short of the city, whose white towers and minarets could be seen jutting up like icebergs from a sea of olive-green.

Everywhere were scenes of the complete debacle of the enemy—the swollen bodies of ponies and mules that had been ridden to death, dead and dying Turks lying around in all sorts of fantastic positions. Hundreds of the enemy were seen squatting or lying apathetically on the ground, too exhausted to move, too stunned to even give themselves up.

A detachment of the regiment took part next day in a triumphal march through Damascus, which sported the Hedjaz flag from every public building, with only an occasional " Jack " here and there, but the inhabitants did not seem quite sure of us, wondering possibly whether our administration with its discipline might not prove more irksome than that of the Turk.

We settled down to a few days' complete rest for man and beast, and richly we deserved it. The total

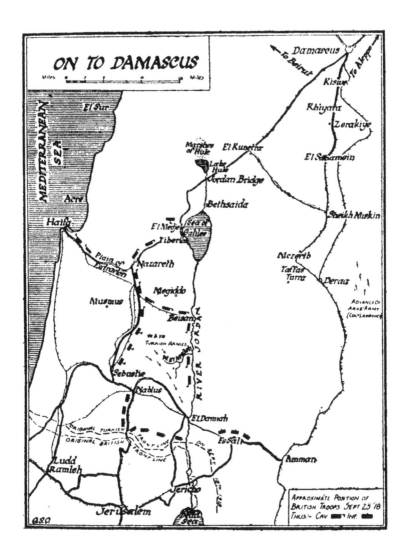

captures accredited to the regiment from September 19th to October 1st were 88 officers, 5000 other ranks, 8 Krupp field-guns, 5 camel-guns, 25 machine-guns, and a large quantity of war material.

And now the inevitable happened ; with the re-action nearly all the old " originals " crocked up. An epidemic of influenza and malaria broke out, and naturally those whose blood had worn thin with four and a half years of war and who had stuck the piece right through, were the first to fall a prey to the ravages of sickness. We lost more men sick and dying in two days than we had lost killed and wounded during the whole of the stunt. It was pitiful to hear daily of the death of some old pal who had roughed and weathered it through, only to die of this new plague when the end of the journey was in sight. If, however, one reached hospital alive and had sufficient strength to pull through, it meant " Blighty " for a cert.

As this story is largely a personal reminiscence I will not dwell in detail of General Allenby's further advance by a flying column which eventually occupied Aleppo with but little resistance, but I would remind readers that the Armistice with Turkey was signed on October 31st, and this withdrawal of Turkey from the War undoubtedly did much to dispirit the already beaten German troops on the Western Front.

This campaign of General Allenby's will surely go down to posterity as one of the most brilliant and dramatic examples of the use of cavalry in the whole history of warfare.

The whole scheme had been most ably conceived by the genius of the Commander-in-Chief, boldly interpreted by his four Corps Commanders, Lt.-General Sir Edward Bulfin, Lt.-General Sir Harry Chauvel, Lt.-General Sir Philip Chetwode, and Major-General Sir Edward Chaytor, and finally enacted by the loyalty, heroism and cheery enthusiasm that conquered all hardships and performed miracles of endurance, of all other ranks in the Palestine Army.

Still weak from a bout of malaria in company with
" Hungry " and Nic, I was well on my way home early
in October, but of the last adventures of the Regiment
abroad I must tell briefly. A whole column took part
in the rapid advance on Aleppo, and returned to
Damascus heavily depleted by sick. Large drafts
arrived to enable the older campaigners to be more
quickly demobilized. There were one or two little
cases of friction, usually amicably settled by the
padre ; but on the whole with sports and joy-rides the
men had a fairly good time. I am told that of the
last draft that reached the Regiment in May, 1919,
" four fell off their horses on the way from the
station," and that the last man of the old originals
who had left England in '15 who remained was our old
friend Jim, the farrier-major. I hope he had some good
fishing and that many a time he was able to " Pooll
him up on the bank."

Riding down to railhead, weak of body, but joyful
of heart at prospect of the homeward journey, and
Old England once again, we three musketeers returning from the wars soon noticed a big Colonial cantering
along towards us. As he drew in alongside we were
aware of a handsome face beaming with an open smile,
which crowned about six feet of sheer brawn. He
commenced to talk volubly.

" Say, cobbers, where are you folk off to ? "

I, thinking to score heavily and swipe him dead, said
airily : " Only to London, that's all."

" Crimes, chum," he shouted with enthusiasm,
" that's where I'm off to, guess I'll row in with you
blokes."

That is how I first made the acquaintance of
Sergeant Roy Macgregor of the New Zealand Mounted
Rifles, one of the happiest, cheeriest characters I have
ever known. He rode to the railhead, came down to
Kantara and finally embarked on the *Kaiser-i-Hind*
with us from Port Said to Taranto. He smilingly
informed us that we'd " better adopt him." He'd no

s

mess tin, no knife, no fork, no money, nothing but a
few spare clothes rolled up in brown paper, a pass to
England and a grin. He was a kind of human whirl-
wind that subsided for a few hours only from midnight till 5 a.m. He was real good company. I have
never enjoyed a journey so much in my life. Nic and
"Hungry" soon took to him, especially when they
found him equally impervious either to Nic's blunt
rudeness, or the veiled impertinence of "Hungry's"
subtle sarcasms. He just laughed at everything.
With a masterful smile he would approach :—

"Here, I want another pound, who do I have it
from this time ? Don't forget I've two hundred
waiting for me at Cook's in London and I'll see you
boys are all right."

Two Japanese destroyers, the "P" and "Q,"
accompanied our convoy to Taranto, and great
excitement prevailed on board as, on the second day
out, a submarine was sighted. "P" seemed to turn
in her own length and swept at full speed around our
bows, throwing out a jet-black smoke screen. "Q"
dashed off at full speed and dropped depth-charges
where the submarine had been seen to dive, and then
hovered about the spot for some time, whilst we continued our zigzag course. I believe the "Q" accounted for our attacker on this occasion.

The sight of land was welcome, but we were somewhat amazed when the boat seemed to head straight
towards the cliffs. As she swung a point, however,
we saw the narrow opening to the great basin harbour
of Taranto. The entrance was so small that it was
like going in a lock ; a crowd of Italians on the foot-
bridge overhead raised a half-hearted cheer in response
to our greeting.

The Bay at Taranto was an interesting sight ; it
was packed with small French and Italian gunboats,
and we remarked that it must have been washing-day,
as the spars and riggings of the ships fluttered with
the laundry of the crews.

After a couple of days we entrained, and by dint of a little soft-soaping of the R.T.O., a young sub. rather prone to flattery, we acquired a carriage for the four of us. There was no door on one side, but that slight defect we eradicated by driving nails into the uprights so that a waterproof sheet could be fitted at will.

I shall long remember the first part of that glorious journey as the railroad ran along the coast of the Adriatic with the white-crested waves dashing on the rocks below. Right up the coast we went to Rimini, where the railway ran inland, through Bologna to Faenza, at which town we enjoyed a whole day's rest from travelling. Englishmen were none too popular in Southern Italy at this time, as the Italians were under the impression that we were doing all we could to prolong the war and that but for our stubborn obstinacy it would have been over long ago. Consequently any attempts at cheery greetings as we stopped at wayside stations were rather coldly and formally returned. It was a constant source of enjoyment to " Mac," however, to watch the little children waving to the train by turning the palm of their hand inwards to the body and opening and closing the fingers.

Nic and " Hungry " had a seat a-piece for sleeping, whereas " Mac " and I shared the floor. I can assure you we were never dull, we played a deal of bridge, arranging a final settlement when we arrived at London, and we found our New Zealander ever resourceful and constantly amusing.

There was no light in our carriage, which meant that bridge or reading had to cease at sunset. At Bologna Mac set out to remedy this defect, and we watched him enter an office on the station marked " Lampada," or some such word. High altercations followed ; we heard him cajolling, bargaining, threatening, and, as the train began to move, we saw him bolting up the station waving what looked like a

brass halo in his hand, closely followed by three irate
Italian porters. It was a lamp of sorts, a circular
ring containing oil, and there was a wick, but, having
nothing to fit the lamp into, we suspended it from the
luggage racks with bootlaces.

To us who had spent such years staring over desert
lands, the scenery from Faenza, along the valley of
the Po, across the plain of Piedmont and through the
Apennines to Genoa was one sheer delight. Then
along the Riviera, the deep blue waters of the Mediterranean sparkling in the sunshine, the waves lazily
lapping the yellow sands, the little white villas so neat,
so trim, so suggestive of love and comfort, nestling
among the dark green foliage on the hill-sides. The
indolent beauty of Mentone, Nice and Monaco, the
shouts and laughter of the children by the wayside,
and the pungent odour of the back streets : we seemed
to have been transported by a magic carpet from all
scenes of battle, murder and the holocaust of war.

We sang all day, the ring of our voices but faintly
echoing the joy and excitement in our hearts as each
day brought us nearer home.

Somewhere near to Monaco, Mac had rather a set-
back, which caused us to roar with laughter till we
cried. The train had stopped near to some tomato
groves and little olive-skinned youngsters were
" scrumping " this ripe fruit and, clambering over on
to the railway, were bartering their stolen goods for
cigarettes. We emptied our kits of stray packets of
" Flag," " Portlight," and " Red Hussar," and
eagerly exchanged such merchandise at the rate of
" one cigaretten—two tom-ar-to." We had almost
filled the rack on one side of the carriage when the
native Scot in Mac suggested a fine idea. Hastily
seizing a couple of packets of " Portlight," he laid
them on the seat and, sitting on them heavily,
squashed them flat. Then, leaning well out of the
window, he began negotiations : " Cigaretten Turkish
—good, good—four tomato—Turkish—four tomato—

Cigarette English—two tomato, but Turkish—Turkish —four tomato." The youngsters fell for it, and in high glee Mac disposed of a packet and a half at the new rate of exchange. The train apparently began to move off at the precise moment that the youngsters discovered the fraud, for Mac was half turning in the window to produce another Turkish, when he received four tomatoes for it—" goods on approval." Two hit him clean in the face, broke, and covered him with pips and juice, and as he spluttered, blinked and swore, the second two arrived, hitting him one clean in the eye and the other spreading the order of the Serbian Eagle across his manly breast.

Mac's quick wit was used to better purpose at Marseilles. It was dusk, and the train was about to move off when a body of troops arrived on the station and the R.T.O., rushing down the train, crammed them in wherever he could find a spare seat. The comparative comfort we had enjoyed with only four to the carriage looked like coming to an abrupt end- ing, but Mac with his head out of the window tumbled to what was happening. He turned round excitedly, " Quick, quick, get your kit-bags and great-coats down—quick, for the love of Mike."

" What the devil for ! "

" Oh, Hell ! don't argue, get your kit-bags down." He grabbed at mine, wrapped my great-coat round it, buttoned it up, turned up the collars and placed a field service hat on top of the guy. Nic and " Hungry " quickly followed suit, and when the R.T.O. rapidly glanced in the carriage as he bustled down the plat form he saw in the dark interior seven soldiers, three dozing heavily. One sleeper was being prodded by Mac, with " Wake up, Bill, here's the porter come to clip your ticket." We breathed freely and guffawed heartily as the train moved out of the station.

Life felt just glorious as the train sped onward through the beautiful Rhine valley, passing Arles, Avignon, Orange and Valence. What more could

man want, but beautiful country all around him,
good companions and the knowledge that after years
of wandering he was going home ?

The train stopped on a bridge in Lyons overlooking a main street, and soon a collection of little
workgirls gathered below and scrambled for the tins of
" bully " and " pork and beans " we threw down to
them. We sang to them and they cheered, smiling
their prettiest, waving their hands and joining in as
we moved slowly off with

> " Good-by-ee, good-by-ee,
> Wipe a tear, baby dear, from your ey-ee."

This song was all the rage just then, and I shall never
hear it without thinking of that final journey through
France where we sang it to crowds at every station,
who welcomed and received us in the friendliest
possible manner, all the more noticeable after the
frigidity of the Italians.

Yet another incident of the journey concerns Mac.
Well after midnight, the train halted for over an hour
at the junction of Dijon. Mac and I had been sleeping
on the floor and had got up to look out of the window
with monkey-like curiosity. We were just settling
down again, when we saw a hand steal in under the
waterproof sheet on the doorless side of the carriage,
grab Mac's only pair of boots, and disappear.

Exclaiming the usual " Well, I'm ——," etc., he
rushed to that side and pulled down the waterproof
sheet, but, needless to say, there was not a soul in
sight.

" That's done it," said Mac. " Have you got a
spare pair, 'Appy ? "

" Yes, I'll get 'em out of my kit-bag in the
morning."

" Aye, but I want 'em now."

" Don't be a b——y fool, it's no good putting 'em
on now."

" Look here, cobber," said he, grinning all over his

face, " give us a hand on those boots of your'n, and I'll show you something real good."

Both Nic and " Hungry " were awake by this time and received the news of Mac's misfortune with high glee. Nothing would satisfy Mac but that I should give him my spare pair immediately, so I had to rake them out from the bottom of my kit. I shall long remember looking on with wonderment and suppressed mirth, as Mac, taking my boots, placed them down by the open flap of waterproof sheet, with the toes invitingly protruding from the carriage. With a look almost of adoration, as if about to participate in some ritual of worship, he knelt down in front of them, carefully drew his bayonet and remained in this posture, with the bayonet poised a nice striking distance above the boots, until the train moved out of the station.

Havre at last, a tramp at night over the cobble stones, then the boat and in the morning rushing on deck to catch the first glimpse of the grey shores of dear old England, through the early mist of dawn.

We could hardly keep still in the train from South-ampton. It was Mac's first visit to England, but we were London boys, and we were going back to that dear old town, our eyes moist with happiness as we watched the haphazard old fields, with broken hedges and old barns thrown here and there, all so different from the neat, immaculate agriculture of the south of France, through which we had so recently passed.

The grey and soot-stained stones of the old Waterloo, and then a taxi to " Cook's " to draw Mac's " dough." As our driver turned into the Strand and we saw the old streets again filled with fine clear-eyed sweet young English girlhood—it was just the grandest feeling ever. Mac wanted to give us most of his money, but we kind of kept him down till we got him to the Petit-Riche, where we ate a luncheon such as we had often dreamed about when hungry in the hills of Judæa.

I took Mac to Hampstead, where my mother promptly adopted him for the whole of his stay in England, and he had just "the time of his life." Apart from occasionally getting into bits of trouble, so that we often had to explain to the local police that we knew him, and nearly causing my sister's engagement to be broken off, and apart from one or two other things, we enjoyed his company immensely and claimed him as a brother.

After a short leave we were sent across to Ireland to the cavalry barracks at Newbridge, and there found many of our Regiment who had been evacuated sick or wounded, or who had not been sent back abroad after leave. One or two old regular sergeants who had seen no active service, but had been in charge of these depots, tried to "put it on us," by sending us to take charge of stables whilst they played billiards or snooker. The first night in the mess they also passed a few gratuitous insults as to " these amateur soldiers." A prompt speech by one of our party pointing out that "they were the professional soldiers, but that when the time had come for them to fight, they'd allowed the so-called amateurs to do it for them. That men who had fought in Gallipoli, Salonica, Sinai and Palestine knew more about the game than those sitting on the fence and wearing rooty medals. That we didn't intend to run the barracks for them and that we'd do no duty till we saw it posted in orders, etc.," and they left us alone.

Among the notables at Newbridge, we met old Charlie again. Overjoyed to see us he came up winking and waving his thumbs worse than ever. In answer to our query as to how he was getting on, he replied : "Dull when I first come 'ere, but I'm doing all right now. Nice little bit I've got shoved away, I can tellyer; 'ere, 'ave a look at this."

He produced a screwed-up greasy roll from the front flap of his riding breeches which, on opening, proved to be a Post Office savings book. He winked about four times in quick succession.

" Yus, dull it was at first, there weren't no one 'ere. When one night I goes into the canteen and there's a new lot all togged up in new khaki and they 'aint half splashing the money about. I listens a bit, and I larns as how they're all young miners and as 'ow they've only just been called up for duty. I larns as 'ow they 'aint half been 'aving a time, earning eight and ten pounds a week. I listens a bit longer and then I says to myself, ' Charlie, you're all right, me boy,' " a pause and a portentous wink, " so I goes away and buys a Crown and Anchor board."

Of myself ; I had been weak and ill from malaria when I left the Regiment, I was covered with septic sores, on account of which an elderly doctor to whom I reported for treatment and who had been reading the kindly articles of Christabel Pankhurst on " Soldiers Home from the East and Venereal Disease," threw me into isolation on The Curragh. One day there and I caught the septic pneumonia that was sweeping the country like the Black Death ; I was removed to a decent hospital by a doctor who knew what " septics " were, and, though despaired of, struggled through to life again.

Of the hospital I have but few recollections except the kindliness and care of the sisters and nurses, and the cheery chats with the doctor who knew my beloved Heath so well. I faintly remember, however, when the poor fellows were being carried out from our ward at the rate of five a day that there was a huge open fireplace at the far end of the ward. When a man became so bad that he looked certain to die, they moved him up by the fire to pass his last hours in greater comfort. One evening under the direction of the Sister, two orderlies came in and moved my bed up to the fire. " You needn't do that, Sister, I'm not going out, I can tell you, not this journey, anyhow," I faintly assured her.

The night Sister, " the thin-lipped American " it amused her to hear me call her, as she was so thoroughly unemotional, saved my life. During my crisis, I seemed to be struggling to keep my mind, and she held my hand whilst I recited all the Shakespeare or other poetry I knew, grappled in the recesses of my memory for algebraic quantities and trignometrical formulæ, anything to keep a grip on things away from that darkness. In the morning my temperature was down, my crisis was over. " Thin-lipped little lady," if ever you should read this, accept my thanks.

There was a rumour that the War was over on the evening of November 10th, and next morning I was astonished to receive a visitor, no other than dear old " Hungry " with a bandage right across his face. His eyes were peeping over the bandage, dancing with laughter as he explained that the rumour of the cessation of hostilities had been so well received in the sergeants' mess at Newbridge, that on his way to his quarters he had fallen on to a heap of broken bottles and almost cut his nose off. An honourable wound, I think, dear Cassius.

I heard the news of the Armistice whilst still very ill in bed, and I cannot describe what a feeling of peace and rest came over my soul. I didn't want to shout out—I think I just wanted to cry, that was all.

Luck came my way, the hospital doctor arranged for my early demobilization, and I eventually arrived back home on Christmas Eve, in time for Christmas service at the old Parish Church and my pre-prandial pint as of old at the Hollybush Inn.

ENVOI

THE Peace has been much harder than the War. Most of us who went out in the full flush of young manhood came back to find ourselves thoroughly out of touch with life in England. Jobs were scarce, the pay was poor, there were vested interests at work to hang on to positions gained by the stay-at-homes whilst " the boys " had been " out yonder." One crept back almost apologetically into the " daily round," and it was hard indeed to knuckle under to regular hours, petty regulations, trivial jealousies, when one had slept for four years on the open desert beneath a canopy of stars. To the ex-soldier the Peace has been sheer disillusionment and disappointment.

In the first flush of victory we were promised a " land fit for heroes " to live in. Never again should the dirt and ugliness of the slums, the blindness and brutality of ignorance, the vile evils of the over-crowding in our big cities retard the growth and pro-gress of our young manhood. We would build the world anew. The peace-day hymn for thousands of our young children was the hopeful, stirring, pro-gressive poem of Blake. What was it they sang in such impassioned chorus ?

> " Bring me my bow of burning gold !
> Bring me my arrows of desire !
> Bring me my shield ; O clouds, unfold !
> Bring me my chariot of fire !
> I will not cease from mental fight,
> Nor shall the sword sleep in my hand,
> Till we have built Jerusalem
> In England's green and pleasant land."

That was the spirit of the nation in 1919. But the statesmen, the politicians, the business men, the financiers have let us down.

Lloyd George ! You were the man with the greatest chance in history. We won the War, but the people of the nation believed that you did. You could have done almost anything you liked, the people would have risen to the greatest heights imaginable under your guidance. Such was the feeling of relief at the cessation of hostilities that had you even called for a " Burn Your War Bonds " campaign, the people would have followed you. They would have given of their war-profits freely and without stint had you shown the way, and thus have rid ourselves and our children of this dreadful burden of taxation for all time.

No other statesman has ever had such a chance of eternal fame. England created a will to win the War, a living flame of purposefulness, that taken and directed to win the peace could have removed all our social evils in a year of time. No, sir, instead of listening to the promptings of your own soul, you hearkened to the mutterings of " big business," the Federation of British Industries, the " get back to pre-war day " merchants, and we,—the lads who did the job,—have never forgiven you. The national mind, taught to throw self on one side, set on one purpose alone the " will to win," was allowed to break and crack into individual streams of self-interest and aggrandisement. The hydra-headed God of Greed took a deep breath once more and raised itself, certain of a million worshippers.

You people of England, these men of whom I have written, by their high endeavour, by their cheerful endurance of hardship, suffering and pain, by the giving up of their sweet young lives failed you not in the time of your stress ; but—you have failed them. On Armistice Day you will pay a shilling or even more for a poppy, you will feel mighty good and

sentimental about them, and then you will shelve
your responsibility for the rest of the year.

Has anyone noticed the most pathetic sight in
London ? I will tell you what it is. Go on a bright
spring morning and watch that glorious military
spectacle of pomp and splendour, the Changing of the
Guard. Outside the Palace Square you will see
visitors from all nations, French and Belgian officers
thrilled with the " snap " and precision of our crack
corps ; clear-skinned, bright-eyed American girls
laughing and joking of " Pop " and " Mama " with
square-shouldered Cyruses and Hirams ; swarthy
Indian and Persian students gazing stolidly through
the railings with that impassivity so characteristic of
the Oriental ; and best sight of all, fine bonny curly-
haired young babies, with the steel-blue eyes and the
flaxen locks of the real Saxon, held high on their
nurses' shoulders as they clap their hands in rhythm
to the music and chuckle with delight at the sight of
the " Solgers."

But you have missed someone. Look again.
There on the fringe of the crowd is a pale white face,
lined with worry and pinched with want. A shabby
cap or greasy bowler half shields his dull hopeless eyes
that glance furtively around as if half-apologizing
for their presence " in such a goodly company." A
threadbare suit with ragged sleeves and trouser-legs
completes the picture. The air is chilly yet he boasts
no great-coat, but has his muffler wrapped high around
his neck ; you would scarcely notice that he wears no
collar.

Now that you look more closely at the crowd about
you, you see many just such another, and you wonder
perchance what fascination that picturesque ceremony
can have for such a " poor fellow," thin, weedy and
wan. Has he no work to do that he can thus idle away
his time on the precious hours of this perfect morning,
even as you are doing ? If he has not, he should be
off looking for it. But wait, his moment is to come.

The ceremony is over and with slow step the band leading the Old Guard marches out of the Palace gates. A few more paces, and " rah rah rah " on the drums, the band breaks into quick step and to the tune of " Colonel Bogey " off goes the Guard on the march back to the barracks. As you stand to watch the departing troops—why, bless my heart and soul, look at that " little fellow " you noticed just now—there he goes down the broadwalk with dozens of his brothers around him. Did you see him square his shoulders, fling back his head ; did you see that back straighten and that step become more firm ? Why, even his arms are swinging now with something of a swagger—well up to the front and back to the rear. There he goes, his eyes are no longer dull, but hold a light of joy as for a brief moment he unconsciously throws himself back to the past, when he too wore the King's uniform and was the honoured servant of the nation. And as he marches he feels around him a little of the old spirit of comradeship and cheerful endeavour of those thousands of " good fellows " who lie in foreign fields, and who went to their death with a song and a jest, that you and I—and he—might live in freedom, peace and happiness in " England's green and pleasant land."

He asked you for bread, but you gave him a stone.

Ingram Content Group UK Ltd.
Milton Keynes UK
UKHW012007160523
421856UK00001B/25

9 781845 749033